CONTAINER PLANTS

for patios, balconies, and window boxes

The colors of oleander
flowers range widely,
from white through
cream, yellow, pink,
salmon, and red to
purple. Here, an
apple-blossom-white,
single-flowered cultivar
from the 'Apple
Blossom' group, with
fimbriated petals veined
with wine red.

CONTAINER
Halina Heitz
PLANTS

for patios, balconies, and window boxes

Consulting Editor: Dennis W. Stevenson, PhD
Director, Harding Laboratory
The New York Botanical Garden

Portraits of the Most
Popular Container Flowers,
Tub Plants, Herbs, and
Vegetables and Instructions
for Their Care.

350 color photos by
Friedrich Strauss and other
plant photographers

120 color drawings by
György Jankovics
and Ushie Dorner

BARRON'S

A spot made for dreaming. Roses and marguerites—the quintessence of warm summer days on the balcony or patio. Container gardeners can easily create such oases themselves. Combinations of beautifully flowering plants are the result of long summer days and tender loving care. Here, the rose has competition from morning-glories and the variegated-leaved flowering maple. Blue Swan River daisies are underplanted at the foot of the marguerite standard. At its left are Swedish begonia and fragrant lavender.

5

CONTENTS

A charming hanging basket—*Convolvulus sabatius* keeps company with nemesia (red, yellow) and blue daisies (blue).

Pink hanging geranium, 'Lachskönigin'.

Important: To keep your pleasure
in your hobby untarnished, please
read carefully the information on
The Law and Safety Precautions
on page 47 and the **"Important
Note"** on page 240.

Demidouble hibiscus flower in
salmon-orange.

A summery flower box
with low, double-
flowered sunflowers
('Teddy Bear') and
Swedish begonia.

PREFACE

A manual for growing plants in pots, boxes, tubs, and other containers—creatively and the year round.

Who does not long to have magnificent green foliage and a riotous, splendidly colored mass of flowers surrounding the house, whether they be on the balcony, patio, or roof garden, at the windows, or beside the front door? An enormous assortment of plants and containers is available to help your wish become a reality, whether you are dreaming of the sunny Mediterranean or just longing to be closer to nature—at all times of year.

Appropriate Plant Care

This gardening guide, with its many color photos and drawings, will help you grow gorgeous plants in pots, bowls, boxes, tubs, or hanging baskets. The keys to success are the right location and the proper care. Only by knowing the origin and living conditions of your plants can you give them the best care and overwintering. Colored drawings on all the How To pages illustrate procedures and provide information on planting, repotting, care, cutting and pruning, overwintering, propagation, and decorating. Drawings that illustrate symptoms make it possible to identify and control pests and diseases quickly. If you are interested in increasing your gardening know-how, look up terms in the Glossary.

It is simply unbelievable what can be grown in large and small containers! In individual plant portraits, illustrated by color photographs and including detailed instructions on care, this book presents to you over 300 of the most beautiful flower box and tub plants, including many new, unusual ones—shrubs, dwarf trees, herbaceous plants, flowering bulbs, and climbing plants, as well as herbs, fruit-bearing woody plants, and vegetables, that are suitable for container culture.

Ideas for All Seasons

Let your imagination be aroused by the captivating color photos and practical suggestions for making your balcony or patio beautiful during every season of the year. You will find suggestions for planting bowls, boxes, tubs, and hanging baskets. Detailed shopping lists and instructions for planting and tending your container garden guarantee that these combinations of plants can easily be duplicated, even by beginners. There are new ideas for experienced gardeners as well:

creating a minipond for the patio, planting a box of scented plants, or using climbing plants to make a privacy screen. If you want to use all your senses to the fullest, you will find suggestions for balconies where herbs, vegetables, and fruits grow, and many other ideas as well. Give yourself a chance to enjoy this kind of mobile gardening. The superb color photos—most of them taken expressly for this book—illustrate how gloriously plants can thrive with appropriate care.

The author and the editors wish you a great deal of pleasure and success with your container garden.

About the Author

Halina Heitz, a successful author of other gardening books (including *Indoor Plants*, the companion of this book) and an authority on ornamental plants, was an editor on the staff of *Mein schoner Garten* for 15 years.

Author and publisher wish to thank photographer Friedrich Strauss for his exceptional photos, many of which were taken especially for this book, as well as György Jankovics and Ushie Dorner for their informative drawings, and Martin Weimar for the beautifully planted containers in the section Planting Ideas for Every Season.

A special note of thanks goes to all our advisors:
Dr. Susanne Amberger-Ochsenbauer, agricultural engineer, Freising.
Wolfgang Eberts, Bamboo Center, Baden-Baden.
Horst Gewiehs, bulb importer, Rotenburg.
Garry Grüber, Ludwig Kientzler AG, Gensingen.
Petra Leithäuser, Benary Seed Cultivators, Hannoversch Münden.
Birgit Obreiter, Weihenstephan Professional School.
Siegfried Stein, Sperling Seeds, Lüneburg.
Dr. Witt, Horticultural School and Research Institute, Bad Zwischenahn.

Magical Harmonies of Color
Cool blue-violet and warm orange colors are displayed by these plants (left to right): Cupflowers, African lilies, a miniature orange tree, and lavender.

Elegance in white: The assortment of plants available is so large that you can decorate your balcony and patio in your favorite color, using many different species. The geometric box spirals and the globe-shaped ligustrum go extremely well with the cool white of the roses, lilies, geraniums, and marguerite chrysanthemums.

ALL ABOUT CONTAINER PLANTS

Who wouldn't like to have magnificent, healthy plants with abundant flowers that are the focus of all attention? Success will come more easily if you know a few little gardening secrets. On the following pages, you will learn all you need to know about container gardening.

Balcony flowers from *Ageratum* to *Zinnia*, tub plants from *Abutilon* to *Yucca*, citrus trees, flowering bulbs, herbaceous plants and woody plants from the garden, wild flowers, potherbs, berry bushes, and vegetables—the range of plants being potted for "mobile gardening" is expanding constantly. Most of them have their origin in warm countries. As container gardening becomes an increasingly popular hobby, however, more and more hardy plants from latitudes, they can be cultivated only in tubs in which they are over-wintered and protected against frost (see pages 28–29).

<u>Classic container flowers</u> are the traditional petunias, geraniums, tuberous begonias, and fuchsias, in addition to numerous summer flowers, climbing plants, and twining plants. Container flowers, which may be annuals, biennials, or perennials, come chiefly from the tropics and subtropics. The annuals and biennials are spent after one or two growing seasons and are then discarded. Perennials can be over-wintered.

Many plant lovers, however, are reluctant to try overwintering, possibly because they have too little space available or because they are afraid they will prove unable to bring the plants through the winter properly. Granted, some plants need to be overwintered in a bright location, and not everyone can provide the level of light they require. Apart from this, however, far too many other thoroughly healthy plants are being thrown away every fall. These plants, given the proper winter care, would flower even more magnificently the following year. The plant portraits (see pages 86–227) and the recommendations for overwintering (see pages 28–29) will show you what kind of overwintering is called for—and will demonstrate that it is not too complicated after all.

<u>Garden plants for container culture</u> are the latest trend. Herbaceous plants, summer flowers, bulbs, potherbs, vegetables, broad-leaved and needle-leaved evergreens, and fruit trees that until recently were grown primarily in gardens now are appearing on balconies and patios and flourishing there, healthy and luxuriant, to the great delight of their caretakers. Many of them, when planted in the ground, are completely hardy; in containers, however, most need protection in winter.

GET TO KNOW YOUR PLANTS

The growing of plants in containers—mobile gardening—was popular even in ancient times. The orange tree and the rosemary plant allegedly were the first exotics introduced in Europe. Today, we grow plants from every climate zone in the world. Their needs are correspondingly diverse.

cool and temperate regions are making an appearance.

Basically, all plants—whatever their origin—that do not grow too large and that form shallow, rather than deep, roots are suitable for container culture. Root growth is a decisive criterion, because the plants, after all, will have to make do with the limited area of soil in the container; in fact, they should even be able to grow luxuriantly there. Because the living space of these plants (with a few exceptions, unusually hardy species and cultivars) is so confined, we have to protect them in winter.

Plants for the Balcony and Patio—The Major Groups

The groups listed below will provide an overview of the variety of plants that can be grown in containers. The plants included in each group have no common botanical background; they are a haphazard mixture, representing extremely diverse origins and ways of life.

<u>Classic tub plants</u> are evergreen or deciduous woody plants, herbaceous plants, herbs, or grasses from tropical and subtropical regions, including the Mediterranean. Most of them are perennials (aside from annual herbs and grasses) and are not resistant to harsh winters. Planted in the open, in a garden, they would survive the cold only under especially favorable conditions. Consequently, in northern

Feet in the water, head in the sun—in its native habitat, the oleander often grows near water.

Native Habitats and Climate Zones

Most of the plants that we grow in containers come from the tropics, subtropics, or warm temperate zones. These three climate belts, extending north and south from the equator, reach around the globe; beyond them, toward the poles, begin the cool temperate zones. Each climate zone, in turn, is subdivided into different regions. Often, the zones overlap, and atypical climate islands, conditioned by geographical peculiarities, may form within the zones.

It Depends on the Temperature

Whether a plant is suited for summer growing outdoors in our area depends on its requirements relative to its native habitat: Does it like continuous warmth or is it accustomed to great variations between daytime and nighttime temperatures? Tropical rain forest plants that need evenly warm temperatures cannot take summer holidays. They

are also known as hothouse or greenhouse plants (see page 14), which means that outside of their natural habitat they are able to thrive only if kept in warm rooms year in and year out. Accordingly, the following are suitable for balconies and patios:
• Plants from tropical mountainous areas where it is hot during the day, but at night, temperatures may drop into the frost range.
• Plants from tropical deserts, exposed to daytime temperatures that reach as high as 122°F (50°C) in the shade by day and often plummet almost to the freezing point at night.
• Plants from the subtropics, with temperatures that are warm by day and drop at night, warm summers, and mild winters. This category also includes plants from the so-called etesian climate. (This term is more often used to mean "Mediterranean climate," which borders the subtropics, but it also applies to central Chile, California, southern Australia, and South Africa.)

• Plants from our own latitudes, which by virtue of their origin are suited to our particular climate.

Other Local Conditions

In addition to the temperatures of their climate zones, in their native habitats plants are subject to other conditions to which they have adapted over the course of their evolution—in short, circumstances that now are the very foundation of their existence and that they urgently need in our care also. For example, the altitude at which a plant lives, the soil it has beneath its roots, and the amount of water it gets are decisive factors. Consequently, botanists break down the climate zones still further, into humid (wet), arid, and semiarid (dry and semidry) regions, as well as tropical high elevations.

Wet regions are found near large expanses of water and on the windward side of mountains. As a rule, the soils tend to be acid. Precipitation exceeds evaporation every month, all year round, and it may fall as rain or as dew. Wet regions exist in parts of Tenerife, East Asia, Central America, southern and southwestern South America, southeastern Australia, New Zealand, Tasmania, and the southwestern and southeastern United States. Plants native to wet regions love high atmospheric humidity (*Lotus, Camellia*), need a great deal of water (*Eucalyptus*), and can tolerate partial shade (*Pittosporum, Trachycarpus*).

Dry and semidry regions occur throughout most of the subtropics and in warm temperate zones. In semiarid regions, during many months the evaporation exceeds the precipitation; in arid regions, evaporation is greater than precipitation every month of the year. Dry, desert, and semidesert regions are found in Israel, Turkey, and southern North America, and on the leeward side of the Andes. Semidry regions occur along the Mediterranean and in Australia and South Africa. The soils tend to be poor. Plants native to dry and semidry regions can store water (*Agave*) or get by on little water (*Yucca*). They need enormous amounts of light, but in terms of their nutrient requirements, they are quite undemanding: These plants seldom need to be fertilized. This category includes plants from Australia and the Mediterranean area.

Tropical high elevations are characterized by warm days and cool nights. The ground may stay warm at night, but at very high altitudes it also can cool down to the frost range. It rains a great deal. The climate permits rapid metabolism of nutrients. Tropical high elevations occur chiefly in Central and South America.

The plants native to tropical high elevations require much light (*Bougainvillea*). With the exception of bougainvillea, they can tolerate low soil temperatures. In case the shoots die when temperatures are low, they can sprout again from the stem (*Passiflora, Datura*). Plants in this group need abundant water and nutrients (see Nightshade Family, page 16).

Cold House and Hothouse

Anyone reading about plants for the house or garden will often run across two concepts that relate to the overwintering of exotic plants. In the past, many container plants entered Europe as immigrants (see page 17) and needed a roof over their heads in winter. During the Renaissance, these shelters at first were primitive wooden sheds. Later, they developed into greenhouses made of glass, which, after the invention of heating, could be temperature-controlled according to the plants' requirements.

A cold house is warm in summer and cool (about 46° to 54°F [8°–12°C]) and bright in winter. In it grow numerous classic tub, conservatory, and balcony plants from the subtropics and Mediterranean regions. It is also suitable for overwintering flora from tropical high elevations.

A hothouse has a year-round temperature over 68°F (20°C) and high relative humidity. It shelters many indoor plants native to tropical rain forests. It is too warm for overwintering most balcony and tub plants.

Individual Life Span

The length of time a plant can live depends on the genetically determined life cycle characteristic of its species.

Annual plants live only one growing season; within a single year, germination takes place and seeds ripen. Only the seeds survive the winter; consequently, annuals cannot be overwintered. Examples: *Calendula officinalis, Lobelia erinus*.

Biennial plants form a shoot with leaves in the first year. During the second year, they flower and fruit, then die. Like annuals, they survive through their seeds. These plants have to be protected for one winter. Example: *Viola* x *wittrockiana* hybrids.

Perennial plants include herbaceous plants and woody plants.

Herbaceous plants have leaves that are not impervious to frost. The foliage dies in the cold season and is regenerated during the next growing season from roots, bulbs, tubers, and rhizomes. Herbaceous plants grow in gardens for many years. If grown in containers, where they have limited space, their life span usually is shorter, because they have no opportunity to fill their storage organs with adequate reserves.

Woody plants also are perennials. They form wood in their stems and branches, and their life span depends on their genetic programing. They are divided into the following categories, according to their growth: trees, shrubs, subshrubs, partly woody, and partly herbaceous. In addition, they are classified, according to their foliage, as needle-leaved woody plants or broad-leaved woody plants, which are further broken down into evergreen and deciduous groups.

What Families Have in Common

In reading the descriptions of the container flowers and tub plants you will note that certain plant families are quite heavily represented there. Inclusion in a family, however, means that these plants usually have identical or similar needs and a common evolutionary origin. Family membership, then, is a good basic guideline for plant care.

One Genus—Many Colors
Abutilon species and hybrids
1 Hybrid 'Pfitzers Rote'
2 Orange-flowering hybrid
3 Hybrid 'Ashford Red'
4 Hybrid 'Golden Fleece'
5 *Abutilon megapotamicum* 'Variegatum'
6 Hybrid 'Kentish Belle'

Low hydrangeas at the partially shaded doorway make a splendid reception.

Aster or Composite Family (Asteraceae or Compositae)

The sun-shaped flowers of these plants serve a symbolic purpose, informing us that these plants, without exception, thrive in sunny locations.

Examples:

Ageratum (*Ageratum*), *Asteriscus*, daisy (*Bellis*), Swan River daisy (*Brachycome iberidifolia*), pot marigold (*Calendula officinalis*), China aster (*Callistephus chinensis*), marguerite (*Chrysanthemum*), dahlia (*Dahlia*), African daisy (*Dimorphotheca*), fleabane (*Erigeron*), blue daisy (*Felicia*), gazania (*Gazania*), creeping zinnia (*Sanvitalia procumbens*), dusty miller (*Senecio*), marigold (*Tagetes*), Dahlberg daisy (*Thymophylla*), zinnia (*Zinnia*).

Nightshade Family (Solanaceae)

Remarkable here is the fact that these plants have a high requirement for nutrients and water. This need has its origin in their native habitat, where it rains a great deal and where abundant light and warmth are available in the daytime to convert the nutrients into plant matter. It is also interesting that toxic alkaloids are produced in this family, and nitrogen is necessary for their formation.

Examples:

Bastard jasmine (*Cestrum*), angel's trumpet (*Datura/Brugmansia*), *Iochroma*, tobacco plant (*Nicotiana*), *Petunia*, painted tongue (*Salpiglossis sinuata*), butterfly flower (*Schizanthus pinnatus*), and nightshade (*Solanum*).

Pea or Bean Family (Fabaceae or Leguminosae)

These plants include trees, shrubs, and vines with particularly magnificent flowers. They have a special talent: By means of nodule bacteria on their roots, they can adsorb nitrogen from the air. For this reason, plants in this family are fed very sparingly with nitrogen.

Examples:

Silk tree (*Albizia julibrissin*), flame bush (*Calliandra*), popcorn bush (*Cassia*), broom (*Cytisus*), coral tree (*Erythrina*), sweet pea (*Lathyrus*), trefoil (*Lotus*), scarlet runner bean (*Phaseolus*), pea (*Pisum*), and scarlet wisteria tree (*Sesbania tripettii*).

Myrtle Family (Myrtaceae)

Except for the Mediterranean myrtle, these plants originate predominantly in Australia and the neotropics (e.g., S. America), where they grow in acid, nutrient-poor soils. This means that they cannot tolerate hard, lime-rich water and heavy fertilization. They need a

great deal of light, in winter as well—not surprisingly, because they are members of the group of evergreen woody plants, which conduct photosynthesis the year round through their leaves, and this process cannot take place without light.
Examples:
Bottlebrush (*Callistemon*), Geraldton wax flower (*Chamelaucium*), eucalyptus (*Eucalyptus*), tea tree (*Leptospermum*), ironwood tree (*Metrosideros*), myrtle (*Myrtus*).

Mint Family (Labiatae or Lamiaceae)
This group includes many extremely tasty potherbs. Because sunlight and poor soil are necessary for the formation of the aromatic substances, these plants should neither stand in the shade nor be overfed. Incidentally, the aromatic substances (from a chemical standpoint, essential oils) are avoided by destructive insects, so Labiatae have little need for pesticides.
Examples:
Lemon balm (*Melissa officinalis*), lavender (*Lavandula*), basil (*Ocimum basilicum*), marjoram and oregano (*Origanum*), rosemary (*Rosmarinus officinalis*), sage (*Salvia*), thyme (*Thymus*).

Historical Facts About Container Gardening
The practice of raising plants in containers, rather than in the ground, satisfies the age-old human drive to cultivate and to tend; it is surely older than we can document. We find container gardening in all the highly advanced civilizations of ancient times. The Hanging Gardens of Semiramis, modeled on the old Babylonian temples that were made up of a series of terraces (ziggurats), were presumably the first roof and terrace gardens, and the Greeks' miniature flower gardens probably were the first gardens to contain potted plants. In the Hellenistic peristyle garden, flowers were cultivated in lead boxes. The Romans, adopting this practice, planted primarily useful plants in stone troughs that were filled with soil up to about 32 in. (80 cm) deep, and raised attractive specimens of woody plants singly in tubs. In the Far East, there was the ancient Chinese Penjing culture, which about A.D. 60 gave rise to the refined Japanese art of bonsai. Both were container cultures.

In the Middle Ages, the fairy tale splendor of the Oriental art of horticulture was mirrored in Europe. The Lion's Courtyard of the Alhambra originally was filled with large, exotically planted tubs. The plantings in the roof gardens of the imperial stronghold (Kaiserburg) in Nuremberg, laid out at the command of Emperor Friedrich II, are said to have been exceedingly luxuriant and exotic.

On the History of Tub Plants
In Europe, this history may begin with rosemary, which Romans or Benedictine monks took with them across the Alps from the sunny Mediterranean lands.
• In 794, rosemary was mentioned in the Capitulare de villis, Charlemagne's law concerning landed estates. A woodcut dated 1518 shows rosemary being grown in a wooden tub.
• As early as the twelfth century, citrus fruits were known in Europe.
• In the thirteenth century, Hildegard von Bingen recommended laurel as a medicinal plant.
• In 1550, sage-leaved rockroses (*Cistus salviifolius*) already were being grown in Silesia.
• In 1583, the first agave reached Stuttgart, and in the same year, the daughter of the Augsburg merchant Jakob Fugger is said to have carried the first bridal wreath of myrtle.
• In 1586, figs and pomegranates grew on the property of Laurentius Scholz in Breslau [Wroclaw].
• In 1597, there were oleanders in the prince bishop's garden in Eichstätt.
• Around 1600, the Portuguese introduced the orange tree to Europe.
• In 1619, one of the first orangeries was described as a "building of timberwork that is erected every year around Michaelmas Day."
• With the flourishing of horticulture in the early seventeenth century, and with the increase in plant imports from the Mediterranean countries and later from the rest of the world, the practice of growing plants of southern origin in tubs was adopted throughout Europe. The favorite of the Baroque period was the orange tree, and large sums were expended to procure and overwinter these trees. Soon, orangeries were so large that they became companion pieces to the palaces or houses of the princes and wealthy middle

class. The orangery of the *roi de soleil* at Versailles, near Paris, can still be admired today, with its sizable collection of old citrus trees. Other famous orangeries were created at Herrenhausen, near Hannover; at Sanssouci, near Potsdam; and at Schönbrunn, in Vienna. On October 11, 1814, the participants in the Congress of Vienna dined in the Schönbrunn orangery, which was almost 200 yards long.

On the History of Container Flowers
Container plants as we know them today grew out of the then-existing practice of gardening in containers, of the need to decorate architectural elements (balconies, balustrades, stairways), and (not least of all) of the availability of suitable flowers. The typical architecture of the houses in Alpine regions, with their rustic wooden balconies usually covered by a roof, soon proved to be an ideal backdrop for geraniums, fuchsias, begonias, and petunias, all flowers that breeders had first adapted during a previous century. Since World War II, the assortment of flowers on the market has been expanded constantly by imports from every country in the world and through intensive breeding efforts. Today, balconies, patios, and conservatories have become major recreation areas where we can enjoy nature at home, without the stress of an automobile trip. Professional gardeners take this wish into account and continue to provide us with new plant immigrants from the most remote corners of the globe.

Real balcony and patio gardeners can scarcely wait to prepare their overwintered plants for a new season (see page 25). Anticipation of the forthcoming splendor of their balcony and tub plants drives them to visit florists, nurseries, garden supply stores, and other such places where it is all too easy to fall into a frenzy of buying. Remember that every newly purchased plant will need space, a container, soil, food, and, above all, loving care. In choosing plants, come in nursery containers that are far too small.

What You Need for Plant Care

- Soil or other potting mediums
- Dibble
- Plastic bucket for mixing soil
- All-purpose garden shears
- Gardening gloves
- Gardener's trowel, hand cultivator, hand spade, hand digging fork
- Sharp knife
- Charcoal powder to disinfect cuts
- Assorted fertilizers
- Watering can (5 to 10½ quarts [5–10 L])
- Irrigation systems

Preparing the Containers

The most important principle is this: If at all possible, use only containers that have a drain hole. In containers that lack such a hole, the drainage layer (see page 26) must be two to three times deeper than usual, and the watering of plants in such containers requires considerable experience and intuitive feeling. If the containers are made of plastic, drain holes can be easily bored or made larger.

Before you begin planting, the container must be cleaned. Wash wooden containers several weeks beforehand, and paint them with a wood preservative (see Glossary) that plants can tolerate. Make sure to obtain the material for the drainage layer (see page 26) well ahead of time also.

Previously used containers, whatever material they are made of, should be cleaned with soft soap, hot water, and a coarse scrubbing brush. Algae and calcium efflorescences can be removed easily with a solution of vinegar and salt water— 2 qt (2 L) of vinegar to 1 qt (1 L) of water, with a handful of coarse table salt added. Apply the solution, give it time to act, then scrub the container with the brush and clean water and rinse well.

New containers made of clay or terra cotta should be soaked in water (in a rain barrel or bathtub) for one or two days before use, to wash out any harmful substances. In addition, this procedure will let the containers become saturated with water and prevent their absorbing too much moisture from the potting soil later.

My Tip: Get some bricks, wooden blocks, or a grid to place under wooden containers. This will permit air to circulate underneath the container and prevent it from rotting.

SUCCESSFUL CARE AND OVERWINTERING

Plants that bloom in profusion, look healthy, and grow magnificently are every gardener's dream, and one that can easily be attained. You just have to know how to use soil, water, and fertilizer properly, and keep a watchful eye on your charges in winter also.

keep in mind the intended location and your decorating needs (see pages 44–73). When it comes to tending your garden, however, the procedures are dictated by the specific requirements of the plants themselves, needs that often can be guessed simply by looking at the leaves (see pages 20–21).

Initial Care After Buying Your Plants

With the exception of outdoor woody and herbaceous plants, most container plants are brought out of greenhouses or glass-covered hotbeds in spring. Before they are planted, they need to become accustomed gradually to fresh air and the spring sunshine.

First, acclimate all your newly acquired plants for several days in a light, cool spot sheltered from the wind, rain, and sun. Placing them outside, where more light is available than indoors, will stimulate their growth and harden them off.

Check the soil ball. If it is dry, water the plant thoroughly, and pour off the excess water after half an hour.

Protect plants from late frost in the spring. This step is essential for flowering bulbs and outdoor woody plants in small containers. In the evening, cover tubs, pots, and boxes with a sheet of bubble wrap, burlap, newspaper, or straw mats.

Repot tub plants. Owing to space limitations and transportation requirements, new plants usually

Window Art—A Harmony of Colors

Balconies in Alpine regions are world-renowned for their decorative flowers, although it is far less warm there than in many other parts of the globe. It must be the light that, intensified by the high altitude, promotes the growth of such a wealth of flowers. Some credit also may be due to the time-tested tips that are passed down from one generation to the next. Petunias, red and pink hanging geraniums, and Swedish begonia are in bloom on the balcony. The window is framed by three geranium standards and numerous impatiens hybrids, with rose globes adding highlights.

Leaves Reveal Many Needs of Plants

Leaves are the vital arteries and the "green lungs" of plants. Important metabolic processes such as photosynthesis (see Glossary) and respiration take place in them, and essential oils and toxic substances can be manufactured there. The diversity of leaf forms, colors, and structures is no accident: It is a sign of adaptation to the habitat, and it tells us something about the needs of the plant.

Silvery, blue-green or gray-green leaves provide protection against light. These plants tolerate a great deal of sun. Examples: *Lotus berthelotii* (1), lavender, olive, dusty miller, rockrose.

Tender leaves with a high water content are typical of forest plants. These plants need filtered light. Examples: *Impatiens* hybrids (2), *Fuchsia,* tuberous begonia.

Leathery leaves have a surface that protects against evaporation. These plants can tolerate dryness. Examples: *Citrus* (3), laurel, Natal plum.

White-and-green or yellow-and-green variegated leaves contain reduced chlorophyll surfaces. These plants always need a site with more light (not sunny) than the green-leaved species or cultivars. Examples: Ivy (4), *Hibiscus,* flowering maple, *Euonymus.*

Large, soft leaves have unprotected evaporation surfaces. These plants need a great deal of water. Examples: Abyssinian banana or angel's trumpet (5).

Small leaves are an indication of reduced evaporation surfaces. These plants tolerate a great deal of sun and warmth, but no standing water. Examples: *Lotus berthelotii* (1), blue daisy, myrtle (6), tea tree, rosemary.

Fleshy (succulent) leaves are water reservoirs. These plants withstand dry periods with great ease. Examples: *Agave,* Livingstone daisy, or rose moss (7).

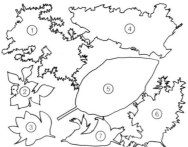

A minipond on the patio. Cypress grass, spiked purple loosestrife, and white iris clearly are enjoying it here.

The Best Potting Soil

An assortment of potting mediums is available. Nevertheless, a good potting soil has to satisfy the specific requirements of the plant and, in addition, meet the following criteria. It must:
• contain adequate amounts of the major nutrients and trace elements.
• give the plants support and stability.
• be able to store and release water.
• remain well aerated and friable.
• be a good buffer in the event of improper watering and fertilization.
• be free of disease-causing organisms, pests, weed seeds, and substances that would harm the plant.
<u>All-purpose soil</u> is a commercial mix basically composed of humus, clay, peat moss, vermiculite, perlite, and in some cases fertilizer and other soil conditioners, such as sand. This soil is formulated to accommodate the requirements of a large variety of plants, thus it is a useful potting mix for most container plants.

<u>Soilless potting mix</u> (also called Cornell mix) generally consists of peat moss, vermiculite, perlite, as well as nutrients and trace elements. This medium is used for seed sowing because it retains moisture and nutrients. Soilless mixes especially formulated for container gardening are also available; these include sphagnum moss and other ingredients that further increase the mix's water-retaining properties.
Important: Soilless mediums are extremely light and need to have soil, sand, or both added to them when used for setting top-heavy plants, like trees or shrubs, in containers.
<u>Special growing media</u> intended for specific types of plants are available in the market; among them are African violet soil, cactus soil, as well as orchid and epiphyte planting materials.
In addition, mediums for hydroculture are offered in the market. These consist of potsherds, balls, pellets, or granules of clay.

Garden soil is best suited for container gardening when it is loamy, rich in humus, and sandy. Its advantages: It is heavy and can keep containers from tipping over even on windy days. People who have gardens can get it absolutely free. Its disadvantages: It is full of weed seeds, insect larvae, and its suitability is not as dependable as that of a packaged all-purpose mix of good quality. Garden owners who need large quantities of potting soil can mix three parts of good garden soil with three parts of well-decayed, sifted compost, two parts of peat, and two parts of sand.
Alternative: Those without a garden can use packaged topsoil (choose one that contains a lot of organic matter) mixed with equal parts of peat moss and sand or perlite.

Watering Plants Properly

How much and how often to water depends on the particular needs of a plant species, the container, the site, the weather, and the season. Basically, all plants can withstand short-term dryness far better than a constantly wet root ball that has no room for air, so that the roots inevitably rot.

The Water

It should be warmed by the sun and not be overly hard. Ideally, fill your watering cans in the morning and let the water stand in them until warm. Tap water, as long as it does not exceed 13 mg/L of dissolved salts is suitable for almost all container plants (your local waterworks can provide this information, if in doubt). If the plants are sensitive to lime (myrtles, rhododendrons, hydrangeas), soften the water. Suspend a bag filled with peat (replace the peat each time if the water contains much limestone) in the water, or use a softening agent (available in some garden- or aquarium-supply stores). Rain water from the barrel is still recommended, despite possible pollution, especially in the case of plants sensitive to lime.

How to Water

As a rule, container plants are watered from above. This method permits the water and nutrient salts (fertilizer) to trickle down gradually so that the fine roots receive sufficient water. For hanging plants, which on hot days often become completely dry in their individual pots, an immersion bath frequently is the best method of watering. Plunge the entire potted ball, along with the container, into a bucket of water until no more air bubbles rise to the surface. This is a sign that the ball is saturated with water. Even limp plants will perk up again in no time. Normal watering often is ineffective, because an extremely dry root ball will let the water run through without absorbing it. On very hot days, there is no need to remove excess water or dripping water in the saucer, unless it is dripping onto a neighboring plant. Some plants, such as angel's trumpet, banana plants, or oleanders, enjoy brief "footbaths" in the middle of summer.
More watering is necessary:
• during the peak growing season in summer.

• in locations with full sun and in windy locations.
• when summer temperatures are high and there is no precipitation (often, plants need water twice a day).
• with loamy and peaty potting soils.
• for plants in clay and terra cotta pots.
Less watering is needed:
• at the start of the growing season in spring.
• in shady spots outdoors that are sheltered from wind.
• in cool, rainy weather.
• for plants with a mulch cover or underplanting.
• for plants in plastic containers.
• during overwintering.

When to Water

The season determines when you should water your plants. In the summer, you can water them in the morning or the evening, but never at midday (temperature shock) and certainly never in the blazing sun (the drops of water act as a magnifying glass causing burning of the leaves).
In the winter, water before noon, so the roots can absorb the water before evening.

Custom-tailored Fertilizing

It is crucial to supply nutrients to plants that are grown in containers with a limited amount of soil. The nutrients contained in the potting soil are depleted quickly and have to be replenished through fertilization.
The chief nutrients that all plants require if they are to grow and flower are nitrogen (N), phosphorous (P), potassium (K), and magnesium (Mg). In addition, trace elements such as iron, copper, manganese, molybdenum, zinc, and boron are essential to the smooth operation of the plants' vital processes.
Compound fertilizers with minerals. The important nutrients and trace elements usually are present in these fertilizers as chemical salts, and in this form they can be absorbed quickly by plants. Compound fertilizers with minerals are available in liquid, powdered, and solid (as fertilizer spikes) forms. They are highly suitable for container flowers, tub plants, vegetables, and ornamental plants during the main growing season, from May to August.
Slow-release fertilizers also contain

minerals. In this case, however, the nutrient salts are bound in such a way that they are released very slowly (over the course of 10 to 12 weeks) as the plants are watered. Consequently, there is no danger that the roots will suffer burn damage. It is best to mix slow-release fertilizer with the potting soil when you set the plants in the containers (see pages 26–27).
Organic and mineral compound fertilizers have the major nutrients and trace elements bound not only to minerals, but also to organic substances. These fertilizers also are appropriate for all the plant groups mentioned under Compound Fertilizers. This category also includes specially formulated organic fertilizers, for flowers, tub plants, vegetables, roses, conifers, rhododendrons, and so on.
Here, too, the major nutrients are precisely formulated for the needs of the specific plant group. This is reflected in the percentages of available nitrogen, phosphorus, and potassium, which should be listed on the package (for example, 14 + 7 + 14 or 14/7/14 means 14% nitrogen, 7% phosphorous oxide, and 14% potassium oxide).
Organic fertilizers such as bone meal, blood meal, horn and hoof meal, or composted manure have only limited usefulness in container culture. Their active ingredients first have to be broken down by microorganisms in the soil. Because these microorganisms are much too poorly developed in the limited soil available, the nutrients often are released somewhat late.

The Golden Rules of Fertilization

• Often and in low doses is preferable to seldom and in high doses, when it comes to applying fertilizer. A low dose is one-half to one-third of the recommended dosage—as a rule, about ½ teaspoon (2–3 g or ml) for 1 qt (1 L) of water. This holds especially true for plants that are sensitive to salt, such as red salvia, Chusan palm, creeping zinnia, *Centradenia, Lobelia*, and snapdragon.
• Newly acquired plants or plants that have been overwintered and then repotted should be fertilized only after four to six weeks.
• Do not fertilize overwintered but not repotted plants until they are sprouting profusely.
• If slow-release fertilizer was

mixed with the potting soil, wait ten weeks after repotting before fertilizing again.
- Fertilize woody plants only until August, so that the wood can mature thoroughly.
- For plants that are sensitive to lime—such as myrtles, rhododendrons, and hydrangeas—use a specially formulated fertilizer.

Appropriate Overwintering

With few exceptions, all plants grown in containers with a limited volume of soil have to be protected from freezing temperatures (see pages 28–29). This applies also to plants that in general are frost-hardy because their root balls are less protected in the container than in the ground, and without proper care they would quickly become nothing more than frozen lumps. Unless winters are extremely mild, exotics accustomed to warmth have to be taken indoors; but garden plants in containers—given proper protection—can stay outdoors, an arrangement that will solve many a problem of space.

The shorter the stay in their winter quarters—which rarely offer optimal conditions—the less the plants will be weakened. Our container plants come from a variety of regions, and some are thoroughly accustomed to extreme cold, which for many is even a necessity. For example, the onset of colder

A Garden High in the Air

This balcony with southern exposure is a good place to grow light-hungry plants such as white bellflowers, clematis, bougainvillea, plumbago, parrot's beak, petunias, Swedish begonia, and marguerite chrysanthemums (left to right), not to mention the Virginia creeper at the arched clerestory window, whose foliage turns a particularly lovely color in fall, with the right light levels.

weather in fall halts growth in all woody plants and thus promotes the maturing of the wood. In spring, cool weather prevents many woody plants (crape myrtle, pomegranate) from prematurely flushing with weak shoots. Consequently, keeping in mind each individual plant's tolerance of cold weather, set appropriate deadlines for moving the plants into their winter quarters and for bringing them outdoors again. This will contribute to your plants' vitality and health.

Some plants cannot tolerate any frost at all, for example tropical specimens and sensitive evergreens, such as Flowering maple, *Bougainvillea, Camellia, Cycas, Cassia, Citrus* species, *Calliandra tweedii, Hibiscus,* banana, passionflower, Brazilian glorybush, and heliotrope. They have to be put inside before frost sets in. Do not bring them back out until after the last frost date in May.

Short periods at temperatures as low as 23°F (–5°C) are tolerable for a few subtropical species from the Mediterranean area, South Africa, South America, and Australia, for example Killarney strawberry tree, *Aucuba,* plumbago, bottlebrush, *Pittosporum, Chamaerops humilis,* carob, olive, and myrtle. Only when temperatures below 23°F (–5°C) persist (high-pressure weather situation) should these plants be brought indoors, and they are ready to return outdoors by the beginning of May. Some important prerequisites: The plants have to be several years old, sturdy, and mature; in their winter quarters, they should not have been weakened by standing in a site that is excessively warm and dark. If the weatherman predicts freezing temperatures at night, protect the large plants with rush mats or bubble wrap, and bring the small pots indoors.

Short periods at temperatures as low as 14°F (–10°C) are acceptable for Mexican orange, Chusan palm, crape myrtle, pomegranate, laurel, and mastic shrub.

If temperatures below 14°F (–10°C) persist, bring these plants in and keep them indoors until mid-April. The restrictions listed above apply to these plants also.

Winter Quarters in and near the House

The ideal winter location for almost all container plants is a place that is

airy and light, with a temperature between 41° and 50°F (5 to 10°C). These conditions, however, truly can be attained only in a greenhouse or a conservatory. In lieu of these places, however, we have more or less ideal sites available: cellars, garages, attics, light wells, or unheated rooms. Warm, dark winter quarters are completely unsuitable. Common container plants that must have light in winter are evergreen coniferous and deciduous trees, species of bamboo, light-hungry plants like bottlebrush, and plants that bloom in the winter, such as camellias.

If need be, some plants can overwinter in a dark place; these are specimens that have been severely cut back and those that shed their leaves. Bulbous and tuberous plants do not need light until spring.

Rule of thumb: The brighter the winter quarters are, the warmer they can be. The darker they are, the cooler they must be.

Spring Maintenance and Acclimation

With the increase in daylight in early March, plants begin to shoot forth anew. At this time, all plants—especially those that were overwintered in the dark—have to get used to the light again. It is time for them to sprout and form new leaves. Now a spring maintenance is also on the agenda:
- Cut off any of the plants' rank growth or parts that were affected by dryness, cold, or excessive heat in their winter location.
- Where recommended (see Plant Portraits, pages 86–227), perform spring pruning.
- If necessary, repot tub plants (see pages 26–27).
- Remove any protective material surrounding the plants.
- Give aquatic plants new soil and new water.

To acclimate the tub plants after moving them back outdoors, put all of them, even those that love sunlight, in a shady spot, sheltered from the wind, for two weeks. This precaution will keep the leaves and shoots from being damaged by sunburn or cold.

The onset of growth should be approached slowly. At the beginning, give the plants only a little water, and increase the amount gradually as they begin to flush.

HOW TO

Spring and Summer Care

Daily pruning, or deadheading, of spent flowers will prevent spermatogenesis, encourage the development of new blooms, and keep the plants healthy and attractive. Break them off at the node (geraniums), cut them off, or pinch them off (other container flowers).

After hard cutting back—by about one-half—petunias will sprout again from below and flower as prolifically as before. Cut them back after the first array of flowers in late July or early August, when the plants develop rank growth and begin to become floppy.

Protection against cold and rain is offered in the spring and from the end of August by hoods made of clear plastic sheets with vents. Tomatoes, peppers, eggplants, and other plants sensitive to cold will still be able to ripen under this covering, and you can prolong your harvest.

Planting and Repotting

The planting and repotting season begins in late February and continues until the end of May. Spring bloomers are repotted after the blooming period. Young plants are set in the soil. Repotting applies to older plants; it is necessary:
• if the plant is completely root-bound.
• if the potting soil is so old and caked that it no longer can absorb water properly when the plant is watered.
• if the plant shows clear symptoms of deficiency or is sickly.
• every year for tub plants in need of nutrients, such as *Datura/Brugmansia*, *Fuchsia*, oleander, marguerite chrysanthemums, and Abyssinian banana!

New soil will dispense more nutrients to the plant and give it stability.

The new container for small plants has to be over ¾ in. (2 cm) larger in circumference than the root ball; for larger plants, use a container 2 to 4 in. (5–10 cm) bigger around than the ball.

Pot them this way: The plants will lift out more easily if you take them out of plastic pots when the root ball is dry, out of clay pots when the ball is wet.
• Shake the old soil off the ball.
• Shorten excessively long roots, and cut off withered or decayed roots.
• The drainage layer (see drawing, Avoid Standing Water) is important. This layer ought to be about 2 in. (5 cm) high in window boxes and at least 4 in. (10 cm) high in tubs. It may consist of sand, gravel, clay granules, or potsherds. On top of this layer, spread a piece of burlap so that it reaches a few inches up the sides of the container. It will prevent the drain hole and drainage layer from becoming clogged by soil.
• Cover the burlap with about 1 or 2 in. (3–5 cm) of potting soil.
• Place the plant in the center. Fill the container with potting soil and press it down.
• Water the plant, and put it in a bright, slightly warm spot.

Avoid Standing Water!

This is how the inside of a container for any relatively large plant should look: Above the drain hole for water is a drainage layer, and between this layer and the potting soil is a piece of burlap to keep soil from getting into the drainage and blocking it.

Cutting the Roots for Repotting

1 Plants that develop profuse roots, such as angel's trumpet or oleander, can be repotted in the same pot.
2 Using a sharp knife, reduce the size of the root ball so as to leave ¾ to 1 in. (2–3 cm) on all sides to accommodate new soil.
3 Put in the drainage layer and some soil. Place the ball in the center. Add more soil, and press it down firmly.

Replacing the Potting Soil for Large Plants

At some point, owing to space constraints, the maximum container size will have been reached; then the plant will need to remain in the same pot, but its soil must be renewed.

Cutting the roots (see drawing, Cutting the Roots for Repotting) will reduce the size of the ball so that the plant has room for new soil, even in the old container. You might also cut the shoots back to preserve the equilibrium between the roots and the shoots.

Replacing the top layer of soil is a temporary measure, to be taken if, for example, the container is too heavy to handle or if you cannot get the plant out of its container. Scraping carefully, remove as much old soil as possible from the surface and replace it with new material to which you have added a slow-release fertilizer.

Pinching Out, Cutting, Pruning

Pinching out (see drawing, Pinching Out Spurs) promotes luxuriant branching and more flower shoots.

Cutting enhances the natural appearance of the plant (see drawing, After hard cutting back) or gives it an attractive shape (see Training and Shaping Plants, page 51). The plant will branch below the place where it was cut. Important: Always angle the cut away from the bud, so that no water can run onto the bud (see drawing, Cutting Correctly).

Pruning (see drawing, Daily Pruning) should be done at regular intervals, daily, if possible. Deadhead spent flowers and remove wilted leaves to help preserve the plant's health. This procedure also will prevent spermatogenesis—the development of male reproductive cells—which would deplete the energies of the plant.

Automatic Irrigation

Balcony and tub plants have to be watered regularly and well, because soil dries out faster in containers than in the ground. If you go away for a weekend or on vacation, use short-term or long-term watering systems (see drawings, Fully Automatic Long-term Irrigation, Short-term Irrigation), available in garden supply stores, to help with plant care. These systems operate on the principle of capillary action. Here are some examples:
- Flower boxes with a water reservoir
- Watering systems with wicks and wick mats
- Drip irrigation systems with ceramic cones or emitters
- Automatic irrigation systems, some of which are computer-controlled

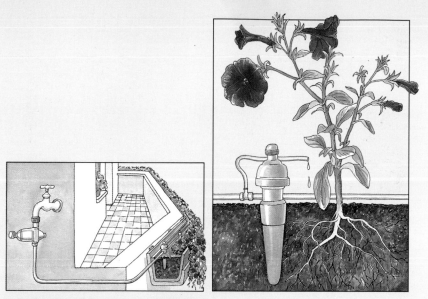

Fully Automatic Long-term Irrigation

1 Water intake from the water lines is controlled by a pressure reducer. The droppers, which are attached to a main pipe, are stuck in the soil.
2 When the soil is dry, suction pressure is created in the ceramic cones and transmitted to a valve, which then opens and lets water drip.

Short-term Irrigation

1 Individual pots can be supplied from an elevated container of water via a wick. Important: The wick should not sag.
2 Several individual pots (made of clay) will obtain moisture over a period of days if they are bedded in water-saturated clay granules or wet sand.
3 Flower boxes with a built-in water storage tank. The water is sucked out of the tank beneath the container's double bottom by means of a wick. The reservoir is replenished via a filler pipe.

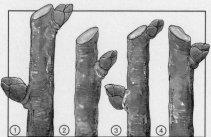

Cutting Correctly

Right: Several millimeters above a bud, make a cut at an angle, slanted away from the bud (1).
Wrong: The distances from the bud are too great (2), too small (3), or the cut is angled toward the bud (4).

Pinching Out Buds for Bushy Growth

1 With young plants, pinch off the main shoot as soon as it has reached the desired height. This will stimulate the formation of side shoots.
2 Keep pinching off the tips of the shoots to encourage further branching.

HOW TO

Moving Indoors and Overwintering

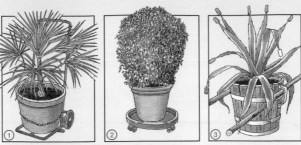

Aids for Moving Plants Indoors

1 For transporting large, heavy pots, there are extremely sturdy dollies with a carrying capacity of about 440 lb (200 kg).

2 A rolling plant stand is practical and a real energy-saver when you are cleaning up and moving plants indoors or outdoors.

3 For heavy tubs there are sturdy carrying bars that are inserted in the tub's handles.

Rules for Overwintering

1 Evergreens and light-hungry plants need to winter over in a bright spot.

2 Heavily-cut-back plants and deciduous plants, as well as species that need a winter rest or will tolerate one if need be, can spend the winter in a dark location.

Winter Protection Outdoors

Insulate the pot from beneath with a thick slab of wood or Styrofoam. Wrap the container with a sheet of bubble wrap. Use fir branches to cover portions affected by frost—for example, the graft points of roses.

Preparations for Overwintering Indoors

Moving the plants indoors is a time-consuming, exhausting task that requires plenty of organization.

• Ahead of time, arrange for equipment to help you move the plants (see drawings, Aids for Moving Plants Indoors), and make sure you have suitable overwintering sites ready.

• Starting in early September, make sure the root ball does not get overly wet; this will reduce the likelihood of the plant's developing rot in its winter quarters.

• If the plants can tolerate it, cut them back before you move them indoors, to gain space.

The Right Time to Move Indoors

Do not move all the plants at once when the temperature first drops below the freezing point (often in late September, at night); take into account each plant's individual tolerance for cold weather (see page 25 and specific entries in individual plant portraits). Rule of thumb: Herbaceous plants generally are more sensitive than woody ones, and evergreen woody plants tolerate cold less well than do deciduous ones.

Care in Winter Quarters

Inspect your plants once a week.

• Periodically remove fallen, dry, or moldy leaves.

• Check the plants for pest infestations and immediately take action to control any damage.

• On frost-free days, give the plants as much fresh air as possible.

• Do not let the root ball dry out completely. Evergreens, in particular, give off water constantly and need to be watered in their winter quarters also.

Overwintering Geraniums Properly

1 Before overwintering, prune the geraniums thoroughly, removing all the flowers and all withered leaves.

2 During the overwintering period, keep removing the rank growth to prevent needless weakening of the plant.

3 After overwintering, cut the plant back to three eyes above the lignified stems. Put it in a bright, warmer spot.

Overwintering Outdoors

All plants grown in large and small containers can spend the winter outside—if they are hardy or almost hardy when grown in the ground. If freezing temperatures threaten to persist, move the containers to a spot that is sheltered from wind and rain. Climbing woody plants on trellises have to be protected.

Large tubs are wrapped: Surround them with a thick sheet of bubble wrap (see drawing, Winter Protection Outdoors) or some other insulating material.

Aboveground plant parts are protected with pine branches or straw if a particular species is sensitive (roses, for example; see drawing, Winter Protection Outdoors) or in areas where cold weather continues for long periods. Otherwise, it is sufficient to toss an old wool blanket over the plant in an extremely hard freeze or to protect it by leaning rush mats against it (see drawing, Protecting Large Woody Plants).

Evergreens such as bamboo or rhododendron need not be covered, and they need to be protected with rush matting only during lengthy spells of frost and intense winter sun (see drawing, Protecting Large Woody Plants). On frost-free days, water the plants with lukewarm water.

Small pots can be sunk in a box or bowl (see drawing, Protecting Small Woody Plants). Put several in the chosen container, and fill the spaces between them with insulating material (Styrofoam chips, wood shavings or chips, newspaper). Cover the top with pine branches.

Boxes with bulbs or hardy container flowers (*Bellis, Viola*) should be set on the floor of the balcony or patio and covered with pine branches.

Overwintering Aquatics

Who would not like to have a small pond in a tub or barrel on the balcony or the patio? Many people, however, are afraid of overwintering. Success in overwintering of aquatic plants depends on the planting. Basically, you should choose robust outdoor aquatics that need a winter rest period in any event. If the containers are fairly small, drain the water before the first frosty spells, cover the plants with wet leaves, and place them—in their containers—in a dark room where the temperature stays just above freezing (garage, cellar, laundry room).

If the containers are extremely heavy (large stone troughs), grow the plants in baskets or other containers inside the heavy ones for greater ease in moving. Simply remove the holders with the plants in fall and overwinter them in large bowls or basins.

Important: Do not allow aquatics to dry out completely in their winter quarters.

Safety Measures

1 When you move citrus plants indoors, the thorns may tear your clothing or scratch your skin. Therefore, tie the crown of leaves tightly together, using stout twine.
2 You can injure yourself on the needle-sharp leaves of agaves. Before moving them indoors, simply stick corks on the tips.

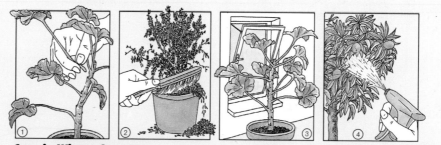

Care in Winter Quarters

1 Immediately remove any leaves that look wilted, moldy, yellow, or brown. This applies not only to geraniums, but also to all other balcony and tub plants.
2 Periodically get rid of fallen leaves to prevent decay.
3 On frost-free days, ventilate for a few hours to prevent fungal diseases.
4 If an infestation of insects occurs, spray plant with a pesticide at once. If necessary, repeat the treatment several times, following the directions on the package.

Protecting Large Woody Plants

Hardy woody plants or climbing plants, as well as bamboo, can be safeguarded against heavy frost and the drying effects of the sun with rush mats leaned at a slant against the wall. Remove the covering on frost-free days.

Protecting Small Woody Plants

Small woody plants can be overwintered in a large crate or basin. Place them on top of a drainage layer. Fill the spaces in between with insulating material (wood shavings or chips, newspaper), and cover the top with fir brush.

FIRST AID FOR YOUR PLANTS

Ladybugs consume vast quantities of plant lice, or aphids, and thus benefit all plants that grow outdoors. Often, however, their numbers are too few on balconies and patios, and the plants are powerless against other pests and diseases. Only prevention and prompt, determined efforts to combat pest and disease attacks can help.

Improper care weakens plants and makes them vulnerable, but it is not the sole cause of diseases and infestations. Environmental factors also play a major role. Weather conditions that vary from region to region and from year to year, the progressive alteration of the landscape by new construction, the destruction of biotopes that keep pests and diseases under control, the use of toxic chemicals, and many other influences ensure that there are years in which invasions of scale, aphids, and miners suddenly increase, bringing about an abominable state of affairs.

Preventive Measures

Prevention is always better than a cure: An optimal location, care that is tailored to the individual requirements of the plant (see Plant Portraits, pages 86–227), proper overwintering, and the observation of an acclimation period are important steps toward protecting your plants. Some additional measures follow:

Proper hygiene for containers and plants: Use only clean containers for your plants. Scrub used ones vigorously with hot, soapy water before putting plants in them again. Periodically remove leaves and flowers that look withered, decayed, or sickly. Disinfect large cut surfaces with powdered charcoal.

Regular plant check-ups: Check your plants at regular intervals all year long, especially when they are in winter quarters (see page 29). Aphids are found frequently at the shoot tips and buds. Keep an eye on the undersides of the leaves also. These measures will help you spot many pests and diseases in the initial stages, when they are easier to control. Glazed, sticky leaves (from the excreta of the insects) are an indication that aphids, scale, or whiteflies are feasting on the sap of the leaves above.

Strengthening plant tissue: During the growth period, water your plants regularly with concoctions prepared from horsetail, nettles, comfrey, or milfoil. The silicic acid they contain will strengthen the plant tissue and make it more resistant to voracious insects. There are also commercially available products that contain a combination of natural fatty acids and plant extracts to effectively bolster a plant's resistance to fungal diseases. Spray the plants—even if they are bare of leaves in the winter—with an aromatic spray made up of essential oils of plant origin. The hormones in the spray will activate plant growth during the growing season, and the essential oils will help control bacteria and fungi the year round.

Valuable minerals and trace elements to strengthen the plants can be supplied by healing earth (one pinch in 1 qt [1 L] of water in your watering can), mineral powder, or brown algae (kelp) extract.

All the products mentioned here can be found in most garden supply stores. The herbs and healing earth also are available in drugstores, pharmacies, health food or natural food stores.

Keeping the leaves dry: If possible, sprinkle water only on the soil surface. Wet foliage is susceptible to leaf eelworms, sunburn, and fungal infections.

The right company: Give your plants neighbors that will help combat pests. Marigolds, calendulas, or morning-glories will attract syrphid flies—beelike or wasplike flies whose larva feed on aphids. Nasturtiums and garden cress also will keep woolly aphids away from small fruit trees in pots. Thyme and garlic prevent fungal infections—in roses and strawberries, for example—and lavender will dispel ants.

An Ounce of Prevention Is Worth a Pound of Cure
Pests and diseases will be less common if, as in this photo, you put individual specimens of totally different species together and make sure that air can circulate around the containers and plants.

Proper plant spacing: Avoid placing the containers too close together, especially in enclosed areas or balconies. Good air circulation—without drafts—is still the best safeguard against fungi.

Appropriate fertilization: Do not overfeed the plants, especially with nitrogen, which makes plant tissue spongy and susceptible to fungal infections. Fertilize woody plants only until August, so that the wood can mature, or harden, and be immune to diseases and pests while the plants are in their winter quarters.

Protection from weather factors: In rainy summers, put plants that have low tolerance for dampness in a covered spot. Protect tender-leaved plants from wind and strong drafts, and give plants sensitive to cold some protection against frost.

Methods of Control

Do not always reach immediately for the poison. In many cases, you can achieve the desired result by "harmless" means.

Hand control will put a stop to the pests' reproduction for the time being. It includes the following:
• Removing afflicted or diseased parts of the plant.

• Picking off or brushing off the creatures. Sclerophyllous plants—plants with thickened, hardened leaves—can also be sprayed with a strong stream of water from the garden hose. Important: Do not spray them in full sun, and make sure the plant has time to dry completely by evening.

Alternative control makes use of several means—not always reliable—favored by organic gardeners:
• Stinging nettle extract (see recipe, page 35) can be used to spray aphids.
• Horsetail broth (see recipe, page 35) is effective against mildew.
• Garlic tea (see recipe, page 35) is useful in controlling fungal infections.
• Wormwood tea (see recipe, page 35) can be sprayed on aphids, leaf-eating beetles, sawyer wasps, apple moths, pea gall gnats, cherry fruit flies, and ants.

Biological pest control among other means consists of employing beneficial insects against pests. This method works best in enclosed areas. Successful outdoors (as well as on balconies and patios) are the following control agents:
• Predatory gall gnats and lacewing flies used against aphids (this defense is not always entirely successful).
• Parasitic nematodes (eelworms) used to control weevils, or snout beetles. In order to develop, however, they need moist soil and temperatures above 55° F (13° C).
• *Bacillus thuringiensis* used to combat caterpillars.

Other biological means are fungicides that contain lecithin; diatomaceous earth, which dries up the larvae of harmful insects and can be dusted on plants to control aphids and other pests; and sprays, mists, and powdered insecticides that contain pyrethrum, derived from the blossoms of a species of chrysanthemum. Insecticides containing this substance are quickly broken down on the plants and in the soil. Pyrethrum is not dangerous to bees, but it is harmful to some beneficial insects—such as ladybugs, syrphid flies, and lacewing flies—and to fish.

Warning: If they touch open wounds or diseased skin or get into the bloodstream, insecticides that contain pyrethrum are also highly poisonous to humans.

Biotechnical pest controls make use of the pests' natural reactions to physical or chemical stimuli. Yellow sticky cards or boards are insect catchers that are coated with glue. By virtue of their color, they attract whiteflies, leaf miner flies, fickle midges, and other flying insects, including some beneficial ones. Consequently, use them only in winter quarters, not outdoors!

Chemical pest controls are used when all other measures have failed, or in the case of extremely valuable plants, when you seek quick action and are unwilling to risk any unnecessary damage.
• Insecticides are effective against insects and can be sprayed, poured, sprinkled on the potting soil, or (if the container is small) stuck into the soil in the form of spikes.
• Acaricides destroy mites.
• Fungicides are antifungal agents.
• Bactericides are not approved for general use in this country.
• Miscible oils—for example, white oils such as paraffin—are chemical agents of natural origin. They clog the respiratory organs of the insects.
• Pesticidal soaps—based, for example, on the potassium salts of natural fatty acids—penetrate the body of the insect. They affect the cell membranes and prevent respiration, so that the pests quickly die.

Natural Pesticides

Algae extract is obtained from a brown alga (*Ascophyllum nodosum*). It contains 70 different substances, such as trace elements, vitamins, hormones, enzymes, proteins, and amino acids, that stimulate growth and strengthen the plant. Like a foliar fertilizer, it is sprayed on the plant.

Diatomaceous earth dries up the larvae of insects and can be dusted on to control aphids, slugs, and other pests.

Essential oils encourage growth and have an antiseptic and fungicidal effect. They are found in aromatic sprays and in preparations containing garlic, sage, thyme, onion, valerian, and camomile.

Silicic acid is a silicum compound that strengthens tissue. It is found in mineral powder, healing earth, and siliceous earth, and in preparations containing horsetail, comfrey, stinging nettle, and milfoil.

Lecithin, known as a nerve-strengthening agent and food additive, is obtained principally from soybeans. Lecithin strengthens the leaf surface and is extremely effective against powdery mildew.

Insecticidal soaps, based, for example, on the potassium salts of natural fatty acids, penetrate the insect's body. They affect the cell membrane and prevent respiration, causing the pests to die quickly.

Paraffin, or white oil, is a refined petroleum product used in pharmacies as a basis for ointments. It blocks the respiratory organs of harmful insects.

Pyrethrum extract is obtained from the flowers of *Chrysanthemum cinerariifolium*, grown as a crop in Africa. The extract affects the nervous system of cold-blooded creatures—insects and arachnids (and fish), for example—but does not harm bees.

Atrium courtyards offer a protective microclimate that many plants find pleasing.

All the chemical products listed (except bactericides) are available in garden supply stores. If you have identified the pest or the disease, you will be offered a product designed to control that particular problem. The drawings (see pages 36–37) depicting various kinds of damage will help you make the correct diagnosis.

Things to Watch Out for
• Do not use highly toxic agents marked with a warning.
• Apply agents that are harmful to bees only in exceptional cases—and then only late in the evening.
• For ecological reasons, use only sprays that contain no chlorofluorocarbons or that employ air as a propellant.
• Follow the directions for use and the dosage instructions exactly. Observe the recommended intervals between spraying, so that you will destroy the next generation of pests as well.
• Do not breathe any of the mist.

• Wear gloves when handling pesticides.
• Keep pesticides in their original packages and out of reach of children and pets. Do not store them along with food or pet foods, and make sure the containers are tightly closed.
• Do not save any leftover substances (the effectiveness of most preparations diminishes rapidly), and do not throw them in your household garbage containers. Instead, take them to your local collection site for discarding toxic substances.

Controlling Physiological Damage
When a plant suffers physiological damage, its roots or leaves may be so impaired that they cannot carry out their tasks (transporting water and nutrients for photosynthesis) as well as they should.
Developmental disturbances: Check the roots. If necessary, remove the damaged parts of the roots (see

below). Move the plant to a better location, and improve the supply of nutrients. Often, air pollution may be the culprit.
Reluctance to blossom: Improper care—such as an excessively dark or cold location, overfertilization with nitrogen, and inappropriate overwintering—should be remedied.
Involuted leaves: Water the plant thoroughly. Remove the excess water and put the plant in a cooler spot.
Pale leaves (chlorosis): Dissolve chelated iron or algae extract in water, as directed, then spray it on the leaves or use it to water the plant. Soften the water. Repot the plant in spring.
Sunburn: Shade the plant at once or change its location. Remove burned leaves.
Root damage: Take the plant out of its pot, remove the diseased (brown) roots with a clean, sharp knife, dust the cut surfaces with charcoal powder, and set the plant in new potting soil.

Controlling Pests

Spider mites: Keep the plant cooler, shadier, and wetter than usual. Water it generously on hot days. Drench it thoroughly with luke-warm water, or spray it several times with a pesticide that kills spider mites. You may need to switch to another preparation later, because the mites develop resistance quickly. Alternatively, spray soft-leaved plants with a pesticidal soap; hard-leaved ones, with a paraffin product (both available in garden supply stores). You may need to repeat the treatment.

Scale, woolly aphids, and mealy-bugs: Scrape off the scales and remove the cocoons. Wash the glazed, sticky honeydew and black, sooty mold off the leaves. Apply paraffin or insecticides.

Aphids: Stinging nettle extract (see recipe, right), wormwood tea (see recipe, right), a pesticidal soap (commercially available), pyrethrum spray, and other insecticides are effective. Watch out for ants, which keep aphids as "milk cows" and fight off their natural enemies.

Whiteflies: Use insecticide and in winter quarters, also yellow sticky cards or boards.

Thrips: Give plants a cooler and damper environment. Apply pesticidal soap (commercially available),

These Climbers and Creepers Have Beautiful Blooms

In a poor location, all these climbing plants are highly vulnerable to aphids.
1 *Passiflora edulis*
2 *Thunbergia alata*
3 *Pandorea jasminoides*
4 *Podranea ricasoliana*
5 *Tecomaria capensis.*

Alternative Home-made Sprays

Stinging Nettle Extract for Controlling Aphids

Steep about 17½ oz (500 g) of fresh stinging nettles (before blooming) in 5 qt (5 L) of water for 12 to 14 hours. Spray on the undiluted liquid, while it is fresh, to combat aphids.

Horsetail Broth for Controlling Mildew

Soak 17½ oz (500 g) fresh or 5¼ oz (150 g) dried field horsetails (scouring rush) in 5 qt (5 L) of water to soften for about 24 hours, then simmer for about 30 minutes. Let cool, put through a sieve, and dilute with water in a 1:5 ratio before spraying. Spray it on the leaves, and water the plant with it.

pyrethrum spray, and other insecticides.

Rose chafers: Spray roses with kerosene before flush begins. If infestation occurs, use pesticidal soap or pyrethrum spray.

Leaf miners: Remove afflicted leaves, where the miners are located. If the infestation is serious, apply insecticide several times, at intervals of 10 to 14 days.

Weevils, or snout beetles: Pick off the bugs in May or June and in August or September. Remove larvae from the root zone. Alternatively, use parasitic nematodes (in a water solution), if the soil temperature is certain to be over 55°F (13°C).

Leaf bugs, or plant bugs: Locate the pests at midday, when they are sunning themselves on the leaves (*Datura/Brugmansia*). Then use insecticide.

Lily beetles: Periodically, pick off the beetles and larvae. If the infestation is serious, use pyrethrum spray or some other insecticide.

Snails: Pick off the creatures in damp morning weather or in the evening. Place beer traps in your garden (cups filled with beer and buried level with the ground).

Winter moth caterpillar: Remove the creatures and the damaged leaves. Use a biological caterpillar spray (*Bacillus thuringiensis*).

Controlling Fungal Diseases

Powdery and downy mildew: Remove and destroy the diseased leaves. Apply horsetail broth (see recipe, above), a fungicide contain-

Garlic Tea for Controlling Fungal Infections

Crush one medium-sized clove of garlic and pour 1 qt (1 L) of boiling water over it. Put the mixture through a sieve and let it cool. Spray undiluted. Also effective against spider mites.

Wormwood Tea for Controlling Insects

Pour 1 qt (1 L) of boiling water on 1 heaping teaspoonful of wormwood. Pass the mixture through a sieve, then let it cool. Spray it undiluted to control aphids, beetles that feed on leaf margins, pea moths, and sawyer wasps, and use it on ant paths.

ing lecithin or some other fungicide specifically for mildew.

Botrytis, or gray mold: Remove affected plant segments. Keep plants dry. Do not overfertilize with nitrogen. If infestation is serious, use special fungicide.

Rust: Remove afflicted leaves. Apply special fungicide.

Sooty mold: Remove heavily covered leaves, wash less-heavily coated leaves with lukewarm water. Get rid of pests (aphids, scale, mealybugs, or whiteflies).

Ascochyta: Immediately stand plant in a spot that rain cannot reach. Cut out the afflicted parts. Spray thoroughly with fungicide to which a dash of detergent has been added.

Leaf spot: Place in a dry spot with plenty of fresh air. Apply fungicide.

Soil fungi: They give rise to root rot, tuber and rhizome rot, brown rot in the roots, stem rot, and blight. Move to a better, drier spot. Remove diseased plants and plant segments. Do not add them to your compost pile!

Controlling Bacterial Infections

Oleander cancer: Immediately remove the afflicted shoots and destroy them. The causative organisms will remain latent, so a definitive cure is not possible.

Geranium wilt: Immediately remove afflicted leaves and shoots. Dust the cut places with charcoal. No cure is possible. Destroy the plants after they have bloomed. Do not add them to the compost pile, and do not propagate them!

HOW TO

Diseases and Pests. What the Leaves Reveal

Healthy Leaf

A healthy leaf has a solid structure, unblemished margins and tip, and color characteristic of the species.

IMPROPER CARE:
Yellow Leaves

Causes: Overwatering, nitrogen deficiency, insufficient light, old age. Remedy: Water less, improve fertilization and location.

Involuted (Curled) Leaves

Causes: Dry root ball, overly hot location, root damage. Remedy: Correct mistakes in care, improve location, repot if necessary.

Pale Leaves (Chlorosis)

The leaf veins retain their green color. Cause: Iron or magnesium deficiency. Remedy: Soften sprinkling water, add chelated iron to water.

Sunburn

Symptoms: Red, brown, or silvery-gray leaf discolorations. Causes: Failure to acclimate, overly sunny location. Remedy: Improve location.

PESTS:
Spider Mites

Symptoms: Webs in the leaf axils and on the shoot tips, whitish-yellow stippling on the upper sides of the leaves. Cause: Dry, warm air that is not circulating. Remedy: See page 35.

Scale

Symptoms: Sticky leaves, brown, waxy scales that conceal lice, leaf drop. Cause: Overly warm overwintering. Remedy: See page 35.

Aphids (Plant Lice)

Omnipresent outdoors. Symptoms: Sticky leaves, leaf deformations. Infestation usually starts at buds and shoot tips. Remedy: See page 35.

Whiteflies

Symptom: On undersides of leaves, small white insects that fly away when disturbed. Cause: Spread by other infested plants (common in fuchsias and tomatoes). Remedy: See page 35.

Leaf Eelworms (Nematodes)

Symptom: Dark spots demarcated by leaf veins. Cause: Wet foliage, which creates susceptibility to infection. Remedy: Keep leaves dry.

Woolly Aphids and Mealybugs

Symptoms: Cottony structures, stunted growth, sticky secretions, soot. Cause: Dry, warm winter location. Remedy: See page 35.

Thrips

Symptoms: Silvery leaves with tiny dots. On undersides of leaves, brownish feeding sites. Cause: Overly warm, dry air in winter location. Remedy: See page 35.

Rose Chafers

Symptoms: Whitish-yellow stippling on rose leaves. On undersides of leaves, greenish-yellow, wingless larvae. Cause: Dry, warm location. Remedy: See page 35.

Leaf Miners (Larvae of Moths and Miner Flies)

Symptoms: Irregular, dark (light, in case of miner flies) channels, or mines, of the caterpillars on the upper surfaces of the leaves. Premature leaf drop. Remedy: See page 35.

Weevils (Snout Beetles)

Symptoms: Circular notches on the leaf margins, sudden wilt—brought about by the feeding of the beetles (leaves) and larvae (roots). Remedy: See page 35.

Leaf Bugs (Plant Bugs)

Symptom: Leaves that, when they unfold, are already riddled with holes. Deformations of leaves and flowers. Remedy: See page 35.

Lily Beetles

Symptom: Notched, streaky feeding sites on leaves of lilies. Remedy: See page 35.

Winter Moth Caterpillars

Symptoms: Tattered leaves or complete loss of foliage. Cause: Green caterpillars that crawl by arching their backs. Remedy: See page 35.

Slugs

Symptoms: Holes eaten in leaves and flowers, trails of slime. Remedy: Hunt for the slugs in the mornings and evenings.

BACTERIA:
Oleander Cancer

Symptoms: Round, yellow-edged spots on leaves, excrescences and bark ruptures, deformed flowers. Cause: *Pseudomonas* infection. Remedy: See page 35.

Geranium Wilt

Symptoms: Wilting and withering of older leaves, stem rot, leaf spots. Cause: *Xanthomonas* bacteria. Remedy: None.

FUNGAL DISEASES:
Powdery Mildew

Symptom: White to dirty-brown powdery deposit on upper and lower sides of leaves. Cause: Fungus spores carried by wind. Remedy: See page 35.

Downy Mildew

Symptom: Brownish gray powdery deposit on undersides of leaves. Cause: Fungus spores carried by wind. Remedy: See page 35.

Botrytis (Gray Mold)

Symptoms: Brownish gray deposit on leaves, stems, or flowers. Causes: Overfertilization with nitrogen; cool, humid weather; placing plants too close together. Remedy: See page 35.

Rust

Symptoms: Small, rust-colored clumps of dust on the undersides of the leaves, light-colored spots on the upper surfaces. Causes: Fungus spores carried by wind; warm, humid weather conditions that persist. Remedy: See page 35.

Sooty Mold

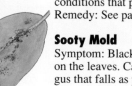

Symptom: Blackish deposit on the leaves. Cause: Fungus that falls as part of the honeydew from aphids. Remedy: See page 35.

Ascochyta

Symptoms: Wilted leaves, bent shoots, reddish-brown spots in the leaf axils. Cause: Infection, usually fostered by continuous rainfall. Remedy: See page 35.

Leaf Spot

Symptoms: Scattered yellow to brown spots, some with clearly outlined spore deposits. Leaf drop. Cause: *Phyllosticta* infection. Remedy: See page 35.

With the rich assortment of young plants available commercially, is it still really worth the effort to raise and propagate them yourself? This question can be answered in various ways. Anyone who lacks room and intends to plant only a few containers will do better to buy seedlings ready for setting. On the other hand, if you want to adorn lengthy expanses of balcony or patio with flower boxes or fill a great number of containers, eco-

RAISING PLANTS YOURSELF

People who like to experiment and have enough time and space can propagate tub plants themselves or raise container flowers with their own hands. It is fun to watch the young plants grow, and, in addition, this creative hobby can save you a great deal of money.

nomic reasons alone are a motive for cultivating your own plants from seeds or cuttings. Additional advantages: A great many exotic plants are available in this country only in seed form that must be ordered from mail-order suppliers. Aficionados of rare and novelty plants are thus able to raise plants that otherwise are virtually unavailable. In the case of vegetables, it is better to grow them yourself, because the young plants available commercially are frequently garden cultivars that are not necessarily suitable for containers. There are two methods of obtaining new plants—sexual propagation (see drawings, page 41) from seeds and vegetative propagation from plant segments (see pages 42–43).

Vegetative Propagation

For many plant species, this is the best way to obtain copies of the mother plant in a relatively short time. With this method, propagation is accomplished by division of an intact plant or by plant segments that have been rooted in water, seed-starting or soilless mix, or another potting soil (see pages 42–43). Vegetative propagation is recommended for woody plants, subshrubs, perennial herbaceous plants, grasses, and bulbs.
Basic Rule: For reproduction, use only segments of healthy, vigorous plants capable of blooming, because the offspring always will be a faithful likeness of the parent plant.

When to Propagate: The right times generally are spring and early summer. The young plants will grow throughout the season when light is most plentiful and can develop better.
Softwood and semihardwood cuttings can be obtained in the course of cutting back in spring, when many plants yield ample material for cuttings, ready to be used at once. Cuttings that are taken in early summer, after the first vigorous flush of growth, also have a good chance to develop. Woody plants can even be cut in summer and fall.
Hardwood cuttings are taken in late fall or early winter. Heel them in sand and keep them cool and free of frost. Plant them in February.
Root cuttings should be taken in December or January.
Division of herbaceous plants is best undertaken shortly before repotting, that is, in early spring.
Tubers are divided at the end of the dormant period, that is, in early spring.
Bulbs are propagated after the foliage dies back.

Propagation from Seed

Seeds can be used to reproduce and start annual and perennial flowers, subshrubs, woody plants, vegetables, and herbs. Container gardeners with little room for the inevitable overabundance of seedlings will do better to limit themselves to plants that need only a brief cultivation period before they are finished and blooming. Plants that take two or more years to flower after the seeds are sown need not only a great deal of care, but also ample room.
Annual plants (for example, many species of summer flowers, grasses, vegetables, and herbs, as well as some climbing plants) have the shortest cultivation period: It takes 8 to 12 weeks from seed grain to finished young plant. You can begin sowing at the following times:
• From January on, in a well-heated greenhouse with double glazing.
• From March on, indoors on a window sill or in an unheated greenhouse, if you have a warm propagating bed.
• From mid-April on, in an unheated greenhouse or a conservatory without additional heating.
• From mid-April to late May, outdoors, depending on the plants' requirements for warmth.

Care and propagation have been successful here: Reproducing blue fanflower, however, is a matter for horticulturists.

Biennial plants (for example, English daisies, English wallflowers, carnations, or pansies) develop only leaves the year they are sown and do not produce flowers until the second year. Sow them in summer in small boxes; in fall, house the young plants in empty flower boxes and leave them on the balcony or patio to overwinter (see drawing, Protecting Small Woody Plants, page 29). Alternatively, put them in a hole dug in the garden, protected with pine brush or straw.

Many herbaceous garden plants also can be raised from seed. The sowing time, the culturing period, and the culture conditions, however, vary considerably from one species to another, and it is preferable to reproduce them by division (see drawing, page 42) or to buy finished young plants.

Woody plants also can be grown from seed, but the culturing period is often lengthy. In addition, the seeds of many hardy species, such as maple, box, barberry, or coto-

neaster require a type of winter handling that is known as stratification, or moist-chilling (see Glossary). Propagation of these plants from seed is better left to fanciers or professional gardeners. Hobby gardeners can reproduce woody plants more successfully from softwood or hardwood cuttings (see drawings, Types of Cuttings, page 42).

What You Need for Propagation

• Seed-starting containers—for example, a bowl with or without a protective hood, or cloche—also, small, simple seed boxes with water drainage, such as fruit boxes, Styrofoam bowls, small clay pots, or multipot flats. Pots made of pressed peat are particularly advantageous. The plants' roots can grow into the pots themselves, and repotting becomes unnecessary.

• Clear plastic bags, which are also used for bagging cuttings (see drawing 3, Propagating Cuttings, page

43), or pieces of plate glass to substitute as covers for seed-starting containers without a cloche.

• Appropriate potting soils, for example, commercially available seed-starting or rooting soil or a 1:1 mixture of peat and quartz sand (not building sand). Compressed peat tablets (see drawing, Sowing in Compressed Peat Pots, page 41) are especially ideal for large seeds or cuttings. Use one plant per peat tablet.

• Rooting bowls that can be heated (mini-hothouses, germinating box) or heating pads to put under the rooting containers to promote the germination of plants that need warmth.

• Plant labels and a waterproof marker for labeling.

• Rooting compound (available in garden supply stores) for rooting cuttings in the potting soil.

• Charcoal powder and fragments to disinfect the water used for rooting some cuttings.

Tips for Successful Sowing

Be alert when buying seeds! Buy seeds from a specialized dealer. Give preference to high-grade seeds (F_1 hybrids, see Glossary), even if they are more expensive. The extra expenditure will pay off in terms of a greater array of blooms; increased vigor, symmetry, and health; and, in the case of vegetables, such as squashes, more fruit. Buy seeds only in stores with a high turnover: The fresher the seed, the better it will germinate—unless it is sealed in a protective bag that you open shortly before sowing.

First, consider your goal! You can save yourself a great deal of involved work by considering, at the time you sow the seeds, how and where you will use the young plants you grow. Different methods of sowing—direct sowing or preliminary culture—are recommended for various kinds of plantings.

Direct sowing. For homogeneous planting (of a flower box, for example), you can sow some species directly in the container (see table, above). After germination, the large group of seedlings is thinned out, so that the tiny plants can grow better. If you have room to spare, transplant the extra seedlings into individual small pots. Direct sowing also is recommended if you want to provide standards with a flowering underplanting. Simply make a layer of soil about ¾ in. (2 cm) deep and sow the flowers there.

Preliminary culture. It is recommended for mixed plantings, where it is important that healthy young plants with their own firm root balls develop, so that they can be combined easily with other plants later.

• Put large seeds, grain by grain, singly onto compressed peat tablets or into pressed peat pots or multipot flats, so that one plant will grow per ball or per pot.

• Very fine seeds, however, cannot be distributed exactly. It is more practical to sow them in rooting bowls. Important: Do not fill the bowls with too much soil; the seeds should be as close as possible to the ground warmth. After sowing, dampen the soil until it is quite soft, using a fine sprinkling nozzle and lukewarm water. As soon as the two cotyledons, or rudimentary leaves, are well developed and proper foliage has formed, transplant the seedlings into individual pots (see drawing, Transplanting Made Easy, page 41).

Container Flowers for Direct Sowing

English daisy, *Bellis* (see page 96)
Pot marigold, *Calendula* (see page 97)
Bellflower, *Campanula poscharskyana* (see page 100)
African daisy, *Dimorphotheca* (see page 108)
California poppy, *Eschscholzia* (see page 109)
Sweet pea, *Lathyrus* (see page 116)
Lobelia, *Lobelia* (see page 117)
Livingstone daisy, *Mesembryanthemum* (see page 118)
Monkey flower, *Mimulus* (see page 119)
Nemesia, *Nemesia* (see page 121)
Portulaca, *Portulaca* (see page 129)
Painted tongue, *Salpiglossis* (see page 131)
Nasturtium, *Tropaeolum* (see page 137)

Tub Plants to Sow

Bottlebrush, *Callistemon* (see page 155)
Rockrose, *Cistus* (see page 163)
Cup-and-saucer vine, *Cobaea* (see page 166)
Banana plants, *Ensete* and *Musa* (see page 172)
Coral tree, *Erythrina* (see page 173)
Eucalyptus, *Eucalyptus* (see page 173)
Ginger lily, *Hedychium* (see page 178)
Hop, *Humulus* (see page 180)
Crape myrtle, *Lagerstroemia* (see page 183)
Mandevilla, *Mandevilla* (see page 190)
Tobacco plant, *Nicotiana* (see page 193)
Canary Island and true date palms, *Phoenix* (see page 196)
Chusan palm, *Trachycarpus* (see page 212)
Petticoat palm, *Washingtonia* (see page 212)

Sow appropriately! Because seeds, too, have very different needs, follow the culture instructions on the packet exactly. They will tell you whether the seed grains have to be covered with soil (dark germinators) or not (light germinators). In addition, you will learn how the seeds should be treated before sowing, as well as their individual germinating temperatures, which can be monitored with a soil thermometer (available in garden supply stores).

Provide high relative humidity. Cover the rooting container with a pane of glass, a transparent cloche, or clear bubble wrap so that "close air" will be created. After germination occurs, lift the cover from time to time. After several days, remove it entirely.

Never let the potting soil dry out.

Subsequent Care of the Seedlings

Seeds are quite diverse. Many plants germinate after only a few days, others take weeks or months. Large seeds are usually the slowest.
As soon as the seedlings are so large that they are touching each other in their container, their development will be inhibited. If the seeds were sown directly in the container, it is time to thin out the seedlings. Tiny plants in seed-starting containers should be transplanted (thinned out) to individual pots (see drawing, Transplanting Made Easy, page 41). Plants that form roots prolifically, such as geraniums, which are usually grown from cuttings, are transplanted twice. Once the ball in the small pot is completely permeated with roots, plant it in a pot of the next-larger size. The root ball will grow even larger and thus provide optimal conditions for magnificent development and flowering in the box.

A great deal of light is necessary for further growth. Put the young plants in a place as bright as possible, but never in the sun. Lack of light will cause the plants to etiolate, or whiten, and unnaturally long intervals will develop between the leaf nodes (see drawing, Rules for Overwintering, page 28).

Pinching out spurs (see drawing, page 27) will encourage many plants to branch prolifically and will cause them to grow bushier and more compact.

Hardening off is important for plants that will stand outdoors later. Put the plants in a cool place (unheated room) as soon as they show, by putting forth new leaves, that they have overcome the shock of being transplanted.

Do not fertilize. The nutrients in the potting soil are completely adequate for the first few weeks. Annuals usually are transplanted into new, lightly fertilized potting soil after two to four weeks. If they stay longer in the rooting container, you can add a small amount of fertilizer four weeks after sowing.

Sowing Botanical Rarities

Growing botanical rarities that cannot yet be bought as plants holds special interest. Here is a small assortment of plants for which small quantities of seeds are available from specialized dealers or by mail order from special suppliers.

Actinotis helianthi: Shrub that grows 12 to 20 in. (30–50 cm) high, has white, tomentose leaves and creamy white flowers that resemble daisies.

Alberta magna: Evergreen shrub from Natal that has lanceolate leaves and orange-colored inflorescences.

Boronia megastigma: Evergreen shrub, which grows up to 39 in. (1 m) high, has needle-shaped, or acerose, foliage and yellow, sweet-scented flowers.

Lawsonia inermis, Henna shrub: Shrub or tree that has ovate leaves and fragrant pink flowers.

Telopea speciossisima: Shrub that is related to *Protea,* grows 10 to over 13 ft (3–4 m) high, has leathery leaves and cone-shaped, red-and-orange inflorescences.

Tips for Successful Propagation of Cuttings

Success depends on hygiene: Use clean containers for growing and sharp, immaculately clean knives or blades for cutting. Do not touch the cut surfaces of the cuttings with your hands. Large, cut surfaces can be disinfected with charcoal. If you are rooting the cuttings in water, put fragments of charcoal in the water. These measures will prevent rot and deter insects.

Rooting aids: If you want to root plants in potting soil, do not hesitate to try rooting products. Before setting the plants, dip the cut surfaces of stem cuttings (not root cuttings) in liquid or powdered rooting agents (available in garden supply stores), which contain growth hormones that will encourage the development of roots.

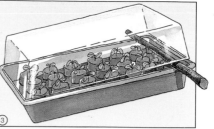

Sowing in Compressed Peat Pots

1 Pour lukewarm water over the peat tablets until they are swollen to full size. Remove excess water.
2 Press one seed grain into each pot ⅜ in. (1 cm) deep. Close the cover.
3 After germination, lift the cover frequently so the plants do not damp off.

Transplanting Made Easy

1 Loosen seedling from the soil with the slender end of a transplanting stick, or widger.
2 Shorten the root tip a little by pinching.
3 With the thick end, bore a hole in the soil of the flower pot, plant the seedling, and press down lightly.

Reduce the evaporation surfaces: For large-leaved cuttings, it is advisable to cut the leaves in half (straight across). With this reduction in the evaporation surfaces, the plant can strike root faster.

Provide bottom warmth: Mini-hothouses that can be heated or heating pads, which are placed beneath the containers (both available in garden supply stores), will provide the necessary bottom heat. Particularly in the case of herbaceous cuttings, either device will prevent rot and make it easier to strike root.

Important—Close air: Put the rooting container in a clear plastic bag (see drawing 3, Propagating Cuttings, page 43). If using a mini-hothouse, close the cover. Humid air will prevent needless evaporation through the leaves. But open the bag or cover now and then to admit fresh air.

Further Care of Cuttings

If tiny new leaves form on cuttings that are being rooted in potting soil, rooting has been successful. Now the evaporation shield (cover or plastic bag) can be removed.

If water is used for rooting, you can watch the roots grow through the glass (see drawing, Rooting in Water, page 42). Once the cutting has developed several small roots, carefully take the plant out of the water—the roots are quite fragile—and set it in a small pot with loose soil.

Light, pinching-out, and hardening-off requirements are the same as for seedlings (see preceding section, Subsequent Care of the Seedlings).

HOW TO

**Vegetative
Propagation
Using Plant
Parts**

<u>Division</u> is used to propagate herbaceous plants that have spread out too much at the sides–for example, bamboo species, and edging box (*Buxus*). Pull the plants apart with determination, but without harming the roots. Best time is when repotting in spring.

<u>Offsets</u> are complete young plants. They proliferate in the case of the agave; even in cultivars, they are exact images of the mother plant. Do not remove them until they have their own roots.

<u>Brood bulbs</u> are side shoots that many flowering bulbs–particularly wild species—use to reproduce on their own in the garden. This rarely succeeds in the limited confines of small planter boxes.

Propagation by Division
See drawing, left.
Plants that grow several shoots, form small stands or runners, or burst their containers may be divided. In spring, take the plant out of its pot, loosen the root ball with your fingers, and, shaking it, separate the roots. With a sharp knife or a spade, cut apart heavily matted root balls or a hard wickerwork of roots. Each portion must have roots and leaf buds of its own. Shorten overly long roots and disinfect injured roots and cut surfaces (in the case of rhizomes) with charcoal powder. Pot the individual pieces.

Propagation by Offsets
See drawing, left.
Offsets are not separated from the mother plant until they are large enough and have many roots of their own. Before being planted, agave offsets should be put in sandy potting soil, quartz sand, or perlite for one to two days. If impatience leads you to remove unrooted offsets, put them in a plastic bag until they put forth roots (see drawing 3, Propagating Cuttings).

Propagation by Brood Bulbs
See drawing, left.
This method of propagation works in containers only if they hold ample soil and only with certain species or cultivars, for example, *Tulipa kaufmanniana, Tulipa fosteriana, Muscari, Scilla,* and *Colchicum.* Dig up the bulbs after the leaves have died back, remove the brood bulbs, store all the bulbs in a dry spot, and plant them again in September or October.

Rooting in Water
A simple method that is successful with cuttings from oleanders, angel's trumpet, or impatiens, for example.

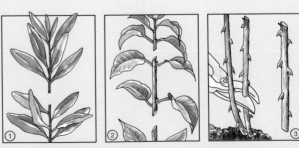

Types of Cuttings
1 Tip cuttings are taken from 1-year-old, flowerless shoot tips. Cut just under a leaf bud. The cuttings should have two to four pairs of leaves and should appear healthy and unblemished.
2 Stem cuttings are taken from the middle and lower portions of the shoot.
3 Hardwood cuttings, with eyes, are taken from the midportion of newly matured shoots. Length: 4 to 12 in. (10–30 cm).

Propagation by Cuttings

A cutting is a piece separated from the mother plant and induced to form a complete new plant.

Tip cuttings (See drawing 1, Types of Cuttings) are taken from 1-year-old, bloomless shoots. These can be soft-wood, semihardwood, or hardwood cuttings, also popularly known as spring, summer, and fall cuttings, after the season in which they are taken. Of these, softwood cuttings are easiest to root, but they rot faster. The cut is taken about ⅕ in. (½ cm) below a leaf node. The cutting should be 2 to 4 in. (5–10 cm) long, and it should have two to four pairs of leaves. Remove the lower leaves, because they would decay in the soil.

Stem cuttings (see drawing 2, Types of Cuttings) have no growth tip.

Hardwood cuttings (see drawing 3, Types of Cuttings) are taken in late fall or in spring from young, but mature, shoots. They should have approximately the circumference of a pencil and should be 4 to 12 in. (10–30 cm) long. Remove the leaves and angle the cut surface on the lower portion, but cut the top straight across, so you can tell top from bottom when placing the cutting into the soil. Each hardwood cutting should have at least one eye at the tip. Lean cuttings at an angle in separate deep tubs or pails. Planting depth: three-fourths of the length of the piece. Alternatively, tie them in a bundle, heel them in a hole in the soil, and plant them in spring. Roses, oleander, and Virginia creeper can be reproduced in this way.

Root cuttings (see drawings 1–4, Root Cuttings) are taken in late fall from herbaceous plants with fleshy roots (*Phlox*) and also from woody plants (*Plumbago*). Stick them in a soil mix of loam, peat, and sand (3:2:1), over-winter them in a frost-free spot with light, and plant them in spring.

Tuber division (see drawings 1–3, Dividing Tubers) is used in particular for tuberous begonias and is successful only with quite large, vigorous tubers. Divide them in spring. Each portion has to have at least one eye to sprout. Disinfect cut surfaces with charcoal powder.

Other Facts You Need to Know

Many plants contain poisons that are released when the plants are cut; they can irritate skin or mucous membranes (see warnings in the individual plant portraits, pages 86–227). Consequently, wear gloves when propagating poisonous plants. While working, do not rub your eyes, and make sure that no plant juices get into open wounds.

Propagating Cuttings in Potting Soil—Geraniums

1 Using a sharp, disinfected knife, cut off a vigorous, healthy side shoot about ⅘ in. (2 cm) below a pair of leaves. Remove the bottom pair of leaves and any buds or flowers, so that all available energy can go toward the growth of the new plant.
2 Set the cutting ⅘ in. (2 cm) deep in the potting soil, press down, and water.
3 Place two curved wires crosswise to create a protective arch over the plant. Cover with a plastic bag and tie it up. Put pot in a very bright place that is warm but not sunny.

Root Cuttings

1 Uncover a piece of root as thick as a pencil and cut it off right at the root neck.
2 Divide the piece of root into smaller segments about 1⅗ in. (4 cm) long. Cut the bottom ends at an angle, the tops straight across.
3 Stick the angled ends into the potting soil so that the tops of the cuttings are flush with the surface of the soil. Cover with soil.
4 Variation: Lay cuttings flat on the potting soil and cover with soil.

Dividing Tubers

1 To force tubers, bed them with the indentation facing up, in small boxes filled with damp peat. Cover with a thin layer of potting soil. Keep in a warm, bright place.
2 As soon as leaf buds are visible, cut each tuber into pieces with a disinfected knife. Each piece should have one leaf bud.
3 Let the cut edges dry in the open air for a few hours. Coat with charcoal powder. Set pieces in separate pots. Keep in a bright, warm place. Later, pinch back the young plants.

Cool, fresh, and exuberant: A summer box filled with *Convolvulus sabatius*, fleabane, petunias, and marguerite chrysanthemums.

PLANTING IDEAS FOR EVERY SEASON

Charming spring flower boxes, prolifically blooming summer plantings, atmosphere for an autumn flower box, and romantic hoarfrost for your balcony in winter. Balconies or patios with a splendid array of blooms in harmonious colors and attractive containers are the result of ingenious ideas, careful planning, and a profound knowledge of plants. On the following pages, you will find tips on decorating and on buying plants, along with ideas for planting containers throughout the year.

If you are interested in realizing your dreams of a flower-filled balcony or patio, first ask yourself this: What location can I offer my plants? The site will define your planning and your choice of plants. In decorating, the available space has a prominent role to play, along with the architectural features of the balcony or the patio. Of course, remember to leave room for a comfortable armchair from which you can enjoy everything!

PLANNING, BUYING, AND DECORATING

Capture the entire gardening year in your containers! Decorative elements used in gardening—such as rose globes and ornamental ceramics—should also make an appearance on balconies and patios. Here we tell you what to bear in mind and how to implement your projects.

Descriptions of Locations

Balconies, outside window sills, patios, gardens, doorways, stairways, driveways, and courtyards are the chief locations for container plants. First, determine the available light and the microclimate.

Locations with full sun have a southern exposure, no buildings to block out the sun, and no roof or canopy overhead. They range from warm to hot.

Bright locations may face east or west. They are warmed by the morning or afternoon sun.

Partially shady and shady locations face north and tend to be cool. Roof-covered balconies or patios with a southern, eastern, or western exposure or bright, warm locations that are partially in the heavy shade of trees or house walls have approximately the same light level.

Wind-sheltered locations are internal courtyards, roof-covered balconies, patios with borders (such as walls or hedges). Here, however, reflected heat from street surfaces or house walls can accumulate.

Windy locations are found primarily on high-rise apartment balconies, roof gardens, and open patios.

Important: The Regional Climate. Do not forget that all these locations are subject to the effects of the regional climate, which has an enormous influence on the plants' well-being and growth. In general, the most ideal conditions for container plants are found in the sunny areas.

Purchasing Tips

Temper your love and enthusiasm for plants, by giving some thought to the costs involved and the care required before making your plant purchases.

Initial considerations:
• In winter, make a sketch of the balcony or patio and indicate where the plants and the furniture of your choosing are to stand.
• Choose only plants that are suited to the location; otherwise, you will not enjoy them.
• If you have small children or pets, from the start exclude from your plans all plants that are poisonous or can cause injury.
• Measure the length of your balcony's balustrade before you buy planter boxes.
• In your planning, keep in mind that you also can use corners, walls, and—if your balcony is roofed—the ceiling to accommodate plants (see drawings, Creating More Room, page 50).
• Consider whether you prefer annuals or perennials in your planting. Annual flowers are more economical if you grow them yourself from seed, although raising them every year takes time and money. Perennial flowers that you purchase are an especially good buy if you are able to overwinter them and cultivate them for several years.
• Consider which boxes can be recycled when it is time for changing seasonal plantings, and decide whether you need additional containers.
• Calculate roughly whether the time you can spare for watering in summer is adequate for the plantings you have in mind, and give some thought to your arrangements for having them watered during your vacation. In many cases, automatic irrigation systems are advisable (see page 27).
• When planning, keep legal regulations in mind (see page 47).

Where Should You Buy Your Plants? The proper source will depend on the group or species to which your chosen plants belong. Most garden centers offer a vast selection, but other specialty plants and seeds are available from mail-order suppliers.

Pillars (*Ipomoea*, *Thunbergia*) and a privacy screen (*Plumbago*) are entwined with climbing plants.

The Law and Safety Precautions

Can you do whatever you want on your balcony or patio? Not entirely. If the balcony is part of a rented apartment, tenants basically can use it as they choose, as long as the rights of other tenants or of the landlord are not encroached upon. Even without obtaining the landlord's permission, tenants normally may put up flower boxes on a balcony and plant them as they wish. This right has limits: The safety of the balustrade may not be jeopardized, and the outside of the building may not be disfigured. The load placed on the balcony by containers, floor coverings, and furniture may not exceed the legal limits. If you plan to use an especially large number of balcony boxes or tubs, the load-carrying capacity and statics of the balcony will have to be checked.

Pay attention to the following details:

• It is preferable to discuss structural alterations—such as attaching flower boxes, trellises for vines and climbing plants, and balcony paneling—or the painting of the balcony's walls and floor with your landlord in advance. If you own the apartment, discuss your plans with the other owners.

• If the containers project beyond the side of the building, make them absolutely secure by using suitable flower box brackets or safety devices (see drawing, Glossary, page 77)—clamps that hold the box in place at the top also.

• If the boxes rest on slanting window sills, put wooden blocks underneath and, as a precaution, fasten each box to a hook screwed into the window frame. Check the holding devices frequently.

• Make certain that when you water your plants or when rain falls, the water does not run down the side of the building, flow onto your neighbor's balcony, or drip onto pedestrians or the sidewalk (slippery ice will form in winter!).

• When spraying pesticides, make sure the mist does not reach your neighbor's property.

Ideas for Plantings

On pages 52 through 73, you will find examples of a variety of plantings—elegant, rustic, charming, extravagant, close to nature—in many colors or tone-on-tone combinations, along with a shopping list for plants, pointers on care, and numerous tips. Have fun duplicating these examples.

The famed terra cotta pots from Tuscany, some of them richly decorated, are also available in this country.

Containers—Important Design Elements

The most important criteria for choosing containers are—besides your personal taste and the environment in which they are to stand—material, weight, form, size, price, and, above all, functionality. A good container must have sufficient room for the plants and drain holes for water. To spend the winter outdoors, the container also must be frostproof.

My Tip: Before planting, soak unglazed containers in water: Submerge small pots and boxes in the bathtub until tiny air bubbles cease to rise to the surface. Stand large and heavy containers out in the rain for a few days.

Important: Expose newly purchased concrete containers to the elements for several weeks before putting plants in them, so that harmful substances will be washed and evaporated out.

Plant containers are made of a variety of natural materials and of plastic. Both types have advantages and disadvantages.

Containers made of fired clay engage in respiration, and their weight usually makes them quite stable. Their earth tones make them a good match for all plants, particularly those from the Mediterranean. Terra cotta tubs, usually richly decorated, may be made by hand or formed in molds based on classical designs. However: The potting soil will dry out and cool off quickly in clay containers. Lime efflorescences develop quite rapidly on the container walls. Clay containers are heavy, and those of good quality are expensive and breakable. They tolerate light frost only if they are dry.

Majolica containers, as a rule, are made of highly fired and hence frostproof earthenware. They are available glazed (large Chinese tubs, for example) or unglazed. No moisture can penetrate the sides of containers that have a glaze, and consequently no efflorescences develop. However: Majolica containers are heavy and expensive.

Wooden containers, like those made of clay, have a long tradition of use. Versailles tubs still are being modeled after fifteenth-century examples, and the beloved wine barrel sawed in half will never go out of fashion. Wood insulates well, and its weight is not excessive. However: Wooden containers, depending on the kind of wood used, are to varying degrees vulnerable to damp and decay. If circumstances require, they have to be given a new coat of glaze or paint. The best way to prevent decay is to line the containers with plastic and set them on bricks or pieces of wood for improved air circulation.

Stone containers are planters hewn from natural stone, for example, vats or troughs made of marble, sandstone, or limestone. These also include the containers so popular in England, produced in Chilstone or Haddonston. Made of pulverized

Almost all plants go well with amphoras, pots, or boxes made of baked clay.

sandstone, these casts are patterned after historic vases, bowls, tubs, or stone baskets. Natural stone containers quickly develop the coveted patina; that is, they are quickly colonized by lichens and mosses. However: They are heavy, scarce, and quite costly.

Artificial stone containers are similar in appearance. Made of ground quartz, white cement, and plastic, they are more affordable.

Concrete tubs are windproof and heat resistant. As already mentioned, they have to be washed before use. However: Concrete containers rapidly become cold in winter. They are quite heavy and are only suitable for use at ground level, not on balconies.

Fiberglass resin containers with a stucco finish are a recent addition. They are light and claimed to be durable. Fiberglass containers are frostproof and have a neutral reaction to plants, but they are not low-priced.

Plastic containers are not only lightweight and durable, they are also inexpensive. They have long been available in a wide variety of shapes and attractive designs. In them plants keep damp longer than in clay containers. Also, they do not cool off as quickly as porous containers. Some are equipped with water reservoirs. However: Their solidity, durability, and resistance to frost depend on the quality of the plastic. Many plastics become brittle in blazing sun or grow so hot that the plants' roots suffer damage.

Metal containers of lead, copper, iron, zinc, or pewter are suitable for direct planting only if their insides are enameled, coated with plastic, or chromeplated.

In the photo above:
Amphora, box, and two decorated tubs of different shapes—all made of terra cotta. The shades may vary.

In the photo below:
An English stone vase. Such a costly container ennobles any plant.

Stone container with hydrangeas.

HOW TO

Decorating with Plants: Suggestions, Aids, and Tips

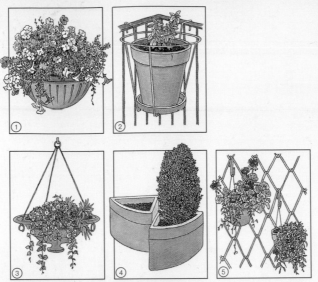

Creating More Room for Plants

1 Semicircular bowls for plants on front and side walls.
2 Corner suspension device for single pots—practical for balcony railings.
3 Go "up in the air" with hanging baskets; put the ceiling to use.
4 Corner containers—a lot of room for plants in a little space. Here, two placed together to form a semicircle allow plants to grow tall right next to the wall.
5 Making the wall green: A strong net mounted on the wall acts as a support for small pots on sister hooks.

Strawberry Jar in Many Variations

Strawberries, herbs, ivy, small succulents such as *Sempervivum* or *Echeveria*, and low summer flowers can be planted in the openings of the soil-filled container. Rotate the jar from time to time.

A Magnificent Array of Blooms in the Tiniest of Spaces

The limited room available on a balcony or patio has to be used ingeniously. Here are some ways to accommodate plants without taking up a great deal of floor space.

The ceiling can be used for hanging baskets (see drawing 3, Creating More Room). Suspension devices with a tackle block to lower the container for watering are handy.

Walls can be used for hanging shelves, semicircular bowls (see drawing 1, Creating More Room), boxes, trellises, and lattices for suspending single pots (see drawing 5, Creating More Room), as well as for attaching taut wires along which plants can climb (see drawing 1, Ways to Help Plants Climb).

For corners, there are specially designed containers with two sides that meet at a right angle, while the third side usually is curved (see drawing 4, Creating More Room). For balcony railings, there are corner suspension arrangements to accommodate single pots (see drawing 2, Creating More Room).

The floor space will be used to greater advantage if you employ containers with room for a great many plants in a small surface area—for example, a strawberry jar (see drawing, Strawberry Jar), a peat wall (see drawing, Flowering Wall), or a plant tower, which consists of plant elements placed one on top of the other.

Training and Shaping Plants

Plants can be induced to take on certain shapes by cutting or by using special holding devices or climbing aids.

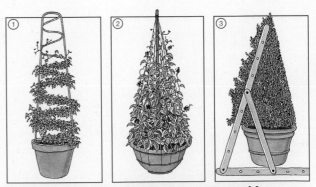

Training and Cutting Plants to Form Pyramids

1 Pyramids of ivy, fuchsias, geraniums, lantana, or tomatoes can be trained on this plant spindle.
2 A tent of scarlet runners: Cords mounted on the edge of the pot taper to a point at the top of a steel tube firmly anchored in the potting soil.
3 By using a template made of wood laths screwed together, you can cut box or conifers into neat pyramidal shapes.

Training standards (see drawing, Training a Standard) takes five years, as a rule. Train several at the same time, because not every attempt will succeed.

To cut a pyramid shape (see drawing 3, Training and Cutting Plants), screw two narrow wooden laths together in such a way that the strips of wood still can move in relation to one another. Set them at the desired angle, then tighten the screw and stabilize the angle with a crosspiece. Use this template as a guide and move it around the tub, cutting the plant along the slanted lath.

Climbing Aids and Plant Supports

Some plants need supports and climbing guides which must be attached at the time the containers are being planted.

Climbing aids for twining plants—such as scarlet runner beans, morning-glory, black-eyed Susan vine, hop, honeysuckle, knotgrass, or birthwort—are poles, taut pieces of stout twine, or climbing wires (with a rough, irregular surface that gives particularly good support). Twining plants grow in spirals around these holding devices, encircling them with their stems and shoots.

Climbing aids for climbing plants— such as sweet pea, cup-and-saucer vine, nasturtium, clematis, and Virginia creeper—are pieces of stout twine, climbing wires, or poles (not too thick, so that the fine tendrils can get a good hold). It is best to position them so as to form a net or a lattice.

Climbing aids for climbing woody plants—such as roses, blackberry vines, and winter jasmine—are trellises and lattices with slats and horizontal laths. An ideal device is the slidable lattice grate (see drawing 2, Ways to Help Plants Climb). Climbing woody plants need help to hold on to the lattice: They have to be tied on.

Root climbers such as ivy, climbing hydrangea, and trumpet creeper, on their own, can attach their anchoring roots to almost any supporting surface.

Privacy Screen and Windbreak

With free-standing screens of climbing plants or flowering walls filled with peat, you can partition yourself off and create a green sanctuary.

Free-standing privacy screen (see drawing, Free-standing Balcony Trellis). If you do not want to build one yourself, you can buy ready-made balcony trellises about 5½ ft. (170 cm) tall, complete with boxes, in garden supply stores.

Peat walls (see drawing, Flowering Wall) have to be built by you (see directions, page 69).

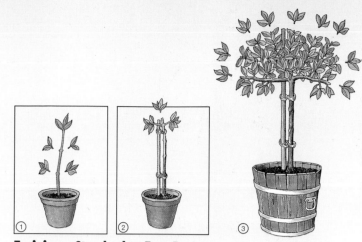

Training a Standard or Tree Form

1 Periodically remove the side shoots of vigorous young plants. At a certain height, put up a supporting stake and attach it with figure-eight loops.
2 Once the main stem is about 4 ft (120 cm) high, cut off the tip. The framework for the future crown will develop from the upper side shoots.
3 Frequently remove the tips of the side shoots, so that they will branch and grow dense foliage.

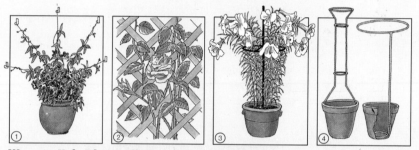

Ways to Help Plants Climb or Stand Upright

1 Climbing wires can simply be attached to wall hooks.
2 Trellises made of wood or PVC are available for walls and free-standing boxes.
3 Holders for herbaceous plants keep tall plants from flopping over.
4 Some plant supports for standards. They are anchored in the pot.

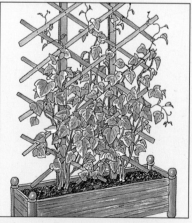

Free-standing Balcony Trellis

For this windbreak and privacy screen, you need a long, stable plant container. On the inside walls of the container, bolt on at least two large, solid laths and attach the trellis to them. Then add potting soil and set the plants.

Flowering Wall for the Patio

You can make this windbreak and privacy screen yourself, from wood laths and screen wire. Fill the frame with coarse-fibered peat and set it from the outside, through the holes in the wire, with small young plants that will develop quickly and cover the surface.

SPRING

Spring is here. Plant multi-colored spring flowers in planter boxes, tubs, pots, hanging baskets, or bowls. There is no lovelier way to inaugurate the season on the balcony or patio.

After the cold and darkness of winter, who is not eager for a little piece of spring—however small? Here are the most important harbingers of spring for container culture on a balcony or patio:

Spring-flowering bulbs, such as snowdrops, crocuses, tulips, daffodils, and many others, have two planting times. In September or October, set the bulbs in containers and overwinter them outdoors with protection or indoors in a bright, cool place. If this is too much trouble, you can buy forced bulbs in pots, starting in January; however, they are suitable only as indoor plants. For balcony or patio culture, it is preferable to wait until March or April, when the largest assortment is available and the planted containers can stand outdoors. The bulbs sold in bloom are hyacinths, low tulips, daffodils, grape hyacinths, bluebells, and snowdrops. Commercial gardeners start these bulbs as early as mid-December, at temperatures between 50° and 68°F (10°–20°C).

Herbaceous plants, such as Christmas roses or the gaily colored primroses, are treated in different ways. It is best to plant Christmas roses in the container in August and let them overwinter outdoors, with protection. Alternatively, in spring, set plants in bloom. They will put forth shoots year after year. Primroses, however, are better planted in the garden after they finish blooming. There they will flower every year and spread on their own. It is not, however, worth the effort to continue growing them in a box.

Biennial spring bloomers, such as English daisies, wallflowers, pansies, and forget-me-nots should be added to the compost heap after the blooming season. Their life cycle is over.

Spring-blooming woody plants, such as pussy willow, periwinkle (see photo, page 55), winter jasmine, and witch hazel are perennials and remain in their containers the year round.

Growing Bulbs in Containers—What You Need to Know

Plant bulbs in bloom on mild days with no sun; they will get used to the fresh air more easily this way. If temperatures below 26°F (−3°C) are predicted, it is best to cover the boxes with a loosely attached "hat" of bubble wrap or newspaper. The planting will last longer if you buy plants full of buds and if the container does not stand constantly in full sun. As a rule, you can enjoy them for over a month.

Continued Culture in the Container

The value of continuing to grow the bulbs in the container depends on your ability to nurse them so that they have enough strength to bloom the following year. This usually is impossible to achieve in the limited soil of a pot or balcony box. The bulbs will be weak and may fail to bloom after overwintering them in the planted box. In large tubs with enough soil, however, continued culture of less-sensitive species can be altogether successful. Proceed as in the garden.

Continued Culture in the Garden

Continued culture in the garden is successful and recommended. Provide bulbs already in the box with one application of special bulb food. Cut off withered and faded flowers (not the entire stem), but let the leaves alone. Lift the plants, along with their root balls, from the containers and plant them in the garden in holes that you have dug. Water

The magic of springtime, in a bowl.

and feed them frequently, so that the bulbs can build up strength again. After the leaves are yellow and dry, they easily can be removed by hand. Now dig up the bulbs and store them in dry peat until the next planting time in September. Alternatively, leave them in the ground, where some species will grow wild or spread on their own.

Other Decorating Ideas

Close to nature, economical, and a delight for the bees—dandelions in a balcony planter box. Violets in bowls are romantic and nostalgic. For the dandelion box, in February dig out a few "fat" dandelion rosettes with the rootstock (depending on the size, three to six dandelions for each 24 in. [60 cm] of the box's length). Set them in balcony boxes with nutrient-rich soil (all-purpose soil or loamy, rich garden soil). Before doing so, shorten the leaves by one-half. Put outdoors in a sunny place and keep well dampened. At first, you may need to protect the plants against late spells of frost. Violets in bowls are a very special kind of salute to spring and are always welcome as a thoughtful gift. For the container, choose a decorated bowl to achieve a romantic effect. Plant it densely with a host of violets (*Viola cornuta*). In spring, they are sold already in bloom. In a cool place, they will last an extremely long time (see Plant Portraits, page 141). Recommended are small-flowered cultivars such as the sky-blue 'Princess Blue', about 4 in. (10 cm) high, or the violet-blue 'Angerland', 6 in. (15 cm) high. Particularly charming is a bowl with sweet violets, *Viola odorata*. If you have them in your garden, simply dig up several plants and set them. Sweet violets create virtual carpets in sites that are not overly sunny, and in a short time they will "fill in" the place where some have been dug out. One of the loveliest cultivars is 'Königin Charlotte'.

A flowering bulb arrangement (see photo, left)
• Bowl: 16 in. (40 cm) in diameter.
• List of plants:
2 snake's head fritillarias, *Fritillaria meleagris*
2 to 3 small pots of low pink tulips, *Tulipa*
3 primroses, *Primula denticulata*
2 cowslips, *Primula veris*
1 *Chionodoxa*

The bees are the happiest of all when the first flowers appear on the balcony.

1 *Puschkinia scilloides var. libanotica*
• Planting and care: This extremely dense, luxuriant planting cannot be prepared in fall. It is made up of forced plants that can be bought in spring. Fill in the drainage layer (see page 26) and put some potting soil on top. Remove the bulbs from the pots they came in, and arrange them so that the low plants are at the edge.

What You Can Prepare in Spring

Spring is the busiest time of year for gardeners. At this time, the basis is laid for the approaching abundance of flowers and fruits. Here is what you have to do between late February and May, including the preparation of the following boxes:
• Sow annual summer flowers, grasses, herbs, and vegetables.
• Force summer bloomers with tubers (begonias, canna).
• Set herbaceous plants.
• Buy and plant container flowers.
• Get new tub plants.
• Plant dwarf conifers.
• Set overwintered plants in new potting soil (perhaps creating new combinations of plants), and starting in April or May, acclimate them to their new location outdoors.

SPRING

Whether multicolored or tone-on-tone, the cheerful colors of spring flowers produce exquisite combinations.

Blue Box with Tulips

Plant in fall, enjoy in spring.
Box length: 24 in. (60 cm).
List of plants:
6 wallflowers, *Cheiranthus cheiri*, multicolored
5 tulip bulbs, *Tulipa*, 'Queen of Night'
1 tulip bulb, *Tulipa*, 'Black Parrot'
Planting and care: Set wallflowers and tulip bulbs in September. Plant the bulbs in the background, about 3 in. (8 cm) deep and in two groups. Overwinter the box outdoors, covered with leaves or straw as protection against frost. On frost-free days, water plants moderately. After the flush of growth in spring, put the box in a spot sheltered from the wind and fertilize weekly.
My Tip: Choose frostproof boxes.

Primrose Box

Quick to plant, cheerful colors.
Box length: 24 in. (60 cm).
Plants:
12 primroses, *Primula vulgaris*, in various colors
Planting and care: From January on, set the box with the finished plants that you have bought, so that they hang slightly over the rim of the box. Water the plants well and feed them weekly. In case of frost, cover the box with newspaper. From May on, set plants in the garden, where they will bloom again the following year. The box can be reused for summer planting.

Multicolored Spring Box

Will bloom until early summer.
Box length: 24 in. (60 cm).
List of plants:
3 wallflowers, *Cheiranthus cheiri*
2 English daisies, *Bellis perennis*
3 forget-me-nots, *Myosotis* hybrids
Planting and care: Buy the plants in spring and set them in box. Plant wallflowers at the side and between the forget-me-not group and the English daisies. Put the box in a sunny to partially shady spot: Water plants regularly and feed them weekly. Deadhead spent flowers. Replace wallflowers and forget-me-nots with summer flowers (for example, geraniums, heliotrope, daisies).

A cheerful box of primroses—an early planting for any location.

A blue box with dark-violet tulips—an enchanting combination for wind-sheltered locations.

Easter Bowl in Shades of Violet

Decorative bowl for indoor use, can stand outdoors after Easter.

Bowl: 10 in. (25 cm) in diameter.

List of plants:

2 primroses, *Primula vulgaris*

3 pots of grape hyacinths, *Muscari aucheri* (about five bulbs per pot)

3 hyacinths, *Hyacinthus orientalis* 'Bismarck'

1 pot of *Chionodoxa gigantea* (several bulbs per pot)

Planting and care: Forced plants are available from January on. Plant in stairstep formation, according to height (primroses and *Chionodoxa gigantea* in front, grape hyacinths in the middle, hyacinths in the background). Do not keep plants overly warm. Outdoors, protect them from frost by covering with newspaper or plastic; alternatively, bring the planter indoors.

Small Willow Stems in a Tub

Long-lasting, honey-producing plants.

Tub: 20 in. (50 cm) in diameter, 18 in. (45 cm) tall.

List of plants:

2 goat willows, or Kilmarnock willow, with pendulous branches, *Salix caprea var. mas* 'Pendula'

10 lesser periwinkle plants, *Vinca minor*

1 Christmas rose, *Helleborus* hybrid

Planting and care: In early spring, buy plants and set tub with them. Two goat willows will form a balanced crown. Put Christmas rose in front, fill remaining area with periwinkles. Stand the plants in partial shade and water them regularly. Overwinter them outdoors, with protection. Feed plants the following spring.

An unusual bowl in shades of violet. A tone-on-tone planting suggestion.

A weeping Kilmarnock willow with underplanting—daffodil bulbs set in fall will bloom promptly at Easter.

A colorful spring box for locations with full sun—also pretty with a forced tulip in the background.

Container plants now can sunbathe and have full scope to display their beauty. Herbs produce their aromatic substances, and fruits begin to ripen.

In summer, container gardeners enjoy what they planned, planted, and sowed in fall. The warm season, however, also gives them a chance to add to or alter the decoration of their balcony or patio, because the assortment of plants available is greatest at this time.

Summer Decorating Ideas

Why not choose a single theme as the guiding principle for decorating your balcony or patio? Consider the following ideas:

The decorative balcony, for example, with a variety of plants, all in your favorite color (white, perhaps; see photo, pages 10–11).

The botanical balcony, as a place to collect plants from a single region (for example, plants native to Australia) or plants from a certain family (for example, a fuchsia balcony; see photo, page 175).

The herb and vegetable balcony (see photo, pages 228–229) can be stocked with fresh ingredients for your kitchen—in complete accordance with your wishes.

The fruit balcony offers a little paradise for snackers. For container culture on balconies and patios, there are running strawberries and everbearing wood strawberries, currants, gooseberries, and blackberries. Blueberry and red whortleberry cultivars also do well in tubs. If you want to raise a little apple, pear, plum, sour cherry, or sweet cherry tree, it is best to contact a nursery or special mail-order garden suppliers and specifically request cultivars that are self-pollinating and grow well in tubs. Depending on the species, the cultivar, and the grafting time, fruit trees in tubs will begin to bear only after one to three years. Fruit trees are overwintered in the same way as roses (see page 29). Cover the aboveground parts with a burlap sack instead of brush.

A minipond in a tub is a water biotope in the smallest of spaces. Wooden vats or half-barrels are most attractive. Soak the wooden receptacles in water for about one week so that they will become saturated and watertight (better, line them with special plastic film for lining pools, available in garden supply stores).

Planting suggestions:
• Container: Watertight receptacle with a diameter of about 20 in. (50 cm) and a depth of 12 to 16 in. (30–40 cm).
• Potting soil: Loam or special pond soil, about 2 in. (5 cm) deep. Cover the soil with a layer of gravel or sand, so that the nutrients stay in the potting soil and do not get into the water.
• Planting: Set 2 blue flags, *Iris sibirica*, and 3 small cattails, *Typha minima*, in the background; in front of them, place 2 horsetails, *Hippuris vulgaris*. In the foreground, plant 2 brooklimes, *Veronica beccabunga*, and 3 moneyworts, *Lysimachia nummularia*. Leave some open water in the middle.
• Fill with tap water to about 2 in. (5 cm) below the rim.
• Location: Partial shade—no blazing sun.
• Care: When evaporation occurs, add water and do not feed under any circumstances.

Scented Box with Tuberoses (see photo, page 240):

Scented plants on a balcony or a patio are a pleasant experience for the senses of sight and smell.

For this composition, it is best to buy finished young plants. The tuberoses, however, are generally available as tubers from mail-order tuber and bulb suppliers, and they have to be started by you.
• Box length: 24 in. (60 cm).
• List of plants:
2 lavender plants, *Lavandula angustifolia*
1 basil plant, *Ocimum basilicum*
2 mignonette plants, *Reseda odorata*
1 heliotrope, *Heliotropium arborescens*
1 scented geranium, *Pelargonium* (here, a cultivar whose leaves are variegated with white; it has the scent of peppermint)
3 tuberose tubers, *Polianthus tuberosa*
• Planting and care: In March or April, put the tuberose tubers in a pot, cover them with soil, and keep them in a bright, dry place protected from frost. Do not water them until the shoot tips pierce the surface of the soil. In May, after the last frost, buy the remaining plants and set the box with them. Put the tuberoses at one end of the box as a background group, and surround them with mignonette and heliotrope. Plant the lavender and basil together at the opposite end, as a counterbalance. Put the scented geranium in the

Black currants, gooseberries, and strawberries thrive here, ready to be picked for a snack fresh from the vine.

foreground, hanging slightly over the rim, as a connecting element. The box needs a sunny to partially shady location, sheltered from wind. Keep the plants well watered, and fertilize them once a week. Overwinter the scented geranium and heliotrope in a warm place indoors; the lavender can winter over outdoors, with winter protection. The other plants will last only one year in the box.

My Tip: Place the box so that it is "at nose level" in the evenings, because tuberose, heliotrope, and mignonette release their scents at this time.

What You Can Prepare in Summer

If you like, start now to lay the foundation for the next year's planting or for fall.
• Take summer cuttings from woody plants.
• Take geranium cuttings.
• Sow biennial summer flowers.
• Collect the seeds of grasses and annual summer flowers.
• Plant autumn crocuses (see box planting, page 66)

In the photo above:
Standards of various berry vines not only look attractive, but also yield an abundance of fruit.

In the photo below:
For planting in vases or hanging baskets, there are special cultivars that bear small fruits.

A riot of strawberries.

SUMMER

Early summer decorating ideas for every taste. Some majestic, some close to nature, some destined for the kitchen.

Roses in a Terra Cotta Tub

A dream combination that will bloom again year after year, if you have a good place for overwintering.

Tub: 16 in. (40 cm) in diameter, 18 in. (45 cm) tall.

List of plants:

1 floribunda rose, *Rosa*
2 flowering maple, *Abutilon megapotamicum*
1 Japanese morning-glory, *Ipomoea nil* (syn. *Pharbitis nil*)

Planting and care: Buy the rose in a container and plant it in May, together with the flowering maple and morning-glory. Stand the plants in sun to partial shade; water them generously and fertilize every two weeks. Keep cutting back the rapidly growing tendrils of morning-glory to keep the rose from becoming too overrun.

In winter, put the entire arrangement in the garage or cellar, or keep it in a cool conservatory at a temperature of 32° to 41° F (0°–5° C), with little watering.

Alternatively, overwinter the rose outdoors, with protection (see page 29) if the container you have chosen is frostproof. The underplanting, however, will freeze, and you will have to replace it the following season.

In spring, replace the topmost layer of soil, and after acclimation (see page 25), stand the tub outdoors again in May.

Little Meadow of Wild Flowers

An economical, unusual decoration—for more than a single summer.

Box length: 24 in.(60 cm).

Plants:

1 handful of commercially available seed mix for a meadow of wild flowers or of herbs

A field of wild flowers—a box that makes learning come alive for children. Sow the seeds in early March, and the flowers will be ready to admire in June.

Even when roses are grown in a tub, they need a location with full sun, where no heat can build up.

58

Planting and care: Gently press down the soil in the box, and sprinkle the seeds over it, not too close together. Cover the seeds lightly with soil and press down slightly with a small board. Water carefully, but well. Stand box in the shade and keep it damp. As soon as the first plants germinate, put box in filtered sunlight, later, in full sun. Always keep well dampened, and fertilize occasionally.

My Tip: If the grass gets too rampant or unsightly, everything can be cut back to a handbreadth. It will grow back quickly.

Pansies and Strawberries

A fragrant box for early summer and a feast for the palate.

Box length: 24 in. (60 cm).

List of plants:

12 pansies, *Viola* x *wittrockiana* hybrids, 'Rokoko Mischung'
6 wild strawberry plants, *Fragaria vesca*

Planting and care: In September, buy the plants, choose a frostproof box, fill it with soil, and plant the two species, intermingling them. Water plants well, keep them moist even in winter. Put container in a sunny, bright spot, but protect plants from frost (see drawing Protecting Small Woody Plants, page 29). After March has begun, remove the protective covering. From May on, feed the plants every two weeks. If the wild strawberries are growing too thick, simply cut off leaves with your shears. They will grow back.

Planting alternative: If you missed your chance in fall, you also can set the plants in spring. The strawberries, however, may possibly bear less well.

Decorative Herb Box

A fine fragrance and fresh herbs for the kitchen.

Box length: 24 in. (60 cm).

List of plants:

2 creeping zinnias, *Sanvitalia procumbens*
1 lavender cotton, *Santolina chamaecyparissus*
1 rosemary plant, *Rosmarinus officinalis*
1 common sage plant, Salvia *officinalis* 'Tricolor'
1 Trye lavender, *Lavandula angustifolia*
1 fleabane, *Erigeron karvinskianus*
4 to 7 common sunflowers, *Helianthus annuus*

Planting and care: In May, set the containers with the plants you have bought, placing the creeping zinnias on the right and left to frame the rest, and putting the plants that grow taller (lavender, rosemary) in the background. Plant the lavender cotton, sage, and fleabane in the foreground, hanging slightly over the rim of the box. Put the sunflower seeds between the plants.

Water the plants, and choose a site with full sun. After the sunflowers' flush of growth, fertilize plants every two weeks. If too many sunflowers appear, thin them out somewhat. Lavender cotton, sage, true lavender, and rosemary are subshrubs or shrubs; they can winter over in a sheltered spot with winter protection (see page 29). Except for sage, they will retain their foliage. You can also attempt to overwinter fleabane—which in its native habitat is an herbaceous plant—if it is well protected. In spring, replace the creeping zinnias, sunflowers, and—to the extent necessary—fleabane.

My Tip: Rosemary, lavender cotton, true lavender, and sage have a fine aroma; therefore, put the box at nose level.

Endearing and nostalgic—pansies and wild strawberries. With good care, the plants will yield berries to nibble well into fall.

Nothing but children of the sun. These Mediterranean herbs will develop their full aroma only in a warm, sunny location.

Enchanting planting suggestions to duplicate—these combinations will display all their beauty in midsummer and late summer.

Elegant Box in Violet and Yellow

Unusual color accents and classical composition.

Box length: 24 in. (60 cm).
List of plants:
1 blue salvia, *Salvia farinacea*
2 heliotrope plants, *Heliotropium arborescens*
3 slipperworts, *Calceolaria integrifolia*
Planting and care: Buy plants in May. Set the container with slipperworts at the edge and toward the front, heliotrope in the center and toward the back, and blue salvia at the very back (as the tallest plant). Water the plants well and fertilize them weekly. Deadhead spent flowers regularly.

Rendezvous for Brightly Colored Flowers

For a change, the geraniums are not present in abundance, but only add a cheery dash of color.
Box length: 24 in. (60 cm).
List of plants:
2 black-eyed Susans, *Rudbeckia hirta*
2 pot marigolds, *Calendula officinalis*
1 red erect geranium, *Pelargonium* x *zonale* hybrid 'Bundeskanzler'
2 dark-blue petunias, *Petunia* hybrids
2 *Convolvulus sabatius*
Planting and care: Buy plants in May and set the box with them. Put hanging plants (*Convolvulus*, petunias) in the middle and in the front, slightly hanging over the rim of the box. Set the geranium in the center as an accent. Place the black-eyed Susans, which grow taller, and the pot marigolds in the background and at the edge, intermingled. After the last frost, bring the box outdoors and stand it in a sunny to partially shady place. Water the plants daily, and fertilize them weekly.

Painted Tongues on Their Own

Filigreed blossoms that last one summer long.
Box length: about 32 in. (80 cm).
Plants:
15 painted tongues, *Salpiglossis sinuata*
Planting and care: Buy the plants in May and set them in soil mixed

All the splendor of summer is captured in this box. Put it in a sunny to partially shady location.

Heliotrope, with its scent of vanilla, and slipperwort will grow this luxuriantly only in a location with full sun and sheltered from rain.

with sand (two handfuls). Put the box in a sunny spot, sheltered from wind and rain. Water plants regularly, and feed them weekly.

Geranium Box
Robust flowers, gracefully arranged.
<u>Box length</u>: 24 inches (60 cm).
<u>List of plants</u>:
3 red erect geraniums, *Pelargonium* x *zonale* hybrids
2 red erect geraniums with white-margined leaves, *Pelargonium* x *zonale* hybrids
2 low marguerite chrysanthemums, *Chrysanthemum frutescens*
2 cornflowers, *Centaurea cyanus*
<u>Planting and care</u>: Buy the plants in May and set them in a box. Those planted in front should hang slightly over the rim. Put the cornflowers in back If the cornflowers are still small, the geraniums

and marguerite chrysanthemums will have to be trimmed occasionally, so that they do not crush them. It is therefore better to buy cornflower plants that are already vigorous. Put the box in a sunny to partially shady location. Water the plants generously, and fertilize them weekly.
My Tip: Deadhead spent blossoms regularly. This will encourage the plants, especially the cornflowers, to bloom again.

Blackberry Wreath
A condensed touch of wilderness. If you want to overwinter it outdoors, choose a frostproof container.
<u>Tub</u>: 18 in. (45 cm) in diameter, 14 in. (35 cm) tall.
<u>List of plants</u>:
1 wild blackberry, *Rubus fruticosus*
7 lesser quaking grass plants, *Briza minor* (or a seed packet to sow)

<u>Planting and care</u>: In May, set the container with blackberry and grasses (underplanting). Put it in a sunny to partially shady location. Water plants generously, and fertilize them every two weeks. Without using poles, twist the long stems around so as to form a green wreath of blackberry vines. Overwinter outdoors, with protection for the pot, or in a cool, bright location at 32° to 41°F (0°–5°C). Lesser quaking grass will spread from seed each year.

Red geraniums keep company with white marguerites and blue cornflowers.

Painted tongue grows slender and wiry; it needs a location sheltered from wind and rain.

If you like, you can put the blackberry tub next to the balcony railing and train the shoots along it.

M elancholy in shades
of red and gold.
Colorful foliage, bright
fruits—before it gets cold,
plants show themselves at
their best one last time. Some,
such as autumn crocuses and
heath, make their big appearance now. And on the table,
springtime is waiting to be
put in pots.

FALL

Fall plantings can be the crowning glory of the gardening year, with their ripening fruits and berries and with the red and gold colors of the dahlias, asters, and chrysanthemums.

Fall atmosphere on balconies and patios is provided either by plantings that you can put in now or by plantings that are at their peak in autumn, as a result of plans you put into action earlier.

Short-term Fall Planting

Do not hesitate to think about undertaking plantings in fall, when the splendor of the summer flowers is almost past. Fall arrangements can be quite versatile and long lasting. It is no happenstance that garden supply stores carry a regular fall assortment.

The Plants. In late summer, the following flowering plants are sold, along with conifers (see page 69):

• *Erica herbacea* in white and violet-pink
• Chrysanthemums, *Chrysanthemum* x *indicum* hybrids in white and in shades of gold, bronze, red, and violet
• China asters, *Callistephus chinensis*, ranging from white, cream, and pink through scarlet and violet to blue
• *Hebe* x *andersonii* hybrids in white, crimson, and violet-blue. *Senecio bicolor,* or dusty miller, lends contrast with its pretty silver-colored leaves

Here's How. Take the annuals, which now are becoming unsightly in any event, out of the summer boxes, clean the boxes, and set them with the new plants. If you had set the summer boxes with perennials and now would like to overwinter them, it is best to buy a new set of balcony boxes for fall. Alternatively, you can carefully lift the summer plants with their root balls out of the containers (first, run a knife around the inside edge of each container to loosen the roots and potting soil). Put the plants in a crate lined with plastic and continue to tend them there. In this way, you can get by with having just one set of containers.

How long will the planting last? Conifers and many evergreens can be overwintered outdoors and will prosper for years in their containers. The fall flowering plants, however, will fade or become unsightly after the first nighttime spells of frost. You can take them out and use the boxes for overwintering summer flowers or for dried arrangements in winter.

Long-term Fall Planting

If well planned, these plantings will last for years, reaching the peak of their splendor each fall.

The Plants. Perennials such as herbaceous plants, grasses, and slow-growing dwarf and needle-leaved woody plants are good choices.

Here's How. Set herbaceous plants, such as *Aster dumosus* hybrids and stonecrop, in late spring or early summer, to give them sufficient time to develop. Set broad-leaved woody plants such as pyracantha hybrids, maple, or locust in spring, because the soil, as it warms up, will spur the formation of roots, and in summer these plants will produce the foliage that is to provide gorgeous fall colors. Apart from these considerations, they need an opportunity to form flowers so that decorative fruits can appear.

How long will the planting last? Almost all these plants can be overwintered outdoors with winter protection; they are long-term investments.

Conifers—Increasingly Popular

Conifers are robust and easily satisfied. Container-grown evergreens, with their ball thoroughly permeated with roots, are available principally in fall. The optimal time for planting them, however—as for all other woody plants that are planted in containers—is not fall, but spring. The plants can grow on into the warm season and form roots more easily. If you plant in fall—which is possible if you are using container-grown plants—the boxes have to stand in a frost-free, bright location in winter. Do not forget to water them, because evergreens continue to lose water through transpiration in winter!

Suitable dwarf conifers for boxes or troughs:

• Blue Colorado spruce, *Picea pungens* 'Glauca Globosa', rounded, spreading growth habit, blue-gray needles
• Norway or common spruce, *Picea abies* 'Little Gem', low and compact in habit, bright-green needles
• Dwarf pine, *Pinus mugo* 'Mops', rounded growth, 12 in. (30 cm) high, dark-green needles
• Chinese arborvitae, *Thuja orientalis* 'Aurea', compact, rounded habit, needles green during flushing, bright green in summer, yellow-green in winter

Autumn dips the locust in liquid gold; it causes dewdrops to glisten in the grasses and bright-colored fruits to ripen.

- *Pinus densiflora* 'Alice Verkade', bushy, 20 in. (50 cm) high, with long, unusually brilliant light-green needles
- Dwarf juniper, *Juniperus communis* 'Sibirica', more out-stretched, slightly overhanging, silvery blue needles
- Silver cypress, *Chamaecyparis pisifera* 'Snow', rounded and bushy, 10 in. (25 cm) high, snow-white needles
For further recommendations of appropriate species and cultivars, (see Plant Portraits, pages 214–215).

What You Can Prepare in Fall
- Buy (or order) bulbs of spring bloomers and set them (September).
- Plant broad-leaved and needle-leaved woody plants in containers (possible on frost-free days until December).
- Summer flowers and grasses that will be used to decorate the boxes in winter can be hung in a shady balcony corner to dry.

In the photo above:
A fall balcony with sunflowers, chrysanthemums, various grasses, Virginia creeper, locust, and cotoneaster, decorated with colorful leaves or fruits.
In the photo below:
Potted myrtle and *Hebe* x *andersonii* hybrids in an oval terra cotta planter.

A symphony in red, green and yellow.

FALL

Entrancing plantings that display their full beauty now, in addition to combinations that quickly capture autumn in a container.

Chinese Lanterns and Currant Tomatoes

An herbaceous, fruity delight for a single season.

Box length: 24 in. (60 cm).

List of plants:

6 Chinese lantern plants, *Physalis alkekengi var. franchetii*

2 currant tomato plants, *Lycopersicon lycopersicum*

Planting and care: Buy plants in May, set the extremely proliferous Chinese lanterns in the background and at the sides so that they do not rob the tomatoes of the necessary light.

After the last frost in late May, put the box outdoors in a sunny location. Water the plants copiously, and fertilize them weekly. If necessary, cut back the Chinese lanterns and support the tomatoes with a stake.

Autumn Bowl

A quick planting with great potential for variation.

Bowl: 24 in. (60 cm) in diameter.

List of plants:

1 cotoneaster with fruits, *Cotoneaster horizontalis*

3 chrysanthemums, *Chrysanthemum x indicum* hybrids

2 dusty miller plants, *Senecio bicolor*

1 cushion bush, *Calocephalus brownii*

Planting and care: The plants are available from late September on. Do not center the cotoneaster; place it so that its decorative branches have room to grow freely. Plant the chrysanthemums together in a cluster as a color focus. The gray of the dusty miller and cushion bush will provide a good transition between the cotoneaster and the chrysanthemums. Any location will do. Keep the bowl evenly damp.

Alternatives: Substitute dog rose or holly with berries for the cotoneaster, and replace faded chrysanthemums with heath.

An autumn bowl with yellow chrysanthemums and the decorative berries of cotoneaster.

Chinese lantern plant and cocktail tomatoes—a delightful mixture of fruit and greenery that reaches a height of at least 39 in. (1 m) in fall.

Box with Autumn Crocuses

A long-lasting, easy-care box. In fall, it blossoms out into a gem.
Box length: 24 in. (60 cm).
List of plants:
8 fescue plants, *Festuca cinerea*
6 autumn crocus bulbs, *Colchicum autumnale*
Planting and care: Best planting time is August, when the autumn crocus bulbs are available. For planting, use some potting soil mixed with sand. Set the fescue plants, then set the bulbs among them, about 1½ in. (4 cm) deep. Water the plants well, feed them lightly. Use any location. Can be overwintered outdoors with protection (see page 29). Do not remove the leaves that appear in spring; wait until they have turned brown.
Warning: Autmn crocuses are poisonous!

Aster Box in Shades of Pink

Various pastel shades, large and small flowers in furious competition.
Box length: 24 in. (60 cm).
List of plants:
6 pink and violet China asters, *Callistephus chinensis*
4 pink asters, *Aster* x *dumosus* hybrids
Planting and care: The plants can be bought from August or September on. Set the box with them, making sure the contours of the planting are solid and even. The small-flowered pink asters lend the box a dainty air. After planting, water the plants well; any location will do.

Sunflowers in a Trough

A handsome perennial planting with potential for variation.
Trough: 27½ in. (70 cm) long, 16 in. (40 cm) wide, 24 in. (60 cm) high.
List of plants:
1 cotoneaster, *Cotoneaster dielsianus*
5 ivy plants, *Hedera helix*
5 sunflower plants, *Helianthus annuus*
Planting and care: In spring, set the perennials (cotoneaster and ivy). In May or June, put young sunflower plants in the background and water them copiously; feed the plants every two weeks. Planting can winter over outdoors in a sheltered spot. Replace sunflowers every year, or substitute other annuals.

Large- and small-flowered asters in shades of pink and violet do well in any location.

Nature in the raw: autumn crocuses growing among blue-green fescue.

Sunflowers grow this large only if they have an abundance of nutrient-rich soil at their base. Choose a location sheltered from wind!

WINTER

Anyone who claims that winter is not a season for the balcony is not familiar with the great variety of plants whose restrained beauty creates atmosphere and transforms the cold time of year into a rich experience of nature.

The balcony or patio does not have to be gray in winter. If you have obtained supplies of grasses, berry-producing woody plants, and evergreens in time, you can enjoy the sight of plants that seem to be sugar-coated with hoarfrost or gaze at snow-covered landscapes in miniature.

Decorating Tips for Winter

Here are several suggestions for anyone who wants to enliven outdoor window areas without spending too much time on the task.

Cut or dried arrangements in boxes: In winter, container gardeners are allowed to cheat a little.

With cut or dried decorations—such as fir or pine branches, cones, thistles, other dried flowers, dried grasses, and fruit-producing branches of cotoneaster, mistletoe, and holly—you can create highly effective focal points without great expenditure. In between them or in large tubs, you can put a few appropriately colored garden globes, which look amusing in little caps of snow. Surrounding yourself with artificial plants may not be to your taste. Nevertheless, evergreens such as needle-leaved woody plants, holly, and box, grow quite slowly as a rule and many gardeners—and their plants—find it painful to sacrifice large portions of their greenery to obtain decorations for winter boxes. Garden centers increasingly are beginning to offer artificial evergreen branches also, as a way to avoid destructive exploitation of living woody plants.

A fir tree at the window: With increasing frequency, spruces or firs grown in nursery containers are being sold as Christmas trees. During the holidays, they can be brought indoors for a short time and decorated. Preferably, however, leave them outdoors where you can see them in their festive decorations. In a heated room, they give off too much water and soon begin to drop their needles, because the root ball, limited by the confines of the nursery container, cannot supply enough water. For the most part, these Christmas trees are young plants of large fir or spruce species, not dwarf plants, so it is advisable to plant them in the garden as soon as the ground is frost-free. If you continue to grow such trees in the container, water them on frost-free days.

My Tip: Immediately after your Christmas tree's "indoor visit," give it some protection against the cold—for example, bubble wrap or newspaper.

Tips on Winter Care

• Except in areas where winters are mild, containers that are to remain outdoors have to be frostproof—whether they hold plantings or not. This also applies to balcony boxes that hold cut or dried winter decorations. Containers that are not frostproof can develop cracks, especially if the soil is wet and expands at freezing temperatures. Keep the containers in a frost-free room.

• Store bags of potting soil indoors as well, to prevent the soil from freezing.

• Frequently, people forget that evergreen woody plants transpire water in winter also and thus need to be watered. Water on frost-free days when the potting soil is not frozen solid, and warm the water slightly beforehand.

• Do not leave watering cans containing water on your balcony or patio, as is usual in summer. A single night of frost can change the water to ice and cause the cans to burst.

• Clear the snow off the plants periodically, so that they do not break or bend under its weight.

• If you sweep snow off your balcony or patio, heap it up around containers in which plants are over-wintering in the open. This offers additional protection against frost.

• Leave balcony linings in place in winter, if plants are being overwintered there. They give added protection from cold, sun, and wind.

• Shut down the water connections on patios. Let the water that is still in the line run off, then turn off the faucet and seal it with a cork so that no moisture can get in.

• During prolonged spells of thaw or rain, make sure no standing water builds up in the containers. It will damage plants that are wintering over outdoors more seriously in winter than in summer.

• Water that overflows from your plant containers can become a special hazard in fall or winter if it runs onto the sidewalk and turns to ice there.

Heath and Broom

Decorative flowers from winter to spring. An unusual transitional planting with potential for variation. Use a frostproof container.

Box length: 24 in (60 cm).
List of plants:
5 heath plants, *Erica herbacea*
2 dwarf broom plants, *Cytisus decumbens*
2 fescue plants, *Festuca scoparia*

Community of Evergreens

A perennial planting that will grow tall, with fruits that provide a rich decorative contrast.

Trough: about 39 in. (100 cm) long, 20 in. (50 cm) wide, 18 in. (45 cm) deep.
List of plants:
1 spruce, *Picea orientalis* 'Aureospicata'
1 cotoneaster, *Cotoneaster dielsianus*
2 ivy plants, *Hedera helix*
1 juniper, *Juniperus communis*

Planting and care: The best time for planting is spring; the plants will have a chance to become well rooted before the next winter. Plant spruce at the side and to the back. Set the cotoneaster with its gently waving branches at the other side as a contrast. The ivy and juniper will form an underplanting and serve as a transition between the other two specimens. Water the plants well and place the trough in partial shade. Continue to water well throughout winter, on frost-free days. In spring, add fertilizer to the water.

My Tip: By all means, choose a frostproof container. Keep in mind that this planting is extremely heavy. Before going shopping, find out about the permissible load on your balcony or roof garden.

Planting and care: Buy the plants in fall, as soon as the heath is available. Mix the soil with some sand. Set the broom plants at a slight angle, so that the branches fall softly over the rim of the box. Place the fescue among the heath plants. Water the planted box well and place it in a sunny to partially shady location. Continue to water the plants throughout the winter on frost-free days. The broom will produce bright yellow flowers in early spring.

Alternatives: Between the heath and the fescue, set a few crocus bulbs (or other bulbs that bloom in spring).

Flowers in the change of seasons. Heath blooms in winter, and broom shows its light-yellow flowerets in early spring.

In fall and winter, the red berries of cotoneaster bring lively color to this planting. In spring, the spruce adorns itself with golden-yellow tips.

Winter in the role of magician. Snowfall during the night—and presto, your balcony is transformed into an enchanted forest! No one decorates more magically than winter. It covers plants with a thick layer of white, makes dry branches with their drops of ice sparkle like necklaces set with diamonds, and uses gleaming white to show just how bright red berries can be.

GLOSSARY

**Horticultural
and Botanical
Know-How**

A

Acaricide
Special preparation that kills mites (for example, spider mites or red spider).

Acclimation
See HARDENING OFF.

Algae
Primitive plants that take up residence on clay pots (and elsewhere) in a damp, bright location and form a dirty green coating. The best way of removing this coating is to scrub it off with a brush, under running water.

Alkaline
Equivalent terms are *basic* or *sweet*, in contrast to *acidic* or *sour*. In plant care, a potting soil is alkaline when its lime content is high and it has a pH VALUE over 7.

Alkaloids
Nitrogenous plant substances that affect the human nervous system. Examples of plants that contain alkaloids: *Brugmansia/Datura* and all members of the nightshade family. Alkaloids frequently are lethal, even in very small doses.

All-purpose soil
A commercial potting medium consisting mainly of peat moss, humus, vermiculite, and sand. It may also include fertilizers and other additives. This potting soil is ideal for many container flowers and tub plants.

Alternating leaves
Arrangement in which leaves do not grow precisely opposite one another, but are spaced at intervals along a spiral (see drawing, page 80). Contrast: OPPOSITE LEAVES.

Anchoring roots
Specialized roots that many plants produce to attach themselves to tree trunks, walls, and the like.

Annual plants (Annuals)
Plants that flower, fruit, and then die within the calendar year when they are sown. Horticulturists call them annuals. Contrast: PERENNIAL PLANTS.

Assimilation
Assimilate = adjust, adapt. In its botanical sense, the term applies to the plant's conversion of foreign substances into its own substances. In carbon dioxide assimilation (see PHOTOSYNTHESIS) for example, the plant synthesizes sugar.

Austral flora
Vegetation that is characteristic of the Australian continent. Typical representatives are many of the Myrtaceae, such as *Callistemon*, *Eucalyptus*, and *Leptospermum*.

Automatic irrigation
Various systems that can be used to water plants in your absence. Also called long-term irrigation or vacation watering (see drawing, page 27).

B

Ball
Term for soil thoroughly permeated with roots (see ROOT BALL) or for a compressed quantity of peat (peat ball).

Ball dryness
Lack of moisture in the root ball of a pot plant, recognizable when the soil draws away from the edge of the flowerpot. Most plants tolerate ball dryness for a very short period.

Bastard
Product of crossing plants of different varieties, subspecies, species, or genera. Bastards are also called HYBRIDS.

Beneficial insects
Insects that destroy pests. They are a biological form of pest control. These insects are available from garden supply stores.

Biennial plants (Biennials)

Plants that form only leaves the first year; in the second year, they flower, fruit, and then die. Examples: English daisies, wallflowers, and pansies.

Biological pest control

Plant protection without chemicals, by means of BENEFICIAL INSECTS, concoctions brewed from plants, and plant tonics. In the broadest sense, it also includes prevention through optimal care.

Biotechnical pest control

Control of insects via natural, chemical, or physical stimuli, for example, bowls painted yellow and filled with water, yellow sticky cards (for aphids, whiteflies, and fickle midges), attractants, and baits. Physical control measures such as picking or washing off insects can also be included in this category.

Bone meal

Popular organic phosphorous fertilizer that promotes root growth and flower development. Ideal in combination with HOOF AND HORN MEAL.

Bonsai

Term for the Japanese art of shaping tiny trees modeled on large ones and for the miniature potted tree itself. From *bon* = pot and *sai* = tree.

Botanical name

Internationally accepted scientific designation of a plant. The botanical name may consist of two or more parts:

1 The name of the GENUS, for example, *Bougainvillea*.
2 The name of the SPECIES, for example, *glabra*.
3 The name of the CULTIVAR (if the plant is garden cultivated), for example, 'Sanderiana'. However, hybrids or crosses between two species or varieties, which generally do not breed true from seed, are usually different from either parent and are often given names without a species name, for example, *Bougainvillea* 'Harrisii'.
4 The x sign may precede the species name when the plant is known to be a true breeding hybrid or is one of a race of like hybrids, for example, *Bougainvillea* x *buttiana*.

Breeding

Attempts to develop, by means of crossing and selection, new cultivars that satisfy certain requirements. Some breeding goals are larger flowers, double flowers, new flower colors, as well as resistance to disease and adverse climate.

Buds

Plant organs from which stem, leaves, flowers, or entire small plants develop. We differentiate between terminal buds at the end of a shoot, axillary buds in the leaf axils, dormant buds (sleeping eyes) which can remain in the bud stage for years and begin to grow only under special conditions, and adventitious buds, which come from meristematic tissue (SEE MERISTEM). Flower and leaf buds develop into flowers and leaves, while brood buds develop into entire plants.

C

Callus

Tissue that an injured plant forms to close a wound. In cuttings, roots cannot develop until callus tissue has formed.

Cambium

Plant tissue that consists of a cylinder of embryonic cells capable of division. The vascular cambium gives rise to annual rings of wood and the cork cambium gives rise to bark.

Capillary action

Physical principle by which water is "raised" in thin tubes over short or long distances. In practice, capillary action is applied in systems for watering plants during vacation.

Carpet-forming

Horticulturists' term for plants with dense, low-lying, spreading growth, also called cushion-forming. Examples: *Alyssum*, *Lobelia*, *Lobularia*.

Chelate

Chemical substance that enables the iron locked in the ground to dissolve better and thus become available to plants. Gardeners use chelated iron, for example. The brownish red powder is dissolved in water and used to treat chlorosis (iron deficiency).

Chemical control

Control and prevention of pests with chemical agents, which when improperly or carelessly used can endanger humans and pets. Therefore, chemical pesticides are classified according to the degree of their active toxicity into toxic or nontoxic. Poisons are accordingly labeled.

Chlorophyll

Green pigment in leaves and stems essential to the process of PHOTOSYNTHESIS.

Climber

Term for a plant that climbs on other branches, tree trunks, limbs, or trellises by using organs developed expressly for this purpose—for example, disk-shaped and other anchoring roots, stem or leaf tendrils, climbing bristles, spines, and thorns—or by winding as it grows.

Climbing aid

Artificial support for a climbing plant. It takes on the role of trees or bushes that climbing plants use under natural growing conditions to work their way up to the sunlight. The type of climbing aid chosen depends on the specific climbing method of the plant in question (minimum distance from the wall: 4 in. [10 cm]). Climbing aids for twining plants are vertical supports such as poles, stout twine, or wires. Aids for climbers are nets made of plastic-sheathed wire, cords, wire mesh, or wood. Climbing woody plants like roses need a framework with as many bars or horizontal laths as possible, while root climbers like ivy need no aid at all.

Close air

Horticultural term for air that has been "trapped" by a clear plastic bag placed over a pot (see drawing 3, Propagating Cuttings, page 43) or by a pane of glass tightly covering a rooting container. Close air reduces evaporation through the leaves, decreases the cooling off of the soil, and promotes germination and the growth of roots.

Cold house

Term for a greenhouse where temperatures in winter do not exceed a range of 36° to 54°F (2–12°C). Plants needing cool overwintering are called cold-house plants.

Common English name

English but also popular name for a plant. Often an Anglicized version of the scientific name—like hyacinth (*Hyacinthus orientalis*). But there are also many plants that do not have English names.

Complete fertilizer

Fertilizer that contains all the major nutrients essential to plant life and often trace elements (see MINERAL FERTILIZER and MICRONUTRIENTS as well).

Conifers

Cone-bearing trees or shrubs (Coniferae), such as spruces, pines, firs, or cypresses.

Contact poison

Plant pesticide that affects insects when they come into contact with it. Respiratory and food poisons and SYSTEMIC CONTROL AGENTS have other modes of action.

Container-grown plants

Woody plants that are raised and sold in plastic pots or plastic bags. Container-grown plants are ideal as tub plants, because they are accustomed to container culture from the outset and have a correspondingly shaped root ball.

Continental climate

The term for the climate typical of a large, closed land mass. In comparison with the MARITIME CLIMATE, it is characterized by greater daily and even greater seasonal contrasts in temperature and by longer periods of high pressure, which, because of the sun and the lack of water, pose hazards for evergreens such as rhododendrons and false cypresses.

Corm

Thickened, more or less fleshy part of a stem or root (see STORAGE ORGANS) of some plants, as the crocus. All corms are storage organs for reserve food.

Crown

See l in drawing on page 82. Point at which the root joins the above-ground part of a plant (stem axis). The crown is extremely sensitive in many plants!

Cultivar

Cultivated variety of a plant species. The cultivar's name is always set in single quotation marks, for example, *Chrysanthemum frutescens* 'Schone von Nizza'.

Cutting back

Necessary measure for shaping a plant, rejuvenating it, encouraging new growth, and promoting bushy growth and good branching (see page 26).

Cuttings

Horticulturists' term for plant segments that are put in soil or water to root. A cutting can be a terminal cutting (tip cutting), a piece of stem, a leaf, or a portion of a leaf (see drawings, pages 42–43).

D

Damping off

Disease of seedlings and cuttings that is caused—especially under crowded conditions—by fungus in the potting medium and results in injury to root tissue. It causes the plantlets to break off.

Dark germinators

Plants whose seeds will sprout only in total darkness. Once sown, the seeds have to be covered to prevent light from reaching them until germination occurs.

Deciduous

Term for plants that lose their leaves at the end of a VEGETATIVE PERIOD.

Defoliation

Loss of lower leaves because of improper care or too dark a location. In many plants, it is characteristic of the species. These plants shed the lower leaves in order to form a trunk. Examples: *Dracaena draco* or *Yucca*.

Dioecious

If the male and female flowers of a species are located on separate and distinct plants of the same species, they are said to be dioecious. Familiar examples are aucuba, palms, and the willow. Contrast: MONOECIOUS.

Division

Method of propagation suitable for plants with several shoots (herbaceous plants, for example).

Dormancy

See REST PERIOD.

Double flowers

Flowers with many petals. They lack stamens, which have been converted—usually through selective breeding—into petals. Contrast: SINGLE FLOWERS.

Drainage

Measure for removal and redirection of water. Drainage is necessary in order to avoid standing water, which is harmful to plants (see drawing, page 26).

E

Efflorescences

Deposits of lime and fertilizer salts on the outer surface of a clay pot. They are caused by watering with hard, or limy, water or by overly frequent fertilizing. Efflorescences can be removed with a solution of vinegar and water and a coarse scrub brush.

Essential oils

As a rule, sweet-smelling, highly aromatic, slightly volatile plant substances that are concentrated in glandular cells or microscopic oil reservoirs.

Etiolation

Horticulturists' term for the formation of long, weak, pale shoots with large intervals between the points where the leaves emerge and with small leaves. Cause: Insufficient light and overly high temperatures.

Evergreens

Plants that do not shed their leaves in fall. These plants, of course, do renew their leaves, but the process usually does not attract attention, because it is not linked to a particular time of year.

Eye

An undeveloped bud on a stem or a tuber.

F

F₁ hybrids

Descendants of the first generation produced by crossing various homozygous parent varieties. Homozygosis is attained through inbreeding over a long period of years. F, from *filia* (Latin: daughter), indicates that these plants are offspring; 1 means: of the first generation. An F_1 hybrid usually surpasses the parent varieties in growth, quality, and health, as well as in the number of flowers and fruits it produces.

Family

In botany, a group of genera in which certain characteristics are identical. Many tub plants, for example, belong to the *Myrtaceae* (myrtle), *Solanaceae* (nightshade), and *Arecaceae* (palm) families.

Family name

Indicates membership in a particular family. Thus for example, the rubber plant to the mulberry family (Moraceae).

Fertile

Technical term meaning capable of producing seeds and fruits. Its opposite is STERILE. Flowers with sex organs (that is, with pistil and stamens) are fertile; flowers that lack these organs are sterile, for example, the enlarged marginal flowers of the climbing hydrangea.

Fertilization

Union of a male sperm with a female egg cell.

Flora

Another term for the plants of a particular region.

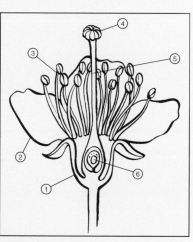

Flower

See drawing, above. In many plants, the most attractive part. It is used for sexual reproduction. Each flower is made up of the following parts:
1 Calyx with sepals.
2 Corolla with petals.
3 The male stamens consist of filaments on which anthers with pollen grains are located. Collectively known as the androecium.
4 Stigma.
5 Pistil.
6 Ovaries are the female parts of the flower. Collectively they are known as the pistil or gynoecium.

Flower box brackets or safety devices

See drawing below. Adjustable supports available in many designs, which are generally made of plastic-sheathed steel or sturdy flat iron. The brackets (left drawing) are used to secure boxes to balcony railings and balustrades. The safety devices (right drawing) keep flower boxes that sit on balustrades or window sills from falling. Both types can be adjusted to fit boxes of various sizes. If the window sills are slanted, it is a good idea to put wooden wedges underneath so that the boxes are level. As an additional precaution, fasten the box to a hook screwed into the window frame.

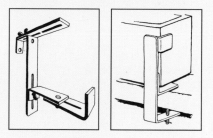

Flowering plants

The most highly developed plants. In technical terminology, they are called angiosperms. Older and less highly developed are the gymnosperms, which include the palm ferns, ginkgo, and conifers; ferns, mosses, lichens, fungi, algae, and bacteria are older yet.

Flush

Emergence of new shoots. An indication that the process of plant growth is getting started again—after the light-poor season, for example.

Fronds

Term for cycad, palm, or fern leaves.

Frost germinators

Plants whose seed—so it once was claimed—germinates well only after a lengthy spell of frost. We now know that the breaking down of substances that inhibit germination is attributable less to frost than to changing temperatures in the range of 28° to 39°F (−2 to +4°C).

Fruiting

Growth stage that follows flowering. Usually, the fruit encloses the seed(s).

Fungicide

Chemical agent for controlling fungal diseases.

Fungus

Plants in one of the lower groups whose bodies consist of threadlike hyphae (mycelium) and contain no chlorophyll. They serve as "garbage eaters" because they can digest cellulose and wood pulp. They are either decay dwellers, parasites (causes of disease in humans, animals, and plants) or live in symbiosis with other plants, for instance orchids and lichens. Some produce important substances for human beings (penicillin) or cause certain processes (such as fermentation). Dampness and specific temperatures are prerequisites for their viability but the pH value and concentrations of oxygen and carbon dioxide in their environment are also determining factors.

G

Garigue

Mediterranean plant community and the continuation of the MACCHIA. The garigue, formed by the destruction and grassing over of the macchia, consists of shrubs up to about 39 in. (1 m) high, among which the bare stones are visible. The index form is *Quercus coccifera*, called garoulia in Provence (hence the name garigue). Other typical plants are rosemary (*Rosmarinus*), lavender (*Lavandula*), thyme (*Thymus*), and sage (*Salvia*).

Genus

Term for plants within a family that have certain characteristics in common.

Genus name

First part of the botanical name of a plant, which is always capitalized. Examples: *Citrus, Lobelia, Pelargonium.*

Germinating temperature

Optimum ground and air temperature for plants to begin to germinate.

Grafting

Method of propagation in which a scion or an eye of a valuable plant is joined to another plant. The two grow together so closely that the stock takes over the supplying of water and nutrients, while the new shoots that determine the appearance of the plant arise from the scion or eye. This method is used, for example, with *Citrus* species, whose seedlings often fail to bloom.

Grapevine-growing climate

Special climate that permits the cultivation of grapevines. Worldwide, grapevines are grown only between 30°N and 50°N and 30°S and 40°S, that is, in the temperate zones, where it is neither too cold nor too hot and dry. Vine-growing regions are characterized by a greater number of sunny days than other regions. Such a climate promotes flower development and wood maturity in tub plants.

Ground covers

Flat-growing or low woody plants that by virtue of their growth properties—when planted in a group—gradually form a closed cover of plants.

Growing season (Growth period)

See VEGETATIVE PERIOD.

H

Habit

Botanical term for the configuration of a plant, the plant's appearance.

Hanging plants

Plants with trailing or creeping shoots that look particularly attractive in a hanging container.

Hardening off

Carefully accustoming the plant to changes in temperature and light conditions. Also called ACCLIMATION.

Hardiness

Term used for a plant's ability to withstand cold in the open air. We distinguish between absolute, genetically determined hardiness and relative hardiness, which can be affected by such factors as location and care. Some woody plants are frost-tender when young; others may be hardy in favorable locations (inner courtyards sheltered from wind and sun). One decisive prerequisite for hardiness is, for example, WOOD MATURITY.

Hardwood cuttings

Lignified pieces of stem. Hardwood cuttings are used to propagate roses, for example.

Hardy

Term applied to plants that can survive the winter in temperate zones without winter protection, unharmed.

Haulm

Stem or stalk herbs. It is either round—and then often hollow (pithy in corn and sugar cane)—or trigonal and filled with pith. Giant grasses, such as bamboo, have the strongest, thickest, and longest haulms.

Herbaceous

Tender plant parts, not woody or lignified, that die at ground level at the end of the growth period.

Herbaceous plants

Perennial nonwoody plants that each year renew themselves from organs under the ground and form leaves and flowers, for example, *Campanula poscharskyana*, a species of bellflower.

Holdfasts

Specialized roots that many plants produce to attach themselves to tree trunks, walls, and the like.

Honeydew

Sticky excretions of aphids and scales. Honeydew attracts ants, but also the fungi that cause sooty molds, which cover the leaves with a black growth. Wash off immediately!

Honey-producing plants

Woody plants, herbaceous plants, or herbs that make excellent sources of nourishment for bees and other insects. They are also called bee plants or bee flora. For example: borage, honeysuckle, Virginia creeper, clematis, lavender, species of wall pepper, balm, and all fruit trees.

Hoof and horn meal

Organic nitrogenous fertilizer with a 14 percent nitrogen component. Can be mixed with the potting soil for plants such as *Datura*, banana, or *Solanum* species, all of which need large amounts of nitrogen. Ideal in combination with BONE MEAL.

Hormone

Substance produced by plants that can, even in small amounts, stimulate or inhibit growth and development. Also called phytohormones.

Humus

Nutrient-rich substrate that consists of decayed and decaying organic material.

Hybrid

Product of crossing plants of different varieties, species, or genera (see BASTARD).

Inflorescence

See drawings, below.
Some plants have flowers that grow singly; in others, several flowers grow at the same site in a certain arrangement. This arrangement is known as the inflorescence. The most important inflorescences are these:
1 Spike
2 Spadix
3 Umbel
4 Panicle
5 Head
6 Raceme.

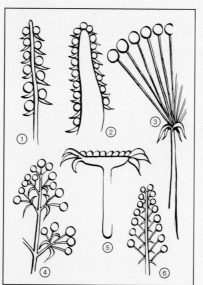

I

Industry-resistant

Criterion for the suitability of woody plants in areas seriously affected by industrial emissions. This property is influenced by other environmental factors such as the specific soil conditions, microclimate, weather patterns, and plant care.

Insecticide

A preparation used to control insects.

Internode

Intervals between leaf nodes on a stem, from Latin: *inter* = between, *nodus* = node.

L

Light

Vital to plant life. It is necessary for PHOTOSYNTHESIS, and it controls the plant's growth, flower development, germination, fall coloration, and leaf drop.

Light germinators

Plants whose seeds need light to germinate. These seeds should not be sown too thickly, and under no circumstances should they be covered with soil. The seeds of light germinators are scattered on the surface of the potting soil and—to make sure that they are touching the soil—pressed down with a board.

Lignification

Storage of lignin (woody substance) in the cell wall. This process results in hard and woody stems.

Lime-hating plants

Plants that have little or no tolerance for lime in water and potting soil. Azaleas, camellias, and miniature orange trees, for example, require a low lime content.

Loam

Type of rich soil that consists of a mixture of clay, silt, and sand. These three components have differing grain sizes. Whichever component is dominant determines the nature of the loam (clay loam, silty loam, or sandy loam).

Long-term fertilizers

See SLOW-RELEASE FERTILIZER.

M

Macchia

Plant community of Mediterranean flora. The macchia has replaced the evergreen oak forests. Its name is derived from the Corsican term for *Cistus*, which is a typical plant of the macchia. In addition, *Arbutus*, rosemary (*Rosmarinus*), and various species of broom are common. The macchia is used in various ways by the local inhabitants. It merges first into the GARIGUE and then, with further destruction and exploitation of the landscape, changes into steppe.

Maritime climate

Climate influenced by the sea. It is characterized by mild, damp winters. Its nature is different from that of the CONTINENTAL CLIMATE and it affects the relative hardiness of plants. Specimens (camellias, for example) that are not hardy in the continental climate may well be so in the maritime at the same latitude and altitude.

Mediterranean

Pertaining to the Mediterranean area. Designates plants belonging to the Mediterranean flora (see SUBTROPICS).

Meristem

Tissue composed of cells still capable of division (formative tissue). It is found in stem and root tips, but is also produced in the callus and root development of cuttings.

Microclimate

Air temperature, atmospheric humidity, radiation, wind, precipitation, and so forth in the immediate vicinity of a plant, in a section of a garden, in an inner courtyard, on a roof-covered balcony, on a wind-sheltered patio, or next to a wall.

Micronutrients

Another word for the trace elements boron, iron, copper, manganese, molybdenum, zinc, and others. Although plants need them only in tiny amounts, lack of them can result in disease.

Mildew

A fungus that attacks plants. There are several types, among them: true mildew and false mildew, which is also called downy or gray mildew.

Mineral fertilizer

Inorganic fertilizer whose nutrients are bound as salts and therefore are immediately available to plants. Danger: Overdosing. Contrast: ORGANIC FERTILIZER, in which the nutrients first must be tapped by microorganisms that later release them into the soil for the plants, a process that takes quite a long time.

Moist chilling

See STRATIFICATION.

Monoecious

When male and female flowers appear on the same plant, it is termed monoecious. Contrast: DIOECIOUS.

Moss build-up

Caused by compacted soil and excessive dampness. It can harm plants that have low tolerance for dampness in the stem area, and it prevents aeration of the soil. Therefore: Carefully loosen the top layer of soil with a fork to avoid injuring the plant or its roots. Remove mossy layer.

Mother plant

Plant that is still nurturing its offsets. Cuttings may be taken from it, or it may serve as a female partner in crossbreeding.

Moving outdoors

Shifting frost-tender plants from their overwintering quarters to a location outdoors. Because of the danger of frost at night, it is best to move plants outdoors only after the last frost date in May.

Mutation

Change in a plant's genetic constitution that appears spontaneously or can be artificially induced by radiation (ultraviolet rays, X rays, and radioactive rays) or by toxins (for example, the poison colchicine from *Colchicum autumnale*) that are employed in breeding.

N

Necrosis

Dead tissue, an injury that in plants can have various causes, such as improper use of fertilizer, overly strong sun, too much or too little water, too low an amount of relative humidity, disease, or pests.

Nitrogen (N)

One of the three most important primary nutrients, which is contained in every complete fertilizer. It is used mainly for synthesis of protein compounds and is responsible for leaf and shoot development.

Node

Point of attachment of a leaf on a stem. Many plants (members of the carnation family, for example) have conspicuously thickened nodes.

NPK

Fertilizer formula for the three main nutrients needed by plants. N = nitrogen, P = phosphorus, K = potassium. The proportion of each that is contained in a specific fertilizer is expressed in numbers (for example: 14 + 7 + 14 or 14/7/14, which means: 14 percent nitrogen, 7 percent phosphorus, 14 percent potassium).

Nutrients

Certain mineral substances that plants require in order to grow and prosper. The principal nutrients include NITROGEN (N), PHOSPHORUS (P), POTASSIUM (K), calcium (Ca), magnesium (Mg), and sulfur (S). The MICRONUTRIENTS or trace elements, are principally heavy metals. Plants receive nutrients from the potting soil and the fertilizer we give them.

O

Offsets

Young plantlets that are produced from the stem form roots; then, they are separated from the mother plant and can be planted. Examples: Agave and screw pine.

Opposite leaves

See left drawing, below. An arrangement in which two leaves are situated opposite one another at a node. Contrast: ALTERNATING LEAVES (see right drawing, below).

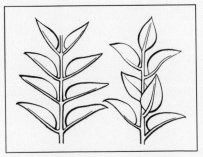

Orangery

Place to overwinter TUB PLANTS.

Organic fertilizer

Fertilizer made from plant or animal substances such as manure, blood meal, horn and hoof meal, stinging nettle broth, or guano. Their nutrients first have to be made available by soil organisms and are not immediately accessible to the plant.

P

Panachure

See VARIEGATION, and drawings, below.

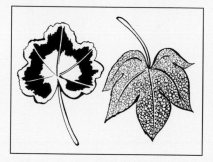

Peat

Soil from bogs, dug out after the bogs have been drained, then ground and packed in sacks. Used for improving the soil in gardens and in producing potting soils. To prevent the depletion of this soil type, which is becoming rarer all the time, it is increasingly being replaced by substitutes such as bark or compost.

Pelletized seed

Special commercially available pellets containing seeds that are small and fine or irregularly shaped. The seeds are surrounded with a coating material made of clay, clay powder, and a binding agent. In this form, they are easier to sow, and there is no need for hobby gardeners to go to the trouble of thinning out.

Perennial plants (Perennials)

Plants that survive several growing seasons. Contrast: ANNUAL PLANTS.

Perlite

Volcanic, industrially processed rock. Like PUMICE, it provides good drainage and aeration, does not decay, and binds few nutrients. Perlite is used as a potting soil for orchids and cactuses and as a propagating soil. It makes an ideal drainage material.

Pesticides

Collective term for all chemicals approved for control of plant pests.

Petals

See FLOWER.

pH value

The pH value (Latin: *potentia hydrogenii*) indicates the concentration of hydrogen ions and is expressed in numbers ranging from 1 to 14. On this scale, 7 = neutral. Numbers below 7 indicate acid reaction, numbers above, alkaline. Many plants do best at a pH of 5.5 to 6.5. The pH value can easily be ascertained with indicator rods (available in garden supply stores and pet stores).

Phosphorous (P)

One of the three chief nutrients for plants. Phosphorous plays a large role in the energy economy of the plant and in its development of roots, flowers, and fruits. It also promotes the processes of maturation.

Photosynthesis

Synthesis of organic substances from inorganic ones with the aid of light (Greek: *photos* = light, *synthesis* = combining or forming). In this process, leaves remove carbon dioxide from the air by means of their microscopic stomata, transform it with the aid of light, chlorophyll, and water into carbohydrates (sugar), and release oxygen (see ASSIMILATION).

Physiological damage

Diseases that occur in plants through some disturbance of the vital processes. Causes: mistakes in care or poor locations.

Pinching out (Pinching back)

Breaking off the tender shoot tips with the thumb and forefinger (see drawing, page 27). It results in better branching and thus in bushy growth.

Pistil

Female organ of the flower. Consists of ovary, style, and stigma (see FLOWER).

Poisonous plants

Plants containing more or less toxic substances that are lethal or injurious to humans or animals. Members of the following plant families are frequently poisonous: pea (bean), dogbane, nightshade. Abide by the warnings in the individual plant portraits (see pages 86–227).

Pollen

All the pollen grains contained in the anther (see FLOWER). The pollen grain is the male sex cell of a plant.

Pollination

Transfer of the pollen to the stigma (see FLOWER) by wind, water, insects, birds, or the human hand, for example, with a brush.

Potassium (K)

One of the three principal nutrients. It positively influences the water content of the cells and is important for various basic life processes: Potassium produces resistance to drought, frost, and certain plant diseases. Potassium is contained in every complete fertilizer. Potassium fertilizers can be given after flowering to all plants that need to enter winter with strong wood.

Preliminary culture

Growing container flowers or other young plants from seed in your house or in a conservatory or greenhouse, from February on.

Pruning

Regular removal of dead plant parts to preclude fungal disease.

Pumice

Porous, stable (that is, it will not decay), mineral volcanic rock with poor capacity for water storage. It ensures good aeration of the potting soil and is also used as drainage material.

Pyrethrum

Natural insecticide from chrysanthemum species that is not harmful to bees and is quickly broken down. According to the latest findings, it is injurious to humans if it gets into open wounds. Through the blood, it can reach and damage the nervous system. Do not use it if you have any unhealed injuries or skin diseases, especially in conjunction with allergies! Even more questionable are insecticides with pyrethroids, that is, synthetic pyrethrum. They last longer and are broken down more slowly.

R

Rainproof

Term for plants whose growth and flower quality are virtually unimpaired by rain. An important criterion for roses and herbaceous plants.

Resistance

Acquired or innate ability to withstand disease and pests (in plants) or chemical substances (in insects). Plays an important role in plant breeding, one goal of which is to produce cultivars capable of resisting pests and diseases.

Rest period

Period in which a plant no longer grows and does not form leaves or new shoots. For many tub plants, the rest period comes in the fall and winter months, when less light is available. During this time, these plants should be given less water, no fertilizer, and a cooler location.

Rhizome

Underground horizontal stem axis (see STORAGE ORGANS) that forms shoots growing upward and roots growing downward. Rhizomes are also called root stalks or rootstocks. They differ from roots in that they grow buds and scales. They also occur in herbaceous plants as organs for overwintering.

Root ball

Term for the soil surrounding pot or tub plants (also *pot ball*); it is completely permeated with roots.

Rooting hormones

Hormone preparations available in the form of powders, liquids, or pastes; they promote rooting of cuttings.

Roots

See drawing, above. In most plants, their role is to anchor the plant in the ground, absorb and transport water and nutrients, and store substances. Specialized root forms are, for example, aerial roots, prop roots, and HOLDFASTS.

Rosette

Particularly dense arrangement of leaves, all of which appear to emerge from a single point on the stem axis. This impression is due to the extreme shortness of the internodes of the stem axis.

S

Salt burn

Caused by overfertilization or by concentration of the fertilizer salts in "old" potting soil. Damage caused by salt may manifest itself as diminished growth, chlorosis (iron deficiency), or dead tissue. Remedy: Replace potting soil or rinse root ball thoroughly with clear water.

Seed

Fertilized part of a flowering plant, able to germinate and bring forth a new plant. It is often provided with a reserve of nutrients and a protective coat.

Seed carpet

A flat mat of seeds based on the same principle as the SEED STRIP. The seeds of various plants are often embedded in it, for example, seeds for an herb garden, a children's garden, or a meadow of wild flowers.

Seed-leaves (Cotyledons)

The primary leaves of a plant. As soon as they reach the light, chlorophyll forms in them and enables the plant to begin to nourish itself through PHOTOSYNTHESIS. Some plants produce only one seed-leaf, others, two.

Seedling

New plant that forms from the fertilized egg cell. The seedling consists of the primary root, seed stem, germ bud, and seed-leaves. It is bipolar: The root system develops from the primary root at the lower terminus, while the stem and leaf develop from the germ bud at the top.

Seed strip

A strip of cellulose or paper about 3 in. (7.5 cm) long and ¾ in. (2 cm) wide, in which the seeds of various vegetables, herbs, or summer flowers are embedded at the proper intervals. It makes it easier to sow seeds evenly and saves you the trouble of thinning out the seedlings. Important: Make sure there is good contact with the soil. Press the strip down firmly, water, and cover with soil.

Selection

Term used in plant breeding to designate the process of discarding plants that do not display the characteristics chosen for perpetuation. Selection also occurs in nature.

Self-cleaning

Horticulturists' term for plants that drop faded flowers on their own, so that they always look tidy. This ability is sought after in new breeds. In roses and geraniums, for example, it is a criterion for quality.

Self-climbing (self-branching) plants

Plants that develop adhesive disks at the ends of the tendrils or anchoring roots, for example, Virginia creeper and ivy.

Self-colored
Having one color only.

Self-pollination
Type of pollination in which a stigma (see FLOWER) is dusted with the pollen of the same flower. Thus only the genetic traits of this selfsame plant are passed on (inbreeding).

Sepals
See FLOWER.

Sexual propagation
Reproduction of a plant from seeds. The offspring need not resemble the mother plant. Contrast: VEGETATIVE PROPAGATION.

Shrub
Plant with lignified shoots, in which several equivalent stems grow from the ground.

Single flowers
As a rule, they possess substantially fewer petals than DOUBLE FLOWERS. Usually, the stamens are visible in single flowers.

Slow-release fertilizers
Give up nutrients to plants slowly and continuously, over a long period of time. Also called long-term fertilizers.

Solitary plant
Plant that, because of its attractiveness, deserves to stand alone. In nurseries, this term is used to designate a shrub several years old or a treelike woody plant with a branched trunk that has been transplanted at least three times and, because it is exceptionally wide, is prepared to stand alone.

Species
Designation for a part of the botanical name of a plant, which as a rule gives some information about its appearance, characteristics, or origin. Example: *Chrysanthemum frutescens. Frutescens* means that this chrysanthemum is a subshrub (Latin: *frutescens* = like a subshrub). A species includes plants that are alike in their essential features.

Spindly (Leggy)
Term for an unbalanced form of growth in plants that lignify, with long stems that grow in a relatively disorderly way. Often develops abnormally under conditions of too low light.

Stalk
Herbaceous branching or unbranching stem, with or without flowers.

Standard
Trained form of a plant, in which side shoots are prevented from developing below a certain height. Thus the main stem is strengthened. Also known as tree form.

Standing water
With few exceptions, fatal for any plant. Occurs when water from irrigation cannot run off and builds up in the soil. If an excess of water squeezes the oxygen out of the soil, the rots suffocate and rot. Therefore: Always make sure that water drains well (SEE DRAINAGE).

Stem
Also called shoot. As a rule, it consists of the stem axis, leaves, and a terminal bud.

Stem cutting
Piece of a stem or stalk—taken, for example, from *Dracaena* or *yucca*—that can be used for propagation.

Sterile
Expression meaning unfruitful or free from germs.

Stigma
Part of the flower (see FLOWER). It is covered with a slimy or sticky layer so that the male pollen will adhere to it.

Stock
A particularly vigorous plant that is used as a base for a scion or eye taken from a plant that flowers or fruits especially well. Example: Japanese bitter orange (*Poncirus trifoliata*) for *Citrus* plants.

Storage organs
See drawing, below. Organs that stockpile water and nutrients, such as
1 rhizomes,
2 corms, or
3 bulbs.

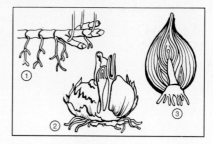

Stratification
Term previously used for the storage of seed from woody plants in layers of damp sand. Today it also refers to the mixing of seed with damp sand or some other medium (moist-chilling). Stratified seeds are put outdoors in fall and have to be exposed to winter temperatures and damp. This attempt to emulate the conditions found in nature results in a kind of pregermination.

Styrofoam chips
Pieces of nonbiodegradable plastic, which are used as a soil additive to improve aeration.

Suberization (Corky growth)
Formation of suberin (corky substance), which is deposited on the cell walls and is largely impermeable to air and water. In some plants it can produce real excrescences of cork (frequently, for example, in hanging geraniums). The cause is excessive humidity in the soil and atmosphere, in combination with an overly dark location. Corky, or suberized, areas are no longer able to assimilate, but they do not harm the plant directly.

Subtropics
Climate regions that border on the tropics north and south of the equator and extend approximately to the forty-fifth parallel. The plants of these zones are accustomed to sharply varying daytime and nighttime temperatures and to alternating periods of drought and rainfall. In the northern latitudes they are coldhouse plants, and as such are overwintered in a cool, almost dry environment.

Succulents

Plants with fleshy, juicy leaves or stems, in which water is stored.

Sucker

Young secondary shoot that grows out of the soil directly next to the mother plant.

Summer oil

Mineral oil product (white oil) used to control scale and other pests. It destroys the waxy layer of the insect's integument and clogs its respiratory organs.

Systemic pesticides

Chemicals that enter the plant through its roots or leaves and are transported throughout the plant in its vascular system. Pests that suck or gnaw on the plant ingest the substances and die.

T

Tendril

Climbing organ of plants. Some tendrils arise from stems, others, from leaves. Stem tendrils are formed by the passionflower and species of grapes. Leaf tendrils are found in peas and vetches.

Terminal cutting (Tip cutting)

Cutting that is taken from the shoot tip (see drawing, page 42).

Thicket-forming plants

They develop numerous shoots, which all come out of the ground and therefore rapidly increase their diameter.

Thinning out

After germination, the seedlings usually are so close together that they have to be thinned out. The weakest seedlings are plucked out to give the strong ones more room to grow.

Topiary art

The cutting of trees and shrubs into ornamental figures and shapes. Suitable plants are yew, for large shapes, and box, for small ones.

Transplanting

Thinning out seedlings (see drawing, page 41); for example, moving them from a seed flat into individual pots.

Trellis

Climbing aid made of wood.

Trimming

A cutting back of the plant that encompasses more than just the growing tip (see PINCHING OUT).

Tropics

Regions of the earth between 15°N and 15°S of the equator. They lie between the Tropic of Capricorn and the Tropic of Cancer on either side of the equator and are also called the hot zone. The average annual temperature is 77° to 81°F (25°–27°C). At the equator it is hot and humid; near the tropics a desert climate prevails. Plants native to these regions are called hothouse plants; they need year-round temperatures that do not drop significantly below 68°F (20°C). In botanical gardens, they are kept in so-called warm houses or tropical houses. Many of them can be cultivated also as indoor plants.

Trunk

Perennial woody, often very thick, branching or unbranching stem that does not die in winter.

Tub plants

Plants that become large relatively quickly and need correspondingly large containers (tubs) and a generous amount of space. Tub plants usually originate in subtropical regions and thrive splendidly only if they spend the summer outdoors in a protected, sunny location. Most of them have to be overwintered in a bright spot at 41° to 50°F (5°–10°C). Some also make good houseplants.

Tuft

Horticultural term for a plant with a closed, fluffy cluster shape or for a clump of several plants of the same kind placed close together.

U

Underplanting

When a standard is grown in a pot, it is best to set the surface of the soil with plants to keep it from drying out. Low, cushion-forming or slightly overhanging plants are quite attractive, such as *Semperflorens* begonias, lobelias, ivy, creeping zinnia, and bellflowers. Compatibility is important; the needs of the guide plant and the underplanting should be approximately the same. Convenient: Annual flowers that only have to be sown year after year.

Useful plants

Term for food plants such as orange trees or tomato plants, plants that produce stimulants or luxuries such as tobacco and cacao, and fodder or forage plants such as sugar beets or clover. Also includes plants that are used in technical processes and provide, for example, wood, fibers, resins, dyes, insecticides, or fuels.

V

Variegation

Also called PANACHURE or mottling by horticulturists (see drawings, page 81). The green leaves have white or yellow spots or patches. In these lighter areas, chlorophyll is absent. Variegation can be caused by MUTATION, BREEDING, or viral infections.

Variety

Abbreviation: *var.* = *varietas*. Also called CULTIVAR.

Vascular bundles

Strands in the plant in which water and dissolved nutrients are carried upward and converted, and processed substances from photosynthesis are carried downward. SYSTEMIC PESTICIDES also travel through them to every part of the plant; these pesticides are conveyed from the inside to the outside of the plant.

Vegetative cones

Growth points of shoot tips, root tips, and buds.

Vegetative period

Also called growth period or growing season. Contingent upon our seasons, the vegetative period for us begins with the increase in light levels in late winter or spring and ends when the days become shorter. The beginning of the vegetative period is discernible by the appearance of new growth.

Vegetative propagation

Asexual reproduction by plant segments, roots, stems, and leaves (see drawings, pages 42–43). The new plant thus obtained is identical to the mother plant in appearance and genetic make-up.

W

Washing out

The use of rain or other water to flush the water-soluble components of a fertilizer or substances such as lime into deeper soil strata or out of a plant container.

Water

Necessity of life for humans, animals, and plants. For nutrients, a means of transport and a solvent. A major factor in PHOTOSYNTHESIS. Without water, the plant wilts, the stigmata of the leaves close, and photosynthesis and transpiration are interrupted. For lime-hating plants (for example, azaleas, camellias, miniature orange trees), soften water that is hard.

Watering space (Head space)

Empty space allowed between the soil surface and the top of a pot, in repotting plants. It prevents soil from being washed over the edge of the pot when the plant is watered.

Water (Aquatic) plants

These include:
1 Herbaceous plants rooted in the bottom, some of which have floating leaves.
2 Submerged water plants rooted in the bottom, with no floating leaves.
3 Floating plants.

Waxy coating (Cuticle)

Extremely thin film or bloom with which many leaves protect themselves against water loss.

White oil

See SUMMER OIL.

Windbreak

Structure that provides shelter from wind and drafts for sensitive plants. Especially important on balconies or patios that are quite exposed to wind or are very high. A windbreak can consist, for example, of trellises covered with foliage, screens made of awning fabric, or glass walls.

Windproof (Windtight)

Term for plants that stay attractive even on a windy, drafty balcony.

Winter protection

Various measures for overwintering frost-tender and not entirely hardy plants, for example, by surrounding them with straw or with air-permeable bast mats, by burying them in holes dug in the soil, by covering them with fir brush (see drawings, pages 28–29). Containers are given frost protection with newspaper, straw, or bubble wrap.

Wood maturity

The hardening of tender green shoots in woody plants through the laying down of layers of lignin (part of woody tissue) in the cell wall. Plants with matured wood are more frost-resistant and less susceptible to disease when overwintered in a spot that is less than ideal. Important: The wood can mature only if no fertilizer is applied from August on.

Wood preservatives

Products with active ingredients that protect wood against wood-destroying putrefactive fungi, fungi that cause bluestain, and insects. All wood preservatives that are brushed on contain solvents whose vapors can harm humans, the environment, and plants. Containers or mounts made of wood, therefore, should be painted at least eight weeks before they are planted, to allow time for evaporation. Under no circumstances should these products be applied indoors. Alternative: Give wood an overcoat of natural-resin-based clear varnish and let everything dry thoroughly for eight days.

Worm compost

Soil that compost worms or muckworms (*Eisenia foetida*) produce when they process organic material. Worm compost contains five times more available nitrogen, seven times more soluble phosphate, and eleven times more potassium than the surrounding soil; it is an especially valuable potting soil.

Y

Yellow sticky cards

Plastic cards coated with an adhesive substance and colored a particular glaring shade of yellow that attracts insects, which then adhere to the glue.

A Mediterranean plant community on the patio: Miniature orange trees with underplanting of parrot's beak, a fig tree, bougainvillea, echeveria, heliotrope, and oleander, along with various *Citrus* species. All in plant-friendly terra cotta containers.

PLANT PORTRAITS AND TIPS ON CARE

The most beautiful plants for small and large containers. Most of them are guests from warm, sunny lands, but some are natives of our own country. On the following pages, you will learn what specific needs they have and how they can be grown successfully.

The Most Beautiful Container Plants

In the following plant portraits, you will become acquainted with the most popular and the newest container plants, along with attractive broad-leaved woody plants, dwarf conifers, and the most beautiful grasses, herbs, and vegetables for balcony and patio gardens. The full-color portraits will familiarize you with the individual growth forms and the sweeping range of flower and leaf colors. The individual descriptions give comprehensive, detailed information on the care plants need the year round, in addition to background knowledge such as each plant's family and origin. The decorating tip at the end is sure to suggest many fine ideas.

Structure of the Plant Portraits

All the plant descriptions are arranged in a clear, well-organized structure, so that information about a plant is available at a glance. Because all the descriptions follow the same format, making comparisons between individual plants is easy. Where will you find the particular plants that interest you? They will be contained in one of the chapters that follow (see box on page 89), arranged according to category and alphabetized under their botanical name.

<u>The English common name</u> appears in large, easy-to-read type directly above the photo. It is the one most familiar to many plant fanciers. If a plant has several names, they too are given.

<u>The botanical name</u>, placed above the English one, is internationally accepted and therefore determines the alphabetical sequence of the plant descriptions.

If only the genus name (for example, *Chrysanthemum* or *Citrus*) appears, several species suitable for container culture are discussed in the instructions on care.

If a species name (for example, *Antirrhinum majus* or *Plumbago auriculata*) is given as the botanical name, the description applies only to this particular species (and its possible cultivars).

The Symbols and Their Meaning

Without having to read through the text, you can tell quickly what location is right for a plant and what kind of overwintering is appropriate for it. At a glance, you will know whether it is poisonous, and you will learn about such important procedures as watering and protection against weather factors.

The plant needs and can tolerate full sun and heat, including midday sun. A location in full sun with southern exposure is important for its flower development.

The plant wants a bright spot, without glaring midday sun. Morning and evening sun—that is, situations with eastern and southern exposure—are tolerated well.

The plant needs partial shade, or, as experience has shown, it also will do well in partial shade.

The plant tolerates or prefers shade.

The plant needs abundant water. On hot days, water thoroughly twice.

Keep the plant only moderately damp. On hot days, water thoroughly once.

The plant needs little water.

The plant is sensitive to rain. It becomes unattractive when wet and has to be protected from prolonged rainfall.

The plant is sensitive to wind and needs a sheltered location.

The plant is an annual or can be cultivated successfully for only one year. These plants consequently need no winter quarters and no winter protection.

The plant has to be overwintered in a bright indoor location.

The plant can be overwintered indoors in a dark location. Of course, bright winter quarters are always better for these plants too.

The plant can winter over outdoors with protection.

The plant is poisonous or contains skin irritants.

Explanation of the Headings

In each case, the instructions on care are preceded by an exact description of the plant. It contains information on the growth form, size, flower shape and color, appearance of the leaves, diversity of the cultivars, and typical characteristics. Cultivars that are reproduced by commercial gardeners and marketed as young plants are listed, along with others that are available in packets for sowing by hobby gardeners themselves. Frequently, information is given about the origin of the name or the history of the plant. In conclusion, appropriate instructions on care are given, arranged according to headings in bold face.

Blooming Season: For most balcony and tub plants, which of course are bought or raised for the beauty of their flowers, this is important information. It has decisive importance in any decorating or landscaping scheme.

Family: Here you will find the family in botanical classification to which the plant belongs.

Origin: This gives the geographical origin.

Location: This is an important criterion in plant care. Here you will learn each individual plant's requirements for light and warmth. Pointers on protection against weather factors are also supplied.

Potting Soil: This indicates suitable soils or soil mixes for use in planting.

Planting: This applies only to container flowers (see pages 90–141), which are generally planted in groups in boxes or which, as in the case of bulbs, may have a particular vegetative rhythm. Under this heading, you also will find information on the time to plant, the planting depth, and the proper spacing of the plants.

Raising: This information is given only for vegetables and herbs (pages 216–227), which hobby gardeners frequently grow themselves from seed.

Watering, Feeding: Under this heading, you will learn how much to water and how often to apply fertilizer. Important: Where "feed lightly or in low doses" is advised, use only one-half to one-third of the manufacturer's recommended quantity for 1 qt (1 L) of water.

Further Care: This will tell you about ways to encourage repeated flowering or to provide support to climbing or floppy plants, as well as about cutting back and plant hygiene.

Overwintering: This provides advice on the proper time for moving plants indoors in regions where frost is likely, procedures for cutting back or trimming before moving them, and the light and temperature levels necessary in their winter quarters. Additional information on care and overwintering is found in the chapter Successful Care and Overwintering (see pages 18–29).

Pests, Diseases: Those listed are the ones to which the plant in question is particularly vulnerable. The causes (if known) of the infestation or disease are also listed. How to remedy them is described in the chapter First Aid for Your Plants (see pages 30–37).

Propagation: The most common methods of reproduction are described. The chapter Raising Plants Yourself (see pages 38–43) will tell you how to put them into practice.

Decorating Tip: Suggestions are offered here for containers or for combinations of plants that are a good match, in terms of color or growth, for the plant described. In addition, the plant's suitability for use in hanging baskets or for training as a standard or a bonsai is noted. For more on design, see the section Planting Ideas for Every Season (pages 44–73).

My Tip: Valuable information derived from the author's own experience is given here.

Warning: This heading appears if the plant contains toxins or substances that irritate the skin. Plants thus designated can be harmful or even lethal to susceptible adults, children, or pets if the plants are ingested or come into contact with the skin or the mucous membranes.

Beware of the Plants— Facts You Should Know

In choosing plants, keep in mind the following criteria if you have small children or pets. Some specimens are to be enjoyed with caution.

Plants can cause allergies. Cases of contact dermatitis (skin inflammation) are known to be caused by phototoxic substances contained, for example, in *Citrus* species or *Tagetes*. Skin irritations may result from handling hyacinth and daffodil bulbs and primrose and clematis species. The *cumarin* in ageratum can give rise to hayfever. Various Compositae, particularly chrysanthemums, are also said to be allergenic.

Plants can cause injuries, for example, through contact with spines, thorns, sharp leaf tips, and thorny leafstalks—as found in the agave, lemon tree, Natal plum, yucca, *Chamaerops humilis*, and petticoat palm.

Plant scents can cause headaches, particularly on almost enclosed, protected patios or balconies. These have an intense fragrance: orange blossom, angel's trumpet, lilies, *Mandevilla laxa*, tobacco plant, and star jasmine.

Plants can contain toxic substances, which can be harmful to the health of humans and animals and, if consumed, can even be lethal. Small children tend to put everything in their mouths, and pets for inexplicable reasons also may nibble on balcony and tub plants.

Danger: Poisonous Plants and Plant Substances

Many plants that we cultivate in gardens and on balconies and patios produce toxic substances. In the plant portraits in this book, the skull-and-crossbones symbol and the heading "Warning" are used to indicate the danger represented by these plants. The following toxins are the most common:

Alkaloids are basic (alkaline), nitrogenous substances that in plants are dissolved in the cell sap as salts of organic plant acids. Usually, one particular amino acid serves as the primary building block. All alkaloids—some 300 are said to exist— bear the name of their plant of origin and end in "-ine." Examples:
• Anemone, *Anemone* = (proto) anemonine.
• Autumn crocuses, *Colchicum* = colchicine.
• Tobacco plant, *Nicotiana* = nicotine.
• Nightshade, *Solanum* = solanine.
• Broom, *Cytisus* = cytisine.
• Box, *Buxus* = buxine.
• Barberry, *Berberus* = berberine.

Glycosides consist of sugar molecules and a noncarbohydrate component, the *aglycon*. The two are chemically linked in a very special kind of bond. Glycosides from foxglove, *Strophanthus*, and lilies of the valley, which affect the heart, have become famous as drugs. Other plants that contain glycosides are wallflower, broom, oleander, and *Thevetia* (yellow oleander).

Terpenes are a group of extremely diverse biogenous substances. *Monoterpenes* occur in essential oils, and *sesquiterpenes* are present in many Asteraceae. *Diterpenes* are found in the heath family, *triterpenes*, in the gourd family and in lantana.

Toxic proteins, along with other toxins, are present in euphorbia and leguminous plants. Examples:
• Castor-oil plant, *Rhicinus* = ricine.
• Bean plant, *Phaseolus* = phasine.
• Locust, *Robinia* = robine.

What You Can Find Where, Quickly

CONTAINER FLOWERS

With boxes, pots, and bowls full of splendidly flourishing foliage and flowering plants that do not grow overly high, spring, summer, fall, and winter will be experiences everyone can enjoy on balconies and patios. Take advantage of the continually expanding assortment of species and cultivars to create a flowery paradise of your own design in the tiniest of spaces and high in the air.

A marvelous combination of pink and violet container flowers. Chrysanthemums, sage, impatiens, and globe amaranth. Add blue lobelias as the prettiest partner imaginable.

If the Langobards had only known what would develop 1,500 years later from the simple *balco*, their word for balcony! First it turned into Romeo and Juliet's *balcone*; later it became the French *balcon* and the English *balcony*. Today, this generally small spot is a plant paradise, a green, flowering outdoor living area, an El Dorado for bees and butterflies, in short, a piece of nature—right under your nose, ready to be touched and experienced. Market analyses, opinion polls, and contemporary architecture offer proof that container gardening for balconies is very much on the rise.

The Assortment of Plants for Flower Boxes

The available assortment of suitable plants for small containers has long since expanded beyond the traditional container flowers such as geraniums, fuchsias, or tuberous begonias. Today, the broad range of offerings includes exotic novelties that cause a sensation as hanging plants or effusive climbers. They are joined by familiar summer flowers, woody plants from the garden, grasses, and flowering bulbs that once were planted only in beds. Now they reveal unsuspected decorative potential for almost every season. Small, compact species and cultivars proved useful immediately, but others first had to be induced—through breeding or horticultural adaptation—to assume a habit appropriate for small containers. On the 52 pages that follow, you will find important information and tips on care not only for container flowers, both the familiar and the new, but also for the "outsiders" that are suitable for flower box culture—bulbs, grasses, and miniature roses, which many people have yet to discover for use on their balconies.

Appropriate Care

Container plants come from all over the world and from the most diverse families. Their growth forms and vegetative rhythms may differ widely from one another. Only by knowing these characteristics can you choose the appropriate plants for your location and make the right combinations of plants. You will no longer see perennials such as herbaceous plants or bulbs as "decorations for a single season"; instead, you will note their individual periods of growth and rest and perhaps become interested in helping them through the winter, to grow and bloom again the following year. Granted, this is not easy with some bulbs, because in the limited soil available they often cannot store enough energy to flower again. The positive experiences of many flower box gardeners, however, are proof that the attempt is always worth making.

Frilly Tutus

Fuchsias, which grow best in partial shade, are among the best-loved container flowers. Here, the double-flowered cultivar 'Ullswater'.

Ageratum houstonianum
Ageratum, Floss Flower

Ageratum comes in many nuances of blue and violet.

☀ 🪣 1 ☠

The botanical name of this subshrub is derived from the Greek *ageraton*. Meaning roughly "that which does not age," it probably refers to the long blooming period of this plant. Depending on the cultivar, ageratum grows 6 to 24 in. (15–60 cm) high, and its leaves range from cordate, or heart-shaped, to ovate, or egg-shaped. The flower heads grow in corymbs, and in the pure species, the flowers range from sky blue to silver-blue. Low, compact F_1 hybrids such as the following are recommended for box culture: 'Blue Danube' (6-8 in. [15–20 cm] high, medium blue), 'North Sea' (6–8 in. [15–20 cm] high, deep blue), 'Pacific' (8 in. [20 cm] high, purple-violet, small-leaved), 'Blue Blazer' (6 in. [15 cm] high, light blue), 'Atlantik' (8 in. [20 cm] high, ultramarine blue).
Blooming Season: May to October.
Family: Asteroceae or Compositae, (aster or composite family).

Origin: Mexico, Guatemala, Belize.
Location: Sunny to partially shady.
Potting Soil: All-purpose soil, plain or enriched with slow-release fertilizer.
Planting: Set purchased or home-grown (see Propagation) young plants 8 in. (20 cm) apart in container.
Watering, Feeding: Water abundantly and feed every 2 weeks.
Further Care: Deadhead spent flowers to stimulate new array of blossoms.
Overwintering: Not applicable.
Pests, Diseases: Spider mites.
Propagation: From seed, from January to March, at a soil temperature of 64° to 70°F (18–21°C).
Decorating Tip: Ageratum is windtight and makes a good match for slipperwort (page 97).
Warning: Ageratum contains cumarin, which can produce irritations of the mucous membranes, hay-fever, and—if ingested—internal bleeding in people sensitive to this substance.

Allium
Allium

Allium moly, golden allium, attracts bees.

☀ 🪣 💧 🏠

The low relatives of allium, which generally are also quite attractive because of their wild appearance, are well suited for flower boxes or bowls.
• *Allium moly*, about 10 to 12 in. (25–30 cm) high, attracts great numbers of bees with its profusion of golden-yellow umbels.
• *Allium oreophilum*, about 8 in. (20 cm) high, frequently also known as *Allium ostrowskianum*, has purple flowers with a dark midline.
All *Allium* species are bought as bulbs and planted in containers in September or October.
Blooming Season: *Allium moly*, May to June; *Allium oreophilum*, June to July.
Family: Liliaceae (lily family).
Origin: Eastern Spain, southwestern France (*Allium moly*); Caucasus, eastern Turkestan (*Allium oreophilum*).
Location: Sunny.
Potting Soil: Loamy, sandy garden soil; all-purpose soil with some sand added.

Planting: Set bulbs in containers in September or October, 6 in. (15 cm) apart and 3 in. (7 cm) deep.
Overwintering: Put planted box in a frost-free, dark, cool spot. Do not let soil dry out. After flush, put in a brighter place.
Watering, Feeding: Keep planted box slightly damp until flush occurs; from then on, water moderately and feed once. Avoid standing water. After the plants lose their blooms, set them—with the root ball—in the garden and feed once more.
Further Care: Deadhead spent flowers.
Pests, Diseases: Thrips, stem eelworms; rust.
Propagation: If grown in containers, not possible. In garden, from offsets (bulblets). *Allium moly* will spread freely on its own, if you do not remove the fruits.

Anemone blanda
Anemone, Mountain Windflower of Greece

Violet *Anemone blanda* with celandine.

In a beech forest, the carpets of white wood anemones (*Anemone quinquefolia*) are harbingers of spring, while *Anemone blanda* brings a springtime atmosphere to the balcony or patio and is one of the early food plants for bees. The plant, which is 4 to 6 in. (10–15 cm) high, renews itself from a tuberous root. The flowers of the pure species are sky blue; those of the hybrids range from white through various shades of pink to blue and violet. Single colors or mixtures are available.

Blooming Season: March or April.

Family: Ranunculaceae (buttercup or crowfoot family).

Origin: Southeastern Europe, Caucasus, Near East.

Location: Bright to partially shady. Protect plants in bloom against late frost.

Potting Soil: All-purpose mix, or loamy, humus-rich garden soil. Likes lime.

Planting: Set the tuberous roots in containers in September, 4 in. (10 cm) apart and 2 in. (5 cm) deep. Place them in water for 24 hours before planting; this will encourage flushing.

Watering, Feeding: Always keep planted box slightly damp; feed twice during growth period.

Further Care: After blossoms fall, plant in the garden and feed once more.

Overwintering: Keep planted box in a frost-free, dark place. Do not let soil dry out. After flush, plants need more light.

Pests, Diseases: Occasionally, tuber rot.

Propagation: If grown in containers, not possible. In the garden, the plants reproduce themselves via daughter tubers.

Decorating Tip: Pink cultivars such as 'Pink Star' or 'Charmer' are an excellent match for blue-flowering crocus.

Warning: All parts of anemones are poisonous.

Antirrhinum majus
Snapdragon

Snapdragons are available in a wide range of colors.

Breeders have developed numerous cultivars with a wide range of colors. The dwarf cultivars, 6 to 10 in. (15–25 cm) high, are suitable for flower boxes. In the dwarf category, there are various mixtures, whose flowers range from white through yellow to pink and red. Still others, such as 'Kimosy Prachtmischung' or 'Floral Carpet', are bicolored. In the garden, snapdragons can survive mild winters, but they usually are treated as annuals.

Blooming Season: June to September. Nursery-grown plants are available in bloom from April on. Once they are slightly hardened off, they can be put outdoors.

Family: Scrophulariaceae (figwort family).

Origin: Original forms, southwestern Europe, northwestern Africa, western Asia.

Location: Sunny to partially shady.

Potting Soil: All-purpose soil, plain or enriched with slow-release fertilizer.

Planting: Set purchased or home-grown (see Propagation) young plants 8 in. (20 cm) apart in container.

Watering, Feeding: Water moderately. Avoid standing water. Apply low doses of fertilizer weekly.

Further Care: None.

Overwintering: Not applicable.

Pests, Diseases: Aphids, spider mites; snapdragon rust, powdery and downy mildew, botrytis.

Propagation: From seed, in February, at a ground temperature of 59° to 68°F (15–20°C). Trim main stems of young plants in order to promote bushy growth.

Decorating Tip: For small or shallow containers, a cultivar known as 'Floral Showers Mix', which forms clusters only 6 in. (15 cm) high, recently became available.

Asteriscus maritimus
Asteriscus

Only the cultivated form is available commercially.

If the Latin botanical name in use today were to be translated literally, this pretty herbaceous plant would have to be called "little beach star" (*asteriscus* = little star, *maritimus* = beach). The wild form is somewhat tricky to cultivate, but the now widespread Australian cultivar 'Gold Coin' is not. It reaches a height of 10 to 12 in. (25–30 cm), grows slightly overhanging, has bright-green foliage, and is profusely covered with sun-yellow flowers, which do not close in bad weather and continue to appear until the first hard frost.

Blooming Season: April or May to October.
Family: Asteraceae or Compositae (aster or composite family).
Origin: Pure species, Mediterranean area, Canary Islands.
Location: Sunny.
Potting Soil: All-purpose mix or loamy, sandy garden soil.
Planting: Set purchased or home-grown (see Propagation) young plants 8 in. (20 cm) apart in container.
Watering, Feeding: Keep evenly damp during growth period, but avoid standing water. Feed weekly until August.
Further Care: Deadhead spent flowers.
Overwintering: In a bright place at 50°F (10°C). Keep relatively dry. Repot in February or March.
Pests, Diseases: Deformation of flower buds caused by aphids.
Propagation: By soft tip cuttings without buds, in summer.
Decorating Tip: *Asteriscus maritimus* is easily combined with all balcony flowers that love sun, and it also has an excellent record as a hanging plant.

Begonia x semperflorens Hybrids
Wax Begonias

Begonia x *semperflorens* hybrid 'Lachsvision'.

Wax begonias are herbaceous plants originally, but they are cultivated only as annuals. There are green-leaved and bronze-leaved cultivars that grow low and compact, as well as large-flowered ones that grow as high as 12 in. (30 cm). The flowers are single or, more rarely, double. The colors range from white through various shades of pink and salmon to deep red. Bicolored wax begonias are quite striking.

Blooming Season: May to October.
Family: Begoniaceae (begonia family).
Origin: Original forms, Brazil.
Location: Sunny to bright.
Potting Soil: Blend of ½ all-purpose soil with ½ peat moss, which can be enriched with slow-release fertilizer.
Planting: Set purchased or home-grown (see Propagation) young plants 6 to 10 in. (15–25 cm) apart in container.
Watering, Feeding: Water generously, but avoid standing water at all costs—danger of root rot. Apply low doses of fertilizer every 2 or 3 weeks.
Further Care: Pinch off faded flowers. After the first profusion of blooms, cut plants back; this will cause them to form additional flowers.
Overwintering: Not applicable.
Pests, Diseases: Powdery mildew.
Propagation: From seed, in late December, at a ground temperature of 68° to 72°F (20°–22°C). Scatter the seeds on the potting soil, do not cover them with soil—light germinator. Difficult for a layman without a greenhouse and artificial light.
My Tip: Wax begonias also do well on windy balconies.
Warning: *Begonia* x *semperflorens* hybrids contain poisonous substances.

Tuberous Begonia

The bright flowers of the tuberous begonia hybrid 'Nonstop Apricot' are visible from a distance.

Tuberous begonias will bloom even in sites that are not very bright. All flower colors except blue and violet are represented. The flowers, up to 4 in. (10 cm) across, are more or less double-petaled, and some resemble roses or anemones. In addition, there are bicolored cultivars with fimbriated or frilled petal edges. The pointed, oval leaves vary in size, are olive green to dark green in color, and have a metallic sheen or green veining. They grow on thick, succulent (thin, in trailing forms) stems. Large-flowered or small-flowered groups—which grow erect in a variety of heights—are available. In addition, there are trailing begonias—which tend to be small-flowered—for hanging baskets. The new garland begonia 'Illumination' deserves special mention. It has long, flexible, decidedly more branched stems and is covered with shallow, salmon-pink blooms.

Blooming Season: May to October.

Family: Begoniaceae (begonia family).

Origin: Original forms, South America.

Location: Bright to partially shady and sheltered from wind. (Bertinii and Multiflora begonias also.)

Potting Soil: All-purpose soil with an equal amount of peat moss added, may also be enriched with slow-release fertilizer.

Planting: Set purchased or home-grown (see Forcing and Propagation) young plants 10 in. (25 cm) apart in container.

Watering, Feeding: During the growth period, water abundantly, but by all means avoid standing water. From August on, reduce amounts of water. Until October, apply low doses of fertilizer every 2 weeks, so that the tubers can regenerate.

Further Care: Support *large-flowered* cultivars with stakes. Deadhead spent flowers. From September on, do not cut off the foliage, but let it slowly turn yellow.

Overwintering: Bring the boxes or pots indoors only after the first nighttime frosts. (In most cultivars, tuber growth is greatest during the short fall days.) Cut off dried or frozen stems and leaves to a length of about ¾ to 1 in. (2–3 cm). Carefully shake the soil off the tubers. If it clings to them, it is better left alone, because the tubers must not be damaged: There is a risk of infection. Store the tubers in well-ventilated wooden boxes or in baskets at 41° to 50°F (5°–10°C), until you force them.

Forcing: In February or March, lay the tubers side by side in crates filled with wet peat, and keep them in a bright place at 64° to 72°F (18°–22°C). Once flushing begins, put the tubers in larger pots or directly into flower boxes. As soon as leaves have formed, move the plants outdoors, but bring them back inside if there is any threat of frost.

Pests, Diseases: Aphids, thrips, soft-skinned mites; powdery mildew, botrytis.

Propagation: By division of tubers, shortly after flush occurs. Disinfect cut surfaces with charcoal powder. In the garden, from seed sown from November to January, at a temperature between 73° and 77°F (23°–25°C) and with additional light (difficult).

Warning: Aboveground and underground parts of tuberous begonias contain poisonous substances.

My Tip: Overwintering modern cultivars often is not worth the trouble, because the tubers usually are still quite small in fall.

The cultivars in the photos:
Left: Snow-white, elegant 'Memory'.
Above: Exotic red-edged beauty, 'Bali Hi'.

Bellis perennis
Daisy, English Daisy

Brachycome iberidifolia
Swan River Daisy

'Pomponette' is one of the best-loved *Bellis* cultivars.

Brachycome is strewn with lightly scented flowers.

All that modern breeds have in common with the modest daisy is the tuftlike rosette of spatulate leaves. The flowers are far more magnificent—double or single, pompons or buttons, and white, pink, or red in color. Well-known, popular cultivars are 'Teppich', 'Pomponette', 'Tasso', 'Super Enorma', 'Habanera', 'Medicis', and 'Roggli'. These compact cultivars, 5 to 8 in. (12–20 cm) high, are raised in summer, and they flower the following spring. For close-to-nature balconies and patios, the long-lasting meadow daisy is now being cultivated and sold once more.

Blooming Season: March to June.
Family: Asteraceae or Compositae (aster or composite family).
Origin: Europe, Asia Minor.
Location: Sunny to partially shady.
Potting Soil: All-purpose mix or loamy garden soil.
Planting: Set purchased or home-grown (see Propagation) young plants 6 in. (15 cm) apart in containers.
Watering, Feeding: Water abundantly during the growth season if the weather is hot; otherwise, water less. Feed weekly.
Further Care: Deadhead spent flowers to prolong the blooming period.
Overwintering: Outdoors, with pine brush as winter protection (see pages 28–29).
Pests, Diseases: Aphids, spider mites; powdery mildew.
Propagation: From seed, in June or July, sown directly in the boxes (light germinator). Some of the plants will start to bloom in fall.
Decorating Tip: *Bellis* looks entrancing when planted close together in rustic ceramic containers, and its beauty is enhanced when combined with blue hyacinths.

Swan River daisies have taken many hearts by storm in recent years. No wonder! This annual forms numerous shoots 12 in. (30 cm) long, branches prolifically, and in a short time produces a multitude of blossoms. The flowers, about 1 in. (2.5 cm) across, have a golden-yellow center and white, pink, blue, or violet petals. They have a pleasant fragrance and soon cover the fernlike foliage.

Blooming Season: July to September.
Family: Asteracae or Compositae (aster or composite family).
Origin: Australia.
Location: Sunny.
Potting Soil: All-purpose soil, plain or enriched with slow-release fertilizer.
Planting: Set purchased or home-grown (see Propagation) young plants 6 in. (15 cm) apart in container.
Watering, Feeding: Keep slightly damp at all times; feed every 1 or 2 weeks. Do not let soil dry out, and avoid standing water.
Further Care: Deadhead spent flowers.
Overwintering: Not applicable.
Pests, Diseases: Whiteflies.
Propagation: From seed, in March, at a ground temperature of 68° to 72°F (20°–22°C). Transplant seedlings once before planting them out. Also from tip and stem cuttings from January to April. They strike root within 2 to 3 weeks.
Decorating Tip: Because it grows in cascades, *Brachycome* is an excellent hanging plant and a pretty underplanting for standards.

Calceolaria integrifolia
Slipperwort, Pocketbook Flower

Slipperwort grows in an attractive, compact shape.

○ 🐿 💧 **1**

The outdoor slipperwort is the small-flowered sister of the large-flowered *Calceolaria* hybrids that are sold as indoor plants. In its native habitat, *Calceolaria integrifolia* is a subshrub that grows 16 in. to almost 4 ft (40–120 cm) high. The modern F_1 hybrids sold for container culture, such as 'Goldari', 'Goldbukett', or 'Leila', seldom reach a height of more than 12 in. (30 cm) and are treated as annuals. The flowers appear in corymbs, free-flowering panicles above the bright-green, oblong-ovate leaves.

Blooming Season: May to September.
Family: Scrophulariaceae (figwort family).
Origin: Chile.
Location: Bright to partially shady and sheltered from rain.
Potting Soil: All-purpose soil, plain or enriched with slow-release fertilizer.
Planting: Set purchased or home-grown (see Propagation) young plants 10 in. (25 cm) apart in container.
Watering, Feeding: Water generously and feed weekly, but not with high doses. The plant has poor tolerance for high concentrations of fertilizer salts.
Further Care: Deadhead spent flowers regularly to ensure reblooming.
Overwintering: Not applicable.
Pests, Diseases: Aphids, whiteflies, spider mites.
Propagation: From seed, from December to February, at a ground temperature of 59°F (15°C). Alternatively, by cuttings taken in January or February or from mid-August to mid-September. Overwinter young plants in a bright, airy place at 46° to 50°F (8°–10°C).
Decorating Tip: The bright signal-light yellow of slipperworts goes particularly well with fire-engine-red geraniums or blue ageratum.

Calendula officinalis
Pot Marigold

The pot marigold cultivar 'Goldschwarze Prinzessin'.

☀ 🐿 **1**

The pot marigold, an annual summer flower, has been grown in many countries from time immemorial as a medicinal and ornamental plant. Its flowers contain essential oil, saponins, bitter constituents, carotenoids, and flavanoids. They are used in medicine and in homeopathy, particularly externally, for wounds that are slow to heal. Cultivars that stay low and compact are best for balcony boxes. Especially recommended: 'Fiesta Gitana', a 12-in.-high (30 cm), early-blooming, double-flowered mix that comes in all shades of yellow and in salmon, apricot, and orange.

Blooming Season: June to October.
Family: Asteraceae or Compositae (aster or composite family).
Origin: Probably the Mediterranean area.
Location: Sunny.
Potting Soil: All-purpose or loamy garden soil. Likes lime.
Planting: Set purchased or home-grown (see Propagation) young plants 8 in. (20 cm) apart in container.
Further Care: Pinch tips to promote bushy growth and deadhead spent flowers regularly.
Watering, Feeding: Remove faded flowers to ensure reblooming.
Overwintering: Not applicable.
Pests, Diseases: Aphids, leaf miners; Powdery and downy mildew.
Propagation: From seed in spring at 57° to 61°F (14°-16°C) (easy). Light germinator.
Decorating Tip: Pot marigolds are most attractive in rustic containers, and they fit in well with other close-to-nature plantings.

Callistephus chinensis
China Aster, Annual Aster

In the well-known 'Pompon-Prachtmischung', the flowers display all the colors of the rainbow.

☼ 🪣 **1**

The name, which means approximately "beautiful wreath" (Greek: *kallos* = beauty, *stephos* = wreath), refers to the flowers, which grow singly on the ends of the branches. China asters are among the most important flowers in commercial gardening. They are widely used as cut flowers and for planting in beds and boxes. Thus, breeders are correspondingly active, and it is difficult to keep up with the large and varied assortment they provide. In addition to an almost inexhaustible choice of high and medium-high cutting asters for the garden, there are a number of lower asters for beds and pots. Most suitable for the flower box are low dwarf cultivars with a bushy habit, such as:
• 'Milady', 10 to 14 in. (25–35 cm) high, semispherical flowers 4 to 5 in. (10–12 cm) across, resembling pot chrysanthemums.
• 'Lüneburger Zwerg', 10 in. (25 cm) high, flowers are tight pompons 2 to 3 in. (6–8 cm) across.
• 'Tausendschön', 6 to 8 in. (15–20 cm) high, large pompons 2 to 3 in. (6–8 cm) across.
• 'Königin', 10 to 14 in. (25–35 cm) high, large pompons of one color.
• 'Love Me', 10 in. (25 cm) high, finely radiate double flowers.
• 'Pinocchio', 8 to 10 in. (20–25 cm) high, dense, small, double stellate flowers.
• 'Comet', 10 in. (25 cm) high, double flowers 4 to 5 in. (10–12 cm) across.
• 'Contrast', 8 to 10 in. (20–25 cm) high, double flowers with petals turned inward like claws.
• 'Dingi', 6 in. (15 cm) high, pompon flowers 2 to 3 in. (6–7 cm) across.
• 'Farbenteppich', 8 in. (20 cm) high, large pompon flowers.
• 'Teisa Stars', 16 in. (40 cm) high, double flowers with visible yellow center.
• 'Stella', 10 in (25 cm) high, double flowers striped with red-and-white.
• 'Nebelungs Troll', 8 in. (20 cm) high, large radiate flowers. Flower colors range from white, cream, and pink through scarlet and violet to blue, with many intermediate shades.

Blooming Season: July to October.
Family: Asteraceae or Compositae (aster or composite family).
Origin: Central, northern, and eastern Asia.
Location: Sunny.
Potting Soil: All-purpose soil, plain or enriched with slow-release fertilizer.
Planting: Set purchased or home-grown (see Propagation) young plants 8 to 10 in. (20–25 cm) apart in container.
Watering, Feeding: Water abundantly in hot weather; otherwise, moderately. Feed weekly. Avoid standing water.
Further Care: Deadhead spent flowers.
Overwintering: Not applicable.
Pests, Diseases: Occasionally aphids; aster wilt (fungal disease), powdery mildew.

Propagation: From seed in March or April.
Decorating Tip: China asters are most attractive when planted tone-on-tone or in a mixture of colors—without companion plants.

Fall atmosphere with heather and autumn crocuses.

Calluna has scaly leaves.

Rising sales figures supply the proof: Heather has become a trend. Over 30 million plants belonging to the *Calluna* and *Erica* species (see page 108)—both important for container gardening—are sold annually throughout the world!
Calluna vulgaris, which in midsummer colors large expanses of moorland in northern Europe a gorgeous pink, is a creeping dwarf shrub with evergreen leaves that are attached like scales. It is the original form from which numerous cultivars with a variety of foliage and flower colors were derived.
In addition to green-leaved cultivars, there are others with golden ('Gold Haze') or gray ('Silver Queen') leaves. The flower colors range from white through pink to dark violet. There are single-flowered and double-flowered cultivars. The blooming period of the cultivars begins at the end of June and lasts until the end of November.

Calluna vulgaris cultivars—grown over a period of years—reach a height of 32 to 36 in. (80–90 cm), but they are sold when about 6 to 8 in. (15–20 cm) high. They most often are sold as seasonal plants (particularly 'Sparkes', 'Red Star', and 'H. E. Beale') for fall planting, but they can be cultivated for several years in troughs or in specially designed window boxes.

Blooming Season: Varies according to cultivar:
• June: 'Caerketton White' (white).
• July: 'Tib' (violet-pink), 'Alportii Praecox' (crimson), 'Decumbens Alba' (white).
• August: 'Kinlochruel' (white), 'J. H. Hamilton' (salmon pink).
• September to October: 'Long White' (white).
• September to November: 'Annemarie' (dark pink), 'Darkness' (crimson).
• September to December: 'Marleen' (lilac-pink).

Family: Ericaceae (heath family).

Origin: Original forms, Europe, Siberia, Asia Minor, northern Morocco.

Location: Sunny to partially shady.

Potting Soil: Rhododendron soil (or equal amounts of all-purpose soil and peat moss) with ⅓ sand.

Planting: Set purchased or home-grown (see Propagation) young plants 10 to 16 in. (25–40 cm) apart in container.

Watering, Feeding: During the growth period, keep them evenly damp. If they are treated as seasonal plants, feeding can be omitted. If grown as perennials, apply organic fertilizer once in spring and early summer.

Further Care: Between mid-March and mid-April, cut back perennials to the old wood.

Overwintering: Outdoors without winter protection. On frost-free days, water little, but <u>do not let plants dry out</u>.

Pests, Diseases: Rare.

Propagation: In August or September, by layers produced by a bed plant (relatively easy) or from 1-in.-long (3 cm), semilignified cuttings (more difficult). Remove lower leaves, set just over ⅓ in. (1 cm) deep. Put pots in plastic bags.

Decorating Tip: A good companion for other moorland plants (such as heath, wintergreen, lavender heath, rhododendrons, and azaleas), grasses. dwarf needle-leaved woody plants, and slow-growing cultivars of maple and broom.

My Tip: You will find unusual cultivars only in good nurseries and through special mail-order suppliers of heather.

If you want to keep your heather longer than a single season, water it with soft water, if at all possible.

Campanula Species and Cultivars
Bellflowers

Campanula carpatica—particularly delicate in white.

Campanula carpatica also may be violet-colored.

Campanula poscharskyana forms long tendrils in hanging baskets.

Along with the well-known semi-hardy species for indoor and balcony or patio use, such as *Campanula isophylla* or *Campanula fragilis*, hardy bellflowers for rock gardens or herbaceous beds are increasingly being grown on balconies and patios in pots, hanging baskets, and boxes. Four examples, two of each type, follow:

• *Campanula carpatica*, Carpathian harebell; tussock bluebell: is thick and bushy in habit, forms large clumps; not proliferous, 10 in. (25 cm) high. Leaves roundish and cordate. Flowers grow singly on long, bare stalks; large, open, bell-shaped blossoms, blue-violet and white. Hardy.

• *Campanula fragilis*, fragile bellflower: is low-growing to pendulous, 12 in. (30 cm) high. Leaves smooth, shiny, with crenated margins. Flowers bell-shaped, usually located at the tips of the stems, blue with white center or white. Semihardy.

• *Campanula isophylla*, Italian bellflower: grows low, slightly pendant, 4 to 8 in. (10–20 cm) high. Leaves almost round to cordate or ovate, margins dentate. Flowers especially numerous at ends of stalks, white or blue. Semihardy.

• *Campanula portenschlagiana*: forms large clumps, dense and bushy; produces threadlike runners. Leaves cordate on thin stems. Flowers abundant, in short corymbs, blue-violet. Hardy.

• *Campanula poscharskyana*: vigorous growth, stays low, but produces threadlike runners up to 20 in. (50 cm) long. Leaves cordate and dentate, long stems. Flowers on branched stalk ends, in blue-violet shades varying in intensity.

Blooming Season: June to July. *Campanula poscharskyana* to September. Precultured plants earlier.
Family: Campanulaceae (bellflower family).
Origin: Siebenbürgen, Carpathians (*Campanula carpatica*), southern Italy (*Campanula fragilis*), all others, Dalmatia.
Location: Full sun (*Campanula carpatica*), all others, bright, without sun.
Potting Soil: All-purpose mix or permeable, lime-rich garden soil.
Planting: Set purchased or home-grown (see Propagation) young plants 12 to 16 in. (30–40 cm) apart in container.
Watering, Feeding: Water moderately. Avoid standing water. Feed every 2 weeks.
Further Care: Remove withered shoots.
Overwintering: Hardy garden bellflowers in frost-free and bright environment, others at 50°F (10°C). Water little.
Pests, Diseases: Spider mites, aphids.

Propagation: By division, cuttings, seed sown in spring.
Decorating Tip: The overhanging, runner-producing species make wonderful hanging plants; the cushion-forming species are admirably suited as underplanting for standards.

Cockscomb, Woolflower

The intense colors of *Celosia*'s "firecracker flowers" are effective from a great distance.

The rich, glowing colors are the hallmark of *Celosia*. They glow like a blazing fire in a bed of summer flowers. The original parent of the cultivars available today for growing in beds and pots is *Celosia argentea*, 6 to 20 in. (15–50 cm) high. This annual plant grows erect and branching. It forms hermaphroditic spikes, which in *C. argentea plumosa* look like plumes, in *C. argentea cristata*, like the comb of a cock. This cockscomb is a compressed inflorescence, in which all the stalks are adnate and bonded together. Similar bondings, caused by a genetic slip-up in the vegetative tip, are also found in foxglove and cristate cactus. In former times, the brilliantly colored "cockscombs," along with their stalks, were cut off and dried in a shady, airy spot. Because they retain their beauty for years, they were used as components of unusual dry bouquets. The leaf shape ranges from lanceolate to oval. For growing in boxes or bowls, the cultivars 8 to 10 in. (20–25 cm) high are especially well suited. For example:
• 'Olympia', 8 in. (20 cm) high, cockscomb flowers in scarlet, yellow, and deep red.
• 'Miss Nippon', 10 in. (25 cm) high, plumed flowers in yellow, pink, and red.
• 'Kewpie', 8 in. (20 cm) high, plumed flowers in golden yellow, orange, and scarlet. This cultivar blooms quite early and is not so dependent on hot summers as the other two plumed cultivars listed.
• 'New Look', 16 in. (40 cm) high, plumed flowers in brilliant, deep red, which rise above the dark foliage. This broad, bushy cultivar, which branches from below, was bred in Europe. In 1988, it was recognized by the AAS (All America Selections) as the best new cultivar. It had been tested exhaustively in 60 test gardens in the United States and Canada in completely different climate conditions. It surpassed all its competitors in terms of the duration of the blooming period, the abundance of flowers, and weather-resistance.

Blooming Season: July to September.

Family: Amaranthaceae (amaranth family).

Origin: Original form, tropical Africa, now common in all tropical regions.

Location: Sunny and hot.

Potting Soil: All-purpose soil, which can be enriched with slow-release fertilizer.

Planting: Set purchased or home-grown (see Propagation) young plants 8 in. (20 cm) apart in container.

Watering, Feeding: Water abundantly and feed weekly. Avoid standing water.

Further Care: Deadhead spent flowers.

Overwintering: Not applicable.

Pests, Diseases: Aphids, downy mildew.

Propagation: In March, from seed, at a ground temperature of about 64°F (18°C). Light germinator.

Decorating Tip: The intensely colored flowers cannot tolerate competition from other flowers, but they look magnificent mixed with each other.

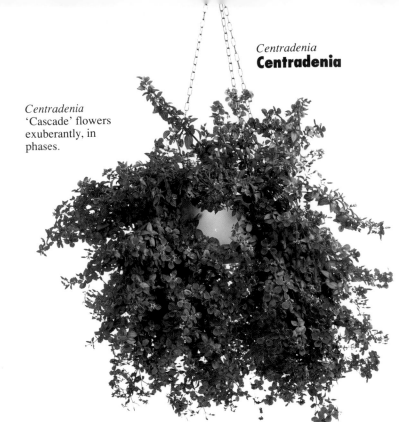

Centradenia
'Cascade' flowers
exuberantly, in
phases.

Centradenia
Centradenia

Cheiranthus cheiri
Wallflower, English Wallflower

Flowers in warm colors, with country charm.

○ 🪴 **1**

Brand new and well on its way to becoming a favorite balcony plant is *Centradenia* 'Cascade', which is not yet widely known under its new, correct name: *Heterocentron*. Its tender, copper-colored foliage is covered with downy hair. The relatively small, delicate, intensely pink flowers have clawlike stamens and appear in large numbers on the slightly pendulous stems. Exuberant blooming phases are followed by brief intervals in which the plant gathers new strength.

Blooming Season: April to September. Main blooming period, May to July.

Family: Melastomataceae (meadowbeauty family).

Origin: Original form, Central America.

Location: Sunny to partially shady.

Potting Soil: All-purpose soil, plain or enriched with slow-release fertilizer.

Planting: Set purchased or home-grown (see Propagation) young plants 8 in. (20 cm) apart in container.

Watering, Feeding: Keep evenly damp in the growth period. By all means avoid standing water and a dry ball. Apply a low dose of fertilizer every 2 weeks.

Further Care: Do not remove withered shoots. Frequently, new buds are formed on the old wood. Pruning and deadheading are unnecessary, because the plant is self-cleaning.

Overwintering: Cut back hard in fall. Put in a bright, frost-free place. Keep only slightly damp. Repot in spring.

Pests, Diseases: Whiteflies.

Propagation: From tip and stem cuttings in early summer.

Decorating Tip: Ideal summer bloomer for relatively small hanging baskets and mixed balcony boxes or as an underplanting for tub plants.

☀ 🪴 🏺 ☠

The honey-sweet fragrance of the flowers alone is enough to convince you to put wallflowers on your balcony or patio. The endearingly old-fashioned and somewhat countrified plant is sometimes treated as a biennial. Breeders have developed cultivars that grow erect and up to 24 in. (60 cm) high for use as cut flowers (stemmed form) and low, branching plants 12 in. (30 cm) high for growing in beds and pots (bush form). The colors of the single or double flowers range from yellow through golden yellow, velvety red, red-brown, brown, and violet to blackish-brown. Most suitable for a balcony box are the cultivars 'Gefüllter Zwergbusch' (12 in. [30 cm] high) or 'Bedder Formelmischung' (10 in. [25 cm] high). Pot plants in bloom are sold from April to June.

Blooming Season: Late April to June.

Family: Brassicaceae (mustard family).

Origin: Southern Europe.

Location: Sunny to partially shady.

Potting Soil: All-purpose mix or loamy, rich garden soil.

Planting: Set purchased or home-grown (see Propagation) young plants 6 to 8 in. (15–20 cm) apart in container.

Watering, Feeding: In the growth period, keep evenly and slightly damp and feed every 2 weeks.

Further Care: Deadhead spent flowers regularly to prolong the array of blooms.

Overwintering: Outdoors (cover boxes with brush). In roof-covered locations, water lightly on frost-free days.

Pests, Diseases: Downy mildew and other fungal diseases.

Propagation: From seed, from May to July, at a ground temperature of about 64°F (18°C).

Decorating Tip: Especially striking in combination with forget-me-nots.

Warning: Wallflowers contain poisonous glycosides, particularly in the seeds.

Chrysanthemum, Marguerite Chrysanthemum, Oxeye Daisy, Pot Chrysanthemum, Feverfew, Shasta Daisy

Chrysanthemum parthenium 'Fortuna'.

Chrysanthemum multicaule 'Kobold'.

Literally translated, the name means approximately gold flower (Greek: *chrysos* = gold and *anthemion* = flower). Thanks to the art of breeding, this flower offers us a multitude of inexhaustible spring, summer, and fall blooms for gardens, balconies, and patios. Most are treated as annuals, but in their native habitats they usually also grow as herbaceous plants or subshrubs. The flowers are single or double, and their diameters (depending on the species and cultivar) may be small, as in the case of the camomile, or as large as daisies.

For boxes and bowls, low, compact species and cultivars are recommended. For example:

• *Chrysanthemum frutescens*, marguerite chrysanthemum, a shrublike plant, is also sold as a small container plant (see page 163).

• *Chrysanthemum x indicum* hybrids. Many cultivars, with single or double flowers (12 to 16 in. [30–40 cm] high, white, yellow, pink, violet, purple, red, and bronze).

• *Chrysanthemum x maximum* hybrids, Shasta daisies. Cultivars: 'Snow Lady' (8 to 10 in. [20–25 cm] high, white), 'Silberprinzesschen' (12 in. [30 cm] high, white, rounded and bushy).

• *Chrysanthemum multicaule* 'Kobold' and 'Goldzwerg' (8 in. [20 cm] high, golden yellow).

• *Chrysanthemum paludosum*, flower box marguerite (10 in. [25 cm] high, white, bushy).

• *Chrysanthemum parthenium*, feverfew, double camomile, matricaria, large camomile. Cultivars: 'Santana' (10 in. [25 cm] high, creamy white pompons), 'Princess Daisy' (10. in. [25 cm] high, white, single-flowered), 'Weisser Stern' (7 in. [18 cm] high, white, double), 'Goldball' (10 in. [25 cm] high, golden yellow) 'Schneeball' (12 to 14 in. [30–35 cm] high, small-flowered, white), 'Weisskrone' (12 in. [30 cm] high, pure white, tightly double), 'Fortuna' (20 in. [50 cm] high, white, intensely double).

Blooming Season:

• *Chrysanthemum x indicum* hybrids, chiefly from September to November, now year round owing to controlled culture.

• *Chrysanthemum x maximum* hybrids from May to July.

• *Chrysanthemum multicaule* from June to September.

• *Chrysanthemum paludosum* from June to October.

• *Chrysanthemum parthenium* from June to September.

Family: Asteraceae or Compositae (aster or composite family).

Origin: Original forms, Europe, Near East, Japan, China.

Location: Sunny.

Potting Soil: All-purpose soil.

Planting: Set purchased or home-grown (see Propagation) young plants (depending on species or cultivar) 8 to 12 in. (20–30 cm) apart in the container.

Watering, Feeding: Keep slightly damp. Feed weekly until August.

Further Care: Cut off spent flowers regularly. In *Chrysanthemum paludosum*, cutting back in August promotes the development of a second blossoming.

Overwintering: Not applicable. Exceptions: *Chrysanthemum x indicum* hybrids and *Chrysanthemum frutescens* can be cut back and overwintered bright, cool, and dry, and in spring they can be forced.

Pests, Diseases: Aphids, spider mites; powdery and downy mildew.

Propagation: From seed in spring. *Indicum* hybrids and *Chrysanthemum frutescens* the year round, by cuttings.

Warning: *Chrysanthemum parthenium* and *Chrysanthemum x indicum* hybrids contain allergens.

Bowl with single and double, large- and small-flowered fall chrysanthemums.

Colchicum autumnale
Autumn Crocus

Autumn crocuses form flowers first, then leaves.

An odd plant—in fall, several violet-pink flowers about 6 in. (15 cm) high, without leaves, grow directly out of the ground. Autumn crocuses get the energy for this growth from a cordate to ovate tuber. The shiny, broad lanceolate to foot-shaped leaves and the fruits appear in spring. *Colchicum* hybrids such as 'Autumn Queen' (white-and-violet marbling or veining) or 'Lilac Wonder' (violet) play a role as garden and container flowers, but the pure species is difficult to cultivate.

Blooming Season: August to October.
Family: Liliaceae (lily family).
Origin: Central, southern, and western Europe, North Africa.
Location: Sunny.
Potting Soil: All-purpose mix or cool, damp, permeable garden soil.
Planting: Set tubers in containers in July or August. Plant them 6 to 8 in. (15–20 cm) apart and 4 to 6 in. (10–15 cm) deep. In late summer, plants are available in bloom, and they should be planted when bought.

Watering, Feeding: During the growth period, keep planted box damp (meadow plant). <u>Avoid standing water</u>. Once the leaves appear, feed every 2 weeks until about June.
Further Care: After the leaves die back, set bulbs in new soil or in the garden. Let them grow there undisturbed, as long as possible.
Overwintering: Put planted box in a frost-free, dark place. <u>Do not let soil dry out</u>. After flush, change to bright location.
Pests, Diseases: None.
Propagation: Not possible in container culture. In the garden, by brood tubers.
Warning: All parts of autumn crocus contain the lethal toxin *colchicine*. If you have children, preferably do without this plant. Wear gloves when planting!

Unusual—the double-flowered *Colchicum autumnale* 'Waterlily'.

Convolvulus tricolor
Dwarf Convolvulus, Dwarf Morning-Glory

Its flowers open and close by the clock.

The tricolored flowers are characteristic of this plant. They open on fine summer days between 7 and 8 AM and close between 5 and 6 PM. In the pure species, the margin of the funnel-shaped corolla is violet. It merges into a white wreath, in the center of which the sulfur-yellow eye stands out. In addition, there are numerous cultivars in colors of rose-pink, various shades of blue, and violet. The dwarf convolvulus is an annual. It grows prostrate at first, then rises to a height of 8 to 16 in. (20–40 cm) and becomes about 12 to 16 in. (30–40 cm) wide. Its stalks are hairy, and the leaves are lanceolate to inversely ovate, almost spoon-shaped.

Blooming Season: June to September.
Family: Convolvulaceae (morning-glory family).
Origin: Southern Europe, North Africa.
Location: Sunny.
Potting Soil: Soilless mix or lime-rich, permeable garden soil.
Planting: Set purchased or home-grown (see Propagation) young plants 16 in. (40 cm) apart in container.
Watering, Feeding: Water moderately and feed every 3 to 4 weeks.
Further Care: Remove the flowers, which last for only a day, after they wilt, in order to encourage the plant to form new buds.
Overwintering: Not applicable.
Pests, Diseases: Occasionally aphids.
Propagation: From seed, from March to April, at a ground temperature of 59° to 64°F (15°–18°C).
Decorating Tip: Also a wonderful hanging plant for baskets and boxes. Especially lovely in combinations: Self-colored neighbors with flowers that have the colors of the funnel-shaped corolla, for example, yellow slipperwort, white petunias, violet verbenas.

Convolvulus sabatius

Convolvulus

This plant, which grows as a perennial or sub-shrub, forms numerous thin, pendulous branches about 39 in. (1 m) long, all arising from a root-stock, with small, rounded ovate leaves of a silvery green color. The solitary, funnel-shaped flowers range from light blue to violet; they close in the evening.

Blooming Season: May to October.

Family: Convolvulaceae (morning-glory family).

Origin: Coasts of north-western Italy, Sicily, northwestern Africa.

Location: Sunny to bright.

Potting Soil: All-purpose mix or loamy, humus-rich garden soil.

Planting: Set purchased or home-grown (see Propagation) young plants 8 to 10 in. (20–25 cm) apart in container.

Watering, Feeding: Keep slightly damp during growth period. Feed lightly each week.

Further Care: Cutting back withered shoots is possible at any time and will result in improved branching and even more profuse flowers.

Overwintering: Cut shoots back by two thirds before moving plant indoors. Keep in bright place, relatively dry, at 50°F (10°C). In spring, repot and keep warmer.

Pests, Diseases: Rare.

Propagation: By cuttings, from fall to spring, or from seed.

Flowering Waterfall
On pillars and in hanging baskets, the shoots can develop unhindered.

Crocus
Crocus

Crocuses are among the first harbingers of spring.

☀ 🔔 🏠

Anyone who would like to enjoy crocuses in a box will find an enormous assortment of species and cultivars, all of which grow 4 to 5 in. (10–12 cm) high. The flower colors include white, yellow, pink, purple, lavender, and violet. In addition, there are cultivars with striated flowers. Suitable for flower boxes are, for example, *Crocus ancyrensis*, *Crocus chrysanthus*, *Crocus tomasinianus*, and *Crocus vernus*.

Blooming Season: Depending on the species or the cultivar, from the end of February to the end of March, *Crocus vernus* and *Crocus chrysanthus* until April.

Family: Iridaceae (iris family).

Origin: Southern and southeastern Europe, Asia Minor.

Location: Sunny. Protect plants in bloom from late spells of frost.

Potting Soil: All-purpose mix (can be enriched with a slow-release fertilizer) or loamy, humus-rich garden soil.

Planting: Set groups of tubers in containers in September or October. Space 4 in. (10 cm) apart, plant 2 to 3 in. (6–8 cm) deep. Alternative: Plant forced, blooming crocuses in spring.

Overwintering: Keep planted box in a frost-free, dark place. Do not let the soil dry out. After flush, put in a bright spot. Not always successful the second year.

Watering, Feeding: Keep planted box slightly damp until flush begins. Thereafter, water moderately and feed once. Avoid standing water. After plants die back, set them with their root balls in the garden and feed once more.

Further Care: Deadhead spent flowers. Remove dead foliage only when it falls off on its own.

Pests, Diseases: Rare.

Propagation: Not possible in container culture. In the garden, from daughter bulbs in early summer.

Cuphea ignea
Cigar Flower, Firecracker Plant

Cigar flower—also delightful as a hanging plant.

☀ 🔔 ➚ 1

This herbaceous plant grows only 12 in. (30 cm) high. It branches profusely and forms thin, somewhat crooked limbs and dark-green, shiny, oval-lanceolate leaves. The bright-red, tubular flowers have at the opening of the tube a black ring with a white zone, which makes them resemble cigars.

Blooming Season: May to September.

Family: Lythraceae (loosestrife family).

Origin: Mexico.

Location: Sunny to partially shady.

Potting Soil: All-purpose soil.

Planting: Set purchased or home-grown (see Propagation) young plants 10 in. (25 cm) apart in container.

Watering, Feeding: Keep moderately damp and feed every 2 weeks.

Further Care: Through trimming, the plant can be kept low, and it still will bloom lavishly.

Overwintering: Not applicable.

Propagation: In March or April from seed, at a ground temperature of about 64°F (18°C). Put three plants in each pot. Shoots obtained through pinching out can be used as tip cuttings.

Pests, Diseases: Aphids, whiteflies.

Decorating Tip: If the plant is allowed to grow undisturbed, the thin branches soon will hang down and create a charming effect in a hanging basket.

Dahlia Hybrids
Dahlias

Low dahlias can be raised from seed.

☀ 🥄 ↗ **1**

Dahlias are sold in a host of cultivars in various flower colors and forms. In the past, breeders were interested primarily in larger flowers and unusual colors, but today efforts are being made to produce low cultivars for flower boxes. The taller dahlia cultivars are forced from overwintered tubers, the dwarf forms, however, usually are treated as annuals, because they are easily grown from seed. Well-known cultivars:
• 'Figaro-Mischung' (12 in. [30 cm] high, double and demidouble).
• 'Mignon-Pracht-mischung' (12 to 16 in. [30–40 cm] high, single-flowered).
• 'Rigoletto-Mischung' (12 to 16 in. [30–40 cm] high, double and demidouble).
• 'Sunny-Serie' (12 in. [30 cm] high, blooms quite early), F_1 hybrids with lovely clear colors in rich red, golden yellow, and dark pink.
Blooming Season: July to October.

Family: Asteraceae or Compositae (aster or composite family).
Origin: Original forms, Mexico.
Location: Sunny and sheltered from wind.
Potting Soil: All-purpose mix (can be enriched with slow-release fertilizer) or loamy, humus-rich garden soil.
Planting: Set purchased or home-grown (see Propagation) young plants 12 in. (30 cm) apart in container.
Watering, Feeding: Water abundantly and feed weekly.
Further Care: Cut off wilted flowers regularly.
Overwintering: Not applicable.
Pests, Diseases: Spider mites, thrips, aphids; botrytis, leaf-spot.
Propagation: From seed in February or March. Sow 2 to 3 seed grains directly in each pot.
Decorating Tip: Dahlias are so strikingly colored that it is best to plant them alone.

Dianthus x *chinensis* Hybrids
Pinks

The cultivar 'Scarlet Charm' goes well with lobelias.

☀ 🥄 💧 **1**

The precursor of these attractive flowers is the China pink, *Dianthus chinensis*. Today, F_1 hybrids are available almost exclusively. They grow 8 to 12 in. (20–30 cm) high and have the typical, narrow carnation leaves and delicately frilled, sometimes red-centered or white-fimbriated flowers on sturdy stalks. Well-known cultivars:
• 'Charm-Serie' (white, salmon, light pink, scarlet, dark red).
• 'Princess-Serie' (same colors as 'Charm-Serie', in addition to violet).
• 'Telstar Crimson' (crimson).
• 'Telstar Mix-Mischung' (scarlet, pink, salmon, with and without colored center).
All the cultivars are sold from May on as young plants and treated as annuals.
Blooming Season: June to September.
Family: Caryophyllaceae (pink family).
Origin: Original forms, China and Korea.

Location: Sunny and sheltered from rain.
Potting Soil: All-purpose mix (can be enriched with slow-release fertilizer) or loamy, sandy garden soil.
Planting: Set purchased or home-grown (see Propagation) young plants 8 to 10 in. (20–25 cm) apart in container.
Watering, Feeding: Water moderately. Avoid standing water. Feed every 2 weeks.
Further Care: Cut off spent flowers.
Overwintering: Not applicable.
Pests, Diseases: Aphids, spider mites; rust.
Propagation: From seed in February or March, at a ground temperature of 59° to 64°F (15°–18° C).
Decorating Tip: These flowers are prettiest when mixed. Make sure the mix includes some white-fimbriated cultivars. They make the planting look frothier.

Dimorphotheca sinuata
African Daisy, Cape Marigold, Star of the Veldt

The flowers of the African daisy shine as if lacquered.

The African daisy (*Dimorphotheca sinuata*) is one of our prettiest summer flowers. It needs, however, a summer of full sun and warmth to unfold its brilliant-orange flowers with their silky gleam. Rainy weather does not agree with it.

Also available commercially are breeds sold under the obsolete synonym *Dimorphotheca* x *aurantiaca* hybrids. These, however, are possibly crossings of *Dimorphotheca sinuata* and *Dimorphotheca pluvialis*. The flowers are white, light yellow, golden yellow, apricot, and dark orange. The plants grow 10 to 12 in. (25–30 cm) high and remain compact.

Blooming Season: July to August, often even to September.
Family: Asteraceae or Compositae (aster or composite family).
Origin: South Africa.
Location: Sunny.
Potting Soil: All-purpose mix or loamy, sandy garden soil.

Planting: Set purchased or home-grown (see Propagation) young plants 6 to 8 in. (15–20 cm) apart in container.
Watering, Feeding: Keep only slightly damp and feed every 2 weeks. By all means avoid standing water and water that strikes the plants from above (rain)!
Further Care: None.
Overwintering: Not applicable.
Pests, Diseases: Rare.
Propagation: From seed sown from March on at a ground temperature of 59°F (15°C). Direct sowing into flower box is possible, but flowering will begin later.
Decorating Tip: Fits in any colorful box with neighboring plants that like abundant sun.

Dimorphotheca pluvialis has bizarre flowers.

Erica herbacea
Heath, Winter Heath

Erica gracilis in white and red cultivars.

Erica is often mistaken for *Calluna* (page 99), and vice versa. On closer scrutiny, however, you will see that their leaves differ. Those of *Erica* are needle-shaped and whorled; in *Calluna*, the leaves are scaly and opposite. *Erica herbacea* (also known as *Erica carnea*) is primarily marketed for planting spring boxes. It is extremely hardy and available in a wealth of cultivars. The best-known are 'King George', or 'Winter Beauty' (violet-pink), 'Snow Queen' (white), 'Vivellii' (deep carmine). In some cultivars ('Aurea', 'Golden Starlet', 'Sunshine Rambler'), the foliage is colored bronze, brass, golden green, or orange-brown in summer and winter.

Blooming Season: Depending on the cultivar, December to April.
Family: Ericaceae (heath family).
Origin: Europe.
Location: Sunny to partially shady.
Potting Soil: Rhododendron soil (or equal amounts of all-purpose soil and peat moss) with some sand added.
Planting: Set purchased or home-grown (see Propagation) young plants 12 in. (30 cm) apart in container.
Watering, Feeding: In the growth period, keep slightly and evenly damp. In spring, early summer, and late summer, apply organic fertilizer or rhododendron food once.
Further Care: Cut off spent flowers.
Overwintering: Without winter protection. Do not allow to dry out.
Pests, Diseases: Fungal infestation possible in extreme dampness.
Propagation: As for *Calluna* (see page 99).
Decorating Tip: Same neighboring plants as for *Calluna* (see page 99).
My Tip: For a seasonal fall planting, the red, frost-tender *Erica gracilis* is also suitable. It can be grown in any kind of potting soil.

Erigeron karvinskianus
Fleabane

Fleabane produces clouds of flowers.

☀ 🖌 🏠

This pretty herbaceous plant for dry stone walls and rock gardens is not entirely hardy, but it frequently reproduces from its own seed in warm, sheltered locations. It owes its name to a German botanist and researcher, Wilhelm Karwinsky von Karwin (1780–1855). This plant tends to spread out as it grows, rather like a creeping plant. It branches profusely and grows no more than 8 to 12 in. (20–30 cm) high. The flowers at first are white and later range from pink to red in hue. They appear in great abundance in solitary capitula, or close heads of sessile blooms. The leaves are obovate and dentate below, elongate and entire above. Well-known cultivar: 'Blütenmeer'.

Blooming Season: May to September.
Family: Asteraceae or Compositae (aster or composite family).
Origin: Mexico to Venezuela. Naturalized in southern and western Europe, Switzerland, and northwestern Africa.
Location: Sunny.
Potting Soil: All-purpose soil.
Planting: Set purchased or home-grown (see Propagation) young plants 8 to 12 in. (20–30 cm) apart in container.
Watering, Feeding: In the growth period, keep moderately damp and feed every 2 weeks.
Further Care: Deadhead spent flowers.
Overwintering: Bright location just above freezing point. Plants that have been hardened off can survive planted in the garden if ground frost is no lower than 25°F (–4°C).
Pests, Diseases: Rare.
Propagation: From seed, from January to March or April, at a ground temperature of 59° to 64°F (15°–18°C). Light germinator.
Decorating Tip: Well suited for a planting with a natural look.

Eschscholzia californica
California Poppy

The California poppy flowers only in fine weather.

☀ 🖌 💧 ↝ 1 ☠

The California poppy, treated as an annual, is decidedly a plant for good weather: Its flowers open only in the sunshine, and then only between 10 AM and 4 PM. Because the blooming period is not long, it is prolonged in garden culture by sowing several times in succession. The California poppy produces a tap root and therefore cannot be transplanted without the pot ball, because the root is easily injured and slow to recover. The bluish-green leaves are finely pinnate. The flowers, which have a silky sheen, grow 2 to 3 in. (5–8 cm) long on stalks 12 to 16 in. (30–40 cm) long. The colors range from creamy white through yellow, orange, and pink to crimson and bronze. Single and double cultivars are sold, usually as a deluxe mix.

Blooming Season: July to September. If sown in fall, they begin to bloom in June.
Family: Papaveraceae (poppy family).
Origin: California, Oregon. Naturalized in central and southern Europe.
Location: Sunny.
Potting Soil: All-purpose mix or loamy, sandy, light garden soil.
Planting: Set purchased or home-grown (see Propagation) young plants 10 in. (25 cm) apart in container.
Watering, Feeding: Keep only slightly damp. Do not feed.
Further Care: Periodically remove seed capsules.
Overwintering: Not applicable.
Pests, Diseases: Rare.
Propagation: From seed in March or April. Broadcast seeds directly in box. Thin out so that seedlings are 10 in. (25 cm) apart.
Decorating Tip: The undomesticated charm of the California poppy is also suitable for the close-to-nature balcony or patio.
Warning: The roots of the plant contain a poisonous alkaloid.

Felicia amelloides
Blue Daisy, Blue Marguerite, Cape Aster

Sun is the elixir of life for blue daisies.

The name by which some people know this plant, Cape aster, refers to its geographic origin and the similarity of its flowers to herbaceous asters.
The plant is usually treated as an annual, but it can be overwintered easily. In its native habitat, the blue daisy grows as a herbaceous plant or a sub-shrub. It reaches a height of 8 to 24 in. (20–60 cm) and produces numerous flower heads about 1⅓ in. (3.5 cm) wide. The contrast between the sky-blue to lavender-blue, radially arranged petals and the yolk-colored disks at their center is quite attractive. The small, oblong-ovate, slightly shaggy leaves can scarcely be seen beneath the wealth of blossoms.

Blooming Season: Year-round. Chief blooming period in summer.
Family: Asteraceae or Compositae (aster or composite family).
Origin: South Africa.
Location: Sunny.
Potting Soil: All-purpose mix or loamy, humus-rich garden soil.

Planting: Set purchased or home-grown (see Propagation) young plants 8 to 10 in. (20–25 cm) apart in container.
Watering, Feeding: Water moderately and feed every 2 weeks.
Further Care: Pinch out central and side shoots throughout the year. This will result in bushier growth and more abundant flowering.
Overwintering: Bright, at 50° to 54°F (10–12°C). Keep moderately damp.
Pests, Diseases: Powdery mildew.
Propagation: By herbaceous cuttings in spring.
Decorating Tip: Quite beautiful in combination with dark-blue lobelias and yellow slipperwort.

Fritillaria meleagris
Snake's Head Fritillary, Guinea-hen Flower

Snake's-head fritillaries are exquisite spring bloomers.

Flowers that look like 2-in.-high (5 cm) upended dice boxes (Latin: *fritillus* = dice box) and are red and white or white with delicate green veining—snake's head fritillaries are spring bloomers of a very special kind! The plants grow 6 to 16 in. (15–40 cm) high and produce narrow, slightly overhanging light-green leaves and nodding flowers. For culture in a balcony box, it is best to treat these plants as annuals, because over the long run they grow best in the garden.

Blooming Season: April to May. Protect plants in bloom against late spells of frost.
Family: Liliaceae (lily family).
Origin: Central, eastern, and southern Europe, Caucasus.
Location: Sunny to partially shady.
Potting Soil: All-purpose mix (can be enriched with slow-release fertilizer) or loamy, humus-rich garden soil.

Planting: Set bulbs, preferably in groups, in containers in September or October. Plant them 4 to 6 in. (10–15 cm) apart, 2⅓ to 4 in. (6–10 cm) deep.
Overwintering: Put planted box in a frost-free, dark location. Do not allow soil to dry out. After flush, put in bright location. Seldom successful the second year.
Watering, Feeding: Keep planted box slightly damp until flush. Thereafter, water regularly, but avoid standing water. Feed once. After plants die back, set them—with their root balls—in the garden and feed once more.
Further Care: Cut off spent flowers.
Pests, Diseases: The bulbs will rot in standing water.
Propagation: Not possible in container culture. In the garden, by brood bulbs.
Warning: All parts of snake's head fritillaries contain poisonous alkaloids.

Fuchsia cultivar with single flowers.

Galanthus nivalis is also available with double flowers.

Fuchsias are sold as young plants in April or May at most garden centers. If you are looking for something out of the ordinary, perhaps cultivars with variegated foliage, you can contact special mail-order suppliers of fuchsia.

Blooming Season: Summer to late fall.

Family: Onagraceae (evening-primrose family).

Origin: Original forms, Caribbean, Mexico, Central and South America, Tahiti, New Zealand.

Location: Bright to partially shady and sheltered from wind. Some cultivars also tolerate sun.

Potting Soil: All-purpose soil.

Planting: Set purchased or home-grown (see Propagation) young plants 8 to 10 in. (20–25 cm) apart in container.

Watering, Feeding: Water abundantly in the growth period and feed weekly until August.

Further Care: Prune plants regularly; at the beginning of the vegetative period, trim them all around.

Overwintering: Bright or dark location at 43° to 46°F (6°–8°C). Water lightly and let fresh air circulate on frost-free days. In spring, remove weak and crossing stems; cut back leaving one to three eyes. With new growth, repot and put plant in a brighter location.

Pests, Diseases: Aphids, whiteflies, spider mites, botrytis, mildew, fuchsia rust.

Propagation: From herbaceous cuttings in spring, from semihardwood cuttings in summer (easy).

Decorating Tip: All the pendulous cultivars make wonderful hanging plants.

My Tip: The "yellow cape fuchsia" that is increasingly being marketed is not a true fuchsia, but a variety of *Phygelius capensis* that blooms from July to October and needs the same care as the true fuchsias.

Snowdrops are the first heralds of spring. Particularly good for container culture is the giant snowdrop, *Galanthus elwesii*, 6 to 8 in. (15–20 cm) high, with broad, gray-green leaves and flowers 1½ to 2 in. (4–5 cm) across. The common snowdrop, *Galanthus nivalis*, 4 to 6 in. (10–15 cm) high, blooms somewhat later and is also available with double flowers.

Blooming Season: *Galanthus elwesii*, February; *Galanthus nivalis*, February or March.

Family: Amaryllidaceae (amaryllis family).

Origin: Western, central, and southern Europe, Asia Minor.

Location: Bright to partially shady.

Potting Soil: All-purpose mix (can be enriched with slow-release fertilizer) or loamy, humus-rich garden soil.

Planting: In September or October, set the small, globe-shaped bulbs in boxes or bowls, preferably in groups, 1 to 1½ in. (3–4 cm) apart and 4 in. (10 cm) deep. Caution: The bulbs should be plump, not dried out.

Overwintering: Keep plants in a frost-free, dark place. Do not let soil dry out. After flush, put in a bright place.

Watering, Feeding: Keep planted box slightly damp until flush begins. From then until the leaves turn yellow, water moderately. Feed twice during the growing season. After the foliage dies back, keep drier.

Further Care: Deadhead spent flowers.

Pests, Diseases: Rare.

Propagation: Impossible in container culture. In the garden, by division.

Decorating Tip: Snowdrops are charming as underplanting for broad-leaved woody plants in large tubs, where they will reappear each year.

Warning: Snowdrops, particularly the bulbs, contain a poisonous alkaloid.

Gazania Hybrids
Gazania, Treasure Flower

The flowers open only in good weather.

Gazanias usually are treated as annuals, but they can be overwintered easily. Only hybrids from various *Gazania* species are available commercially. Recommended for the flower box are the ministar gazanias, the Chansonette mix, or the Morgentau dwarf mix. The cultivars, which grow almost cushion-shaped, are only 8 to 10 in. (20–25 cm) high. They are available in white, yellow, and light orange. The narrow leaves are green on the upper surface, and the undersides are silvery and matted.

Blooming Season: July to September.

Family: Asteraceae or Compositae (aster or composite family).

Origin: Original forms, South Africa.

Location: Sunny.

Potting Soil: All-purpose soil.

Planting: Set purchased or home-grown (see Propagation) young plants 8 in. (20 cm) apart.

Watering, Feeding: In the growth period, water moderately and feed weekly. By all means avoid standing water.

Further Care: Cutting back spent flowers promotes the formation of new buds.

Overwintering: In a bright and frost-free location. The plant can tolerate light frost. Do not let the ball dry out completely. In spring, remove withered parts, and cut shoots back by one half.

Pests, Diseases: Botrytis after lengthy periods of rainfall or in overly damp location.

Propagation: From seed, February to April, at a ground temperature of 64° to 68°F (18°–20°C).

Decorating Tip: Self-colored cultivars are a good match for all balcony flowers with the same needs, for example, snapdragons (*Antirrhinum*), *Asteriscus*, or *Chrysanthemum* x *indicum* hybrids.

Gomphrena globosa
Globe Amaranth, Gomphrena

Globe amaranth is white, pink, or violet-purple.

Globe amaranth is cultivated in fields for use as a cut flower and dried flower. This plant attracts particular attention with the lacquerlike shine of its flowers, which retain the intensity of their color even in a dry bouquet. The annual, slightly hairy plant, which produces oval, vibrantly green leaves 2⅓ to 4 in. (6–10 cm) long, grows about 12 in. (30 cm) high. The flower heads grow singly or in groups. Depending on the cultivar, they are white, pink, or violet-purple. The 'Buddy' cultivars, which come in white and wine red, grow in bushy mounds only 6 in. (15 cm) high. They are particularly appropriate for boxes.

Blooming Season: July to October.

Family: Amaranthaceae (amaranth family).

Origin: Tropical and subtropical America.

Location: Sunny and sheltered from rain.

Potting Soil: All-purpose mix (plain or amended: 2 parts soil, 1 part sand, with some slow-release fertilizer); loamy, sandy garden soil.

Planting: Set purchased or home-grown (see Propagation) tall cultivars 10 in. (25 cm) apart, 'Buddy' cultivars 8 in. (20 cm) apart.

Watering, Feeding: Water lightly and feed lightly every 2 weeks until August.

Further Care: None.

Overwintering: Not applicable.

Pests, Diseases: Powdery mildew.

Propagation: From seed in March at a ground temperature of 64°F (18°C).

Decorating Tip: 'Buddy' cultivars are extremely attractive in individual clay pots of simple design, because they grow in neat, spherical mounds.

Helianthus annuus
Common Sunflower

The dwarf breed 'Teddy Bear', next to violet sage.

☀ 🪣 ⤵ **1**

Tall sunflower cultivars can grow 6½ to 10 ft (2–3 m) high—assuming they have abundant fertilizer and sun. These giants are not suitable for the flower box. There are, however, dwarf breeds that stay considerably smaller, such as the cultivar 'Teddy Bear', also called 'Dwarf Sungold'. It reaches a height of only 16 in. (40 cm) and produces beautiful golden-yellow double flowers. 'Gelber Knirps' grows 24 in. (60 cm) high, and 'Helios' attains a height of about 28 in. (70 cm). Owing to the excellent statics of the sunflower, all of these cultivars grow upright, even in a box. They all are annuals.

Blooming Season: July to October.
Family: Asteraceae or Compositae (aster or composite family).
Origin: Western and central North America, northern Mexico.
Location: Full sun, warm, sheltered from wind.
Potting Soil: All-purpose mix or loamy, rich garden soil with some sand added.
Planting: Set purchased or home-grown (see Propagation) young plants 8 in. (20 cm) apart.
Watering, Feeding: Water abundantly, but avoid standing water. Feed weekly until August. High nutrient requirement.
Further Care: Stake plant in sites with extreme wind exposure.
Overwintering: Not applicable.
Pests, Diseases: Aphids.
Propagation: From seed (easy) in April. Sow one seed grain per pot. Needs no bottom warmth.

Heliotropium arborescens
Heliotrope, Cherry Pie

Light-hungry—the vanilla-scented heliotrope.

☀ 🪣 💧 ⤵ 🏠 ☠

Most often grown is the cultivar 'Marine' compact, bushy, and only 20 in. (50 cm) high. It has large, dark-blue umbels that smell of vanilla and dark, wrinkled foliage. The pure species grows more than 39 in. (1 m) high and has green leaves.

Blooming Season: May to September.
Family: Boraginaceae (borage family).
Origin: Peru.
Location: Sunny and sheltered from wind.
Potting Soil: All-purpose mix or sandy garden soil.
Planting: Set purchased or home-grown (see Propagation) young plants 10 in. (25 cm) apart.
Watering, Feeding: In the growth period, water moderately, but never allow to dry out, and feed weekly. Once leaves have drooped from lack of water, they will be slow to recover. Usually, brown spots are left on the leaves.
Further Care: Regularly cut off spent flowers.
Overwintering: Not really worthwhile (because in the second year, the compressing agent that is responsible for the compact growth will have exhausted itself), but possible. Move this cold-sensitive plant indoors promptly. Keep in a bright location at about 53° to 59°F (12°–15°C). Water little. Repot in spring.
Pests, Diseases: Whiteflies.
Propagation: From seed (light germinator) from early February on, at a ground temperature of 68°F (20°C). Alternatively, take cuttings, beginning in January, from mother plants that have been overwintered in a warm location.
Decorating Tip: Heliotrope can be trained as a standard, if the main stem has support from stakes. This generally takes 5 years.
Warning: Heliotrope contains poisonous alkaloids.

Young heliotrope plants that you raise from seed often will grow much stronger and taller than the mother plant.

CONTAINER FLOWERS

Hyacinthus orientalis
Hyacinth

Hyacinthus orientalis 'City of Harlem'.

☀ 🪣 💧 🏠

Our garden hyacinths derive from *Hyacinthus orientalis*. They grow 8 to 12 in. (20–30 cm) high, form sturdy stalks, and produce somewhat fleshy, strap-shaped leaves.

Blooming Season: April to May.

Family: Liliaceae (lily family).

Origin: Eastern Mediterranean region, southwestern Asia.

Location: Sunny to partially shady. Protect plants in bloom against late spells of frost.

Potting Soil: All-purpose soil with $^1/_3$ sand added or more sandy than loamy garden soil.

Planting: Set the plump bulbs in deep containers in early October, 6 in. (15 cm) apart and about 6 to 8 in. (15–20 cm) deep. Alternative: Buy forced plants in spring and set them.

Watering, Feeding: Until flush begins, keep planted box slightly damp. Thereafter, water moderately and feed once. Avoid standing water. After plants die back, set them, with the root balls, in the garden and feed once more.

Further Care: Cut off withered stalks. Remove foliage only when it is completely dried up.

Overwintering: Keep planted box in a frost-free, dark place. Do not let soil dry out. After flush, put in a bright place. Seldom successful the second year.

Pests, Diseases: Bulb rot due to excessively damp soil.

Propagation: From daughter bulbs (matter for horticulturists).

Warning: Hyacinth bulbs may induce skin irritations in susceptible people.

Impatiens Hybrids
Impatiens, Busy Lizzie, Patient Lucy, Patience

New Guinea hybrids in brilliant colors.

○ 🪣 💧 🏠

Container gardeners have two busily flowering "Lizzies" available:

• *Impatiens* x *wallerana* hybrids grow about 8 in. (20 cm) high. Well-known cultivars are the series 'Belizzy', 'Accent', and 'Super Elfin'. With the exceptions of yellow and true blue, all flower colors from white to violet are represented. In addition, there are white-starred cultivars as well as varieties 10 in. (25 cm) high with roselike double flowers.

• The New Guinea hybrids, *Impatiens*, which have *hawkeri* in their ancestry, display intensely colored shades of orange, pink, and violet. Cultivars such as 'Spectra' and 'Tango', can be grown from seed.

Blooming Season: Outdoors from June to October.

Family: Balsaminaceae (touch-me-not or balsam family).

Origin: Original forms, tropical East Africa, Ceylon, India, and New Guinea.

Location: Sunny to shady.

Potting Soil: All-purpose soil, enriched with slow-release fertilizer.

Planting: Set purchased or home-grown (see Propagation) plants 8 to 10 in. (20–25 cm) apart.

Watering, Feeding: Keep quite damp during growth period and apply low doses of fertilizer weekly until August.

Further Care: Trim plants now and then to promote branching.

Overwintering: Only young plants can be overwintered—in a bright place at 54° to 59°F (12°–15°C)! Keep moderately damp.

Pests, Diseases: Mites, aphids, whiteflies, slugs.

Propagation: By cuttings in spring or from seed in February or March (both easy).

Elegance in a Strawberry Jar

Double-flowered *Impatiens balsamina* hybrids, here in combination with ivy cultivars with different leaf shapes and colors.

Iris reticulata
Small Iris

Blue *Iris reticulata* and yellow *Iris danfordiae*.

Iris reticulata is one of the irises that have bulbs. It grows to a maximum height of 8 in. (20 cm). The grassy, narrow leaves tower above the violet-purple flowers, which draw attention through a yellowish patch and an orange central stripe.

Blooming Season: March.

Family: Iridaceae (iris family).

Origin: Caucasus, Asia Minor, Iraq, Iran.

Location: Sunny to partially shady.

Potting Soil: All-purpose mix or loamy, sandy garden soil.

Planting: Set the box with the small bulbs in fall, or set forced plants in spring, spaced 4 in. (10 cm) apart and at a depth of 2 to 3 in. (5–8 cm).

Watering, Feeding: Keep planted box slightly damp until flush begins. From then until the leaves turn yellow, water regularly. Avoid standing water—danger of rot! Feed twice during the growth period. Keep drier after the foliage has turned yellow.

Further Care: Protect plants in bloom against late spells of frost. Deadhead spent flowers. In fall, remove yellow leaves carefully; do not tear them off! After *Iris reticulata* stops blooming, it can be planted, along with its root ball, in the garden.

Overwintering: Frost-free and bright location. Do not let soil dry out.

Pests, Diseases: Rare.

Propagation: Not possible in container culture. In the garden, from young bulbs in fall.

Decorating Tip: Gorgeous in combination with *Iris danfordiae*, the small yellow iris, which needs the same care.

Warning: *Iris reticulata* can contain iridine, a poisonous substance with a strong taste.

Lathyrus odoratus
Sweet Pea

A deluxe mix of sweet peas, made up of low cultivars.

The English have even created a special society for lovers of this charming annual climber. On squared stalks 39 to 79 in. (1–2 m) long, the sweet pea forms elliptical leaves and loose racemes of 3 to 7 marvelously fragrant solitary flowers in white, pink, red, violet, and blue. Recommended for the balcony box are bushy cultivars that need no climbing aid, for example, 'Super Snoop' (16 in. [40 cm] high) and 'Little Sweetheart-Prachtmischung' (8 to 10 in. [20–25 cm] high).

Blooming Season: June to September.

Family: Fabaceae or Leguminosae (pea or bean family).

Origin: Southern Italy, Sicily.

Location: Sunny and sheltered from wind. The sweet pea has low tolerance for blazing midday sun and accumulated heat.

Potting Soil: All-purpose mix or crumbly, rich garden soil.

Planting: Set purchased or home-grown (see Propagation) young plants 4 in. (10 cm) apart.

Watering, Feeding: Keep evenly damp and feed weekly. High nutrient requirement.

Further Care: Cut off spent flowers regularly, so that new buds will form.

Overwintering: Not applicable.

Pests, Diseases: Spider mites; powdery mildew, botrytis.

Propagation: From seed sown in individual pots in February or March or directly in the flower box from mid-April on.

Decorating Tip: If you want to create a sweet-smelling wall, sow deluxe mixes of one to three tall cultivars and let them climb taut wires or pieces of stout twine.

Warning: Sweet pea seeds are poisonous.

Lobelia erinus
Lobelia

Lobularia maritima
Sweet Alyssum

There are hanging and erect cultivars of lobelias.

White sweet alyssum next to Dahlberg daisies.

☼ ⟋ **1**

The annual lobelia grows to 10 in. (25 cm) high; it has bright-blue flowers, which in some cultivars have a white eye. There are also pure white types. These are available commercially:

• Erect Compacta cultivars that grow 4 to 6 in. (10–15 cm) high, for example, 'Cambridge Blue' (sky blue), 'Kristallpalast' (dark-blue flowers, bronze foliage), 'Pumila Splendens' (deep blue with white eye), 'Kaiser Wilhelm' (cornflower blue).

• Trailing lobelias, equipped with long stems, such as 'Pendula Saphir' (deep blue with white eye) or 'Hamburgia' (dark blue).

Blooming Season: May to August.
Family: Campanulaceae (bellflower family).
Origin: Cape Province of South Africa.
Location: Sunny to partially shady.
Potting Soil: All-purpose soil.
Planting: Set purchased or home-grown (see

Propagation) young plants 8 in. (20 cm) apart.
Watering, Feeding: Water abundantly and apply a low dose of fertilizer weekly. Sensitive to salt.
Further Care: After the first array of blooms, cut back by one third. The plant then will begin to grow again and often will flower into fall.
Overwintering: Not applicable.
Pests, Diseases: Rare.
Propagation: From seed (light germinator) from January to March. Thin out, put in pots in bunches.

Decorating Tip: Lobelias make an exceedingly beautiful underplanting for standards in containers, where they keep the surface of the soil from drying out. Because they spread in billowing masses, always plant them toward the front of the box, so that they can grow trailing over its edge.

☼ ⟋ **1**

Lobularia is surely more familiar to most people under its old name, *Alyssum maritimum*. This undemanding annual does splendidly in low flower boxes with little soil, and it even braves the first spells of frost in fall. It forms cushions 3 to 6 in. (8–15 cm) high, composed of large numbers of stalks that curve upwards and are densely covered with narrow leaves. Depending on the cultivar, the flowers are white, pink, or lilac. Alyssum will continue to flower all summer in racemes 1 to 2 in. (2.5–5 cm) long with a honeylike fragrance.
Blooming Season: June to October.
Family: Brassicaceae (mustard family).
Origin: Azores, Canary Islands, southern Europe, Mediterranean region.
Location: Sunny to partially shady.
Potting Soil: All-purpose mix or loamy, sandy garden soil. Tolerates lime.
Planting: Set purchased or home-grown (see

Propagation) young plants 6 in. (15 cm) apart.
Watering, Feeding: Water moderately and feed once, only after cutting back.
Further Care: Cutting back after the first array of blooms promotes the growth of new shoots and buds.
Overwintering: Not applicable. The flowers often seed themselves in any case.
Pests, Diseases: Powdery and downy mildew.
Propagation: From seed in March or April (easy). Use pots measuring 2 to 2⅓ in. (5–6 cm); put five seed grains in each pot.
Decorating Tip: Sweet alyssum makes an excellent underplanting for standards and for the foreground in combinations including taller, erect plants in a flower box (*Pelargonium* x *zonale* hybrids, African daisies, heliotrope).

Lotus berthelotii
Parrot's Beak, Winged Pea, Coral Gem

Mesembryanthemum criniflorum
Livingstone Daisy

Never let parrot's beak dry out!

The flowers of the Livingstone daisy gleam like silk.

Lotus berthelotii, a splendid plant for hanging baskets, is increasingly available for sale in spring. This herbaceous plant produces lignifying procumbent or down-arching branches with fine leaves up to ⅘ in. (2 cm) long and covered with silvery hair. The axillary flowers, which grow in aggregates at the ends of the branches, are about 1 in. (3 cm) long and scarlet red in color. New on the market is the yellow and copper *Lotus maculatus* 'Golden Flash'. In contrast to *Lotus berthelotii*, it flowers all summer long.

Blooming Season: March or April.

Family: Fabaceae or Leguminosae (pea or bean family).

Origin: Cape Verde Islands and Canary Islands.

Location: Bright to sunny.

Potting Soil: All-purpose mix (can be enriched with slow-release fertilizer) or loamy, humus-rich garden soil.

Planting: Set purchased or home-grown (see Propagation) young plants 12 in. (30 cm) apart.

Watering, Feeding: During the growth period, keep evenly and slightly damp, but not wet under any circumstances. When ball is dry, leaf drop results immediately. From February to October, feed weekly. High nutrient requirement.

Further Care: Repot after blooming season.

Overwintering: Move indoors before frost begins—sensitive to cold. Keep in a bright place at a temperature no warmer than 50°F (10°C). Water lightly.

Pests, Diseases: Aphids.

Propagation: From tip cuttings in February through March or August through September, at a ground temperature of 68° to 77°F (20°–25°C). They strike root readily.

Decorating Tip: Because of its silvery foliage, which proliferates in summer, *Lotus berthelotii* is an attractive plant—even after the blooming season—for hanging baskets, pedestals, or balustrade flower boxes.

The bizarre flowers of *Lotus maculatus* 'Golden Flash'.

Beyond doubt, Livingstone daisies are among the loveliest bloomers in the plant kingdom; in a flower box, they are always extraordinary. These annual summer flowers spread out rapidly and grow 2 to 6 in. (5–15 cm) high. A coating protects their succulent leaves against evaporation. The brilliantly colored, daisylike flowers, 1 in. (2.5 cm) across, open only in good weather. Their colors include white, yellow, orange, pink, red, and violet. The seed is usually sold as a mix. In current nomenclature, the Livingstone daisy is called *Cleretum bellidiforme*, but it still goes by the more familiar name *Mesembryanthemum*, which in literal translation means midday flower (from Greek: *mesembria* = midday and *anthemion* = flower).

Blooming Season: July to September.

Family: Aizoaceae (carpetweed family).

Origin: Cape Province of South Africa.

Location: Sunny, hot, and sheltered from rain.

Potting Soil: All-purpose soil with a large amount of sand; also sandy garden soil.

Planting: Set purchased or home-grown (see Propagation) young plants 4 in. (10 cm) apart.

Watering, Feeding: Keep fairly dry and do not feed.

Further Care: None.

Overwintering: Not applicable.

Pests, Diseases: Fungal infections due to standing water or lengthy periods of rainfall.

Propagation: From seed in March or April at a ground temperature of 64°F (18°C). Sow directly in pots, because the poor root development makes transplanting difficult.

Decorating Tip: Suitable for low boxes and bowls with small soil volume.

Mimulus Hybrids
Monkey Flower

Muscari
Grape Hyacinth

Monkey flowers need large amounts of nutrients.

Grape hyacinth is available with white or blue flowers.

Like an actor or a con-jurer, the genus _Mimulus_ is a master of the art of transformation. Its flowers present themselves as large or small, now with a charming country air, now exotically striped or spot-ted. Commercially avail-able are F_1 hybrids of different varieties from _Mimulus luteus_ and _Mimulus guttatus_; these are classified _Mimulus_ x _hybridus_ and are also known as _Mimulus_ x _tigrinus_ because of its tiger markings, for example:
- 'Grandiflorus', 12 in. (30 cm) high, large-flow-ered, spotted, in all colors.
- 'Malibu', 6 in. (15 cm) high, grows compact, wide, and rounded, in yellow and orange.
- 'Royal Velvet', 8 to 12 in. (20–30 cm) high, brownish-red with spotted yellow throat.
- 'Viva', 8 in. (20 cm) high, large-flowered, golden yellow and brown stripes.
- Mixes with creamy white, golden-yellow, orange, red, and wine-red cultivars.

Blooming Season: June to September. _Mimulus_ hybrids in bloom are sold between April and July.
Family: Scrophulariaceae (figwort family).
Origin: Original forms, North and South America.
Location: Bright to par-tially shady, airy and cool.
Potting Soil: All-purpose soil, which can be en-riched with a slow-release fertilizer.
Planting: Set purchased or home-grown (see Pro-pagation) young plants 6 to 10 in. (15–25 cm) apart.
Watering, Feeding: Keep slightly damp at all times and feed weekly. High nutrient requirement.
Further Care: Cut back after first array of blooms to stimulate reblooming.
Overwintering: Not applicable.
Pests, Diseases: Aphids, powdery mildew.
Propagation: From seed. Preliminary culture from February to April, or sow seeds directly in the box in April.
Decorating Tip: The tiger-striped cultivars look good with outdoor ferns.

Of the 40 to 50 known species, _Muscari armeniacum_ and _Muscari botryoides_—which are similar in appearance—and their cultivars are most suitable for con-tainer culture. These two species, which grow 4 to 8 in. (10–20 cm) high, form narrow, grassy leaves and conical racemes in incom-parable shades of blue and, in 'Album', also in white.
Blooming Season: March to May.
Family: Liliaceae (lily family).
Origin: Central and southern Europe, Asia Minor, Caucasus.
Location: Sunny to par-tially shady. Protect plants in bloom from late spells of frost.
Potting Soil: All-purpose mix or loamy, sandy gar-den soil.
Planting: Set bulbs grouped in boxes in Sep-tember or October, 2⅓ to 4 in. (6–10 cm) deep. Alternative: In spring, buy and set forced plants already in bloom.

Watering, Feeding: Keep planted box slightly damp until flush begins. From then on, water mod-erately and feed once. After flowering ceases, plant in the garden and feed once more.
Further Care: None.
Overwintering: Put planted box in a frost-free, dark place; after flush, put in a bright place. Do not allow soil to dry out. Seldom successful the second year.
Pests, Diseases: Rare.
Propagation: Not pos-sible in container culture, in garden by offset bulbs.

Myosotis sylvatica
Forget-me-not

Narcissus
Daffodil

Forget-me-nots love partial shade.

Daffodils are easy to grow in bowls.

The forget-me-not is a perennial that is treated as a biennial. This compact, profusely branching plant grows 6 to 10 in. (15–25 cm) high, depending on the cultivar, and is covered with soft, short-haired leaves.

Well-known cultivars: 'Blauer Korb' (deep blue, large-flowered, 10 in. [25 cm] high), 'Indigo' and 'Blauer Strauss' (dark blue, 12 in. [30 cm] high), 'Blauer Ball' (bright blue, 6 in. [15 cm] high, mounded, compact growth).

Blooming Season: May to July.

Family: Boraginaceae (borage family).

Origin: Europe, Asia Minor, Central Asia, northwestern Africa.

Location: Bright, partially shady to shady.

Potting Soil: All-purpose soil, which can be enriched with slow-release fertilizer.

Planting: Set purchased or home-grown (see Propagation) plants 6 in. (15 cm) apart.

Watering, Feeding: Keep evenly damp, but not wet—and do not feed: Forget-me-nots are woodland plants.

Further Care: None.

Overwintering: Not applicable to purchased plants. Young plants, in bright and frost-free location. Outdoors with winter protection of fir brush; indoors without it.

Pests, Diseases: Aphids; botrytis, powdery mildew.

Propagation: From seed in July at a ground temperature of 64°F (18°C). After four weeks, transplant out into individual pots.

Decorating Tip: Would you like a nostalgic spring box? Plant forget-me-nots and pansies together.

Small wild daffodils are gaining in popularity because of their natural charm. They are also excellent candidates for the flower box. Ask for:

• *Narcissus bulbocodium*, 4 to 8 in. (10–20 cm) high.

• *Narcissus cyclamineus*, 4 to 8 in. (10–20 cm) high, 2 to 4 flowers per stalk.

• *Narcissus poeticus* 'Actaea', 16 in. (40 cm) high, white with orange center.

• *Narcissus pseudonarcissus*—only the small-flowered varieties that grow no higher than 16 in. (40 cm) are suitable.

Blooming Season: Depending on the species, March to May.

Family: Amaryllidaceae (amaryllis family).

Origin: Central, western, and southern Europe, Algeria.

Location: Sunny. Protect plants in bloom against late spells of frost.

Potting Soil: All-purpose mix (to which some sand may be added, along with slow-release fertilizer) or loamy, sandy garden soil.

Planting: Set bulbs in deep containers in fall, 4 in. (10 cm) apart and 2 to 4 in. (5–10 cm) deep, depending on the size of the bulb. Alternative: Set forced, already blooming plants in spring.

Watering, Feeding: Keep planted box slightly damp until flush begins. From then on, water moderately and feed once. After the plants cease to bloom, set them in the garden and feed once more.

Further Care: Do not remove foliage until it is completely dried out.

Overwintering: Put planted box in a frost-free, dark spot, somewhat brighter after flush. Do not allow soil to dry out. Often not successful the second year.

Pests, Diseases: Root rot due to wet ground.

Propagation: Not possible in container culture. In garden by offset bulbs.

Warning: Daffodil bulbs are poisonous.

As exotic as orchids—Nemesia flowers.

Cupflowers make good underplanting.

Do you like motley colors? Then you should put nemesia, with its flowers of many colors, on your balcony or patio. The flowers, which grow on the stalks in corymbs, range from white through yellow, orange, scarlet, and crimson to blue. Approximately 1 in. (3 cm) across, they have a glossy shine. The plants currently available commercially are hybrids of *Nemesia strumosa*. The blue shades were created by crossing with *Nemesia versicolor*. Best-known are the deluxe mix 'Karneval' (10 in. [25 cm] high, large flowers) and 'Triumph' (8 in. [20 cm] high, large-flowered, compact growth).

Blooming Season: June to August or September.

Family: Scrophulariaceae (figwort family).

Origin: Original forms, South Africa.

Location: Sunny to partially shady and sheltered from wind.

Potting Soil: Soilless mix or all-purpose potting soil.

Planting: Set purchased or home-grown (see Propagation) plants 6 to 8 in. (15–20 cm) apart.

Watering, Feeding: Keep moderately damp and feed only once after cutting back. Low nutrient requirement.

Further Care: Cutting back after the first array of blossoms will stimulate further flowering.

Overwintering: Not applicable.

Pests, Diseases: Rare.

Propagation: From seed in March or April. Transplant once and set in bunches in 4-in. (10 cm) pots. Alternatively, from mid-May on, sow seeds directly in the flower box.

Decorating Tip: Because of the great wealth and showiness of nemesia's colors, only a restrained companion will do. A very pretty one: midnight-blue lobelias.

The cupflower owes its botanical name to Juan Eusebio Nieremberg, a Spanish Jesuit and natural scientist. With their golden-yellow throats, the numerous flowers, which grow singly, do indeed resemble dainty dessert cups. The foliage of this herbaceous plant—in its native habitat originally a perennial—is bright green and delicate. The violet-blue variety, 3 to 12 in. (8–30 cm) high, is the one most often available today, as a seasonal plant. Also on the market are new breeds 6 to 8 in. (15–20 cm) high, such as 'Purple Robe' (wine red) or 'White Robe' (white).

Blooming Season: June to October.

Family: Solanaceae (nightshade family).

Origin: Argentina.

Location: Sunny and warm.

Potting Soil: All-purpose mix (which may be enriched with slow-release fertilizer) or loamy, humus-rich garden soil.

Planting: Set purchased or home-grown (see Propagation) young plants 8 in. (20 cm) apart.

Watering, Feeding: During the growth period, keep evenly and slightly damp; feed weekly.

Further Care: Deadhead spent faded flowers.

Overwintering: These plants, which in the cool climates are annuals, cannot be overwintered, although cuttings taken from them can be: bright, airy spot at 46° to 50°F (8°–10°C).

Pests, Diseases: Aphids.

Propagation: From seed in February or March at a ground temperature of 64°F (18°C). Alternatively, by cuttings in late summer. Pinch out promptly so that plants will be nice and bushy.

Decorating Tip: Extremely beautiful as underplanting for standards with the same needs, such as *Lantana* or *Laurus*.

Warning: Cupflower belongs to the poisonous nightshade family.

Pelargonium x *peltatum* Hybrids
Hanging Geraniums, Ivy Geraniums, Ivy-leaved Geraniums

'Lachskönigin' has been cultivated for decades.

☼ 🐿 ⌂

In its native habitat in the coastal regions of South Africa grows the ancestress of our present-day "hanging geraniums," a slightly pendulous shrub with squared branches, shield-shaped (peltate), fuzzy or hairless succulent leaves, and rose-red flowers. From it, breeds such as the violet 'Galilée' and the pink 'Lachskönigin', which are still cultivated, were produced through crossing with other wild species around the turn of the century. The currently available assortment consists of hanging and semihanging geraniums with double, demidouble, or single flowers and, in some cases, fleshy leaves. The Cascade cultivars constitute a group of their own. These are single-

Flowers upon Flowers
The self-cleaning Cascade hybrids guarantee an abundance of flowers well into fall, in boxes and in hanging baskets.

flowered but extremely free-flowering geraniums, which are also self-cleaning. Well-known cultivars include the following:
• 'Ville de Paris', pink, single-flowered, stems up to about 5 ft (1.5 m) long, foremother of the Cascade cultivars.
• 'Feuercascade', flaming red, single-flowered, stems almost 5 ft (1.5 m) long, weather resistant.
• 'Amethyst', dark lilac, demidouble, short stems.
• 'Sugar Baby', light-pink cultivar for devotees, flowers small and double, stays small, somewhat sensitive to rain.
• 'Mexikanerin', white with red margins, large double flowers, hanging, also does well in partial shade.
• 'Schöne von Grenchen', bright red, demidouble, semihanging, weather resistant, robust, easy to reproduce.
• 'Solidor', salmon pink with dark-red eye, hanging, bushy, weather resistant.
• 'Tavira', bright red, large double flowers, slow

growing, quite weather resistant.
New are hanging geraniums that can be propagated from seed, such as the 'Summer Showers' F_1 hybrids, which have a wide color range.

Blooming Season: April to October.
Family: Geraniaceae (geranium or cranesbill family).
Origin: Original forms, South Africa.
Location: Sunny to partially shady.
Potting Soil: All-purpose mix or loamy, humus-rich garden soil.
Planting: Set purchased or home-grown (see Propagation) plants 8 in. (20 cm) apart.
Watering, Feeding: Water abundantly in the growth period, but by all means avoid standing water. Feed weekly until late August.
Further Care: Deadhead spent flowers regularly (in cultivars that are not self-cleaning).
Overwintering: Do not move indoors with a wet ball. Beforehand, remove

withered and yellowed parts and shorten overly long stems. Put in a bright place at 41°F (5°C). For Cascade cultivars, it is preferable to overwinter cuttings. Water lightly from time to time. In February, cut back to 3 or 4 nodes on a green stem and set in new soil.

Pests, Diseases: Aphids, spider mites, whiteflies; botrytis, geranium wilt.
Propagation: By cuttings, from August to March at the latest. F_1 hybrids, from seed—December to January at a ground temperature over 68°F (20°C).
Decorating Tip: Pink hanging geraniums, for example, look especially pretty with cardinal-red zonal cultivars, or lilac *peltatum* hybrids with erect geraniums.

Geraniums in hanging baskets should be taken down daily on hot days and plunged in a bucket of water until air bubbles have ceased to rise.

Pelargonium x *zonale* Hybrids
Zonal Geraniums, Erect Geraniums, Horseshoe Geraniums

The cultivar 'Champagner' produces large flowers.

'Fidelio' is frequently used also in beds.

Geranium or pelargonium—which is correct? Strictly speaking, the latter. When merchants introduced the first pelargoniums to Europe from South Africa around 1700, the plants at first were termed *Geranium*. In 1789, French botanist Charles Louis L'Héritier de Brutelle assigned them to the pelargoniums. Nevertheless, popular usage has stayed with the name "geranium." The zonal geraniums, which grow to a height of 14 in. (35 cm), are descended from the zoned geranium, *Pelargonium zonale* (*zonale* = belt, stripe), *Pelargonium inquinans* (scarlet geranium), and other species. They have fleshy, slightly hairy stems, which with increasing age lignify in their lower regions. The fuzzy, hairy, or smooth leaves are roundish or only slightly lobed, and they may have more or less pronounced ring-shaped, dark leaf markings. The colors of the single, demidouble, or double umbels range among all the shades of red and pink. Less common are salmon-colored and pure white cultivars. Yellow geraniums are a breeder's dream.

Popular cultivars commercially available: 'Rio' (light pink with dark-pink markings, single, weather resistant), 'Bolero' (bright red, double, weather resistant), 'Casino' (dark salmon, large-flowered, double), 'Flirtpel' (pink, demidouble), 'Cabaret' (red-orange, large-flowered, demidouble), 'Champagner' (light pink with white, large-flowered, single), 'Kardinal' (purple, large-flowered, single, tolerates light shade), 'Stadt Bern' (bright red, small-flowered, single, tolerates shade). Now on the market are F_1 hybrids of zonals that can be reproduced from seed, such as 'Red Elite' (scarlet), 'Bright Eyes' (red with white eye), 'Smash Hit Lachs' (salmon pink), and 'Happy End' (salmon pink, dark, ring-shaped zones on the green leaves).

Blooming Season: April to October.
Family: Geraniaceae (geranium or cranesbill family).
Origin: Original forms, South Africa.
Location: Sunny to partially shady.
Potting Soil: All-purpose mix or loamy, humus-rich garden soil.
Planting: Set purchased or home-grown (see Propagation) young plants 8 in. (20 cm) apart.
Watering, Feeding: Water abundantly during growth period, but by all means avoid standing water. Feed weekly until late August.
Further Care: Deadhead spent faded flowers regularly.
Overwintering: Do not move indoors with wet ball. Beforehand, remove wilted and yellowed parts. Put in a bright place at 41°F (5°C). Water lightly from time to time. In February, cut back to 3 or 4 nodes on a green stem and set in new soil.
Pests, Diseases: Aphids, spider mites, whiteflies; geranium rust, botrytis, geranium wilt.
Propagation: By cuttings, from August to mid-March at latest. F_1 hybrids, from seed, December to January at a ground temperature over 68°F (20°C).
Decorating Tip: Tone-on-tone combinations of white and red hanging geraniums with white or red zonal cultivars are especially beautiful. Pink or lilac tones are also lovely with silver-leaved or variegated hanging plants (for example, *Plectranthus coleoides*).

Scented-leaved Geraniums

Pelargonium fragrans has a pine scent.

Pelargonium crispum releases the scent of lemons.

☼ 🪣 ⌂

Geraniums with scented leaves are a pleasure for the nose and a fragrant, delicate complement to the bright hues and country air of the "flower box geraniums." Anyone who is not intent on having masses of flowers will find in the *Pelargonium* genus charming representatives with leaves of diverse appearance that often release a scent of mint, roses, lemons, or herbs only upon contact. Here are a few recommendations:

• *Pelargonium crispum* 'Minor' has curly leaves and compact growth. Lignifies slightly; is suitable for box planting; has a lemon scent.

• *Pelargonium filicifolium* is distinguished by fernlike, finely laciniate foliage that, along with the sticky, glandular stems, has a strong scent of rue. Suitable for training as miniature potted trees.

• *Pelargonium fragrans* has delicate leaves; its growth makes it suitable for use in hanging baskets; gives off an intense scent of pine.

• *Pelargonium fragrans* 'Lilian Pottinger' is also suitable for hanging baskets; is pineapple-scented.

• *Pelargonium graveolens* 'Grey Lady Plymouth' smells of roses, with a hint of peppermint and cinnamon. It grows smaller than the pure species, including the leaves, which have blue-green or cream-colored margins.

• *Pelargonium odoratissimum* is small-leaved and creeping, which makes it suitable for hanging baskets. It smells of lemon and apple.

• 'Pink Pet' (herb-scented) and the cultivars 'Princess Ann' (lemon-scented), 'Clorinda' (herb-scented), and 'Queens of Lemon' also prosper in flower boxes.

• *Pelargonium tomentosum*, the peppermint geranium, grows as an herbaceous plant or a subshrub with outspread, branching, softly matted stems and thick, dark-green, slightly hairy leaves that look as if covered with white hoar-frost.

For these precious plants you may have to contact specialty garden suppliers.

Blooming Season: Summer.

Family: Geraniaceae (geranium or cranesbill family).

Origin: South Africa.

Location: Sunny; *Pelargonium odoratissimum* prefers partial shade.

Potting Soil: All-purpose mix or loamy, sandy garden soil.

Planting: Set purchased or home-grown (see Propagation) young plants 16 in. (40 cm) apart.

Watering, Feeding: Water moderately, feed every 2 weeks until August.

Further Care: None.

Overwintering: As for *zonale* and *peltatum* hybrids.

Pests, Diseases: White-flies, aphids.

Propagation: By cuttings in summer.

Decorating Tip: Very pretty as a resting point for the eye between hanging and erect geraniums. *Pelargonium crispum* is also suitable for bonsai shaping, and *Pelargonium cunarifolium* easily can be trained as a standard.

The hybrid 'Scarlet Pet' has brilliant red flowers and is orange-scented.

Pelargonium
Variegated-leaved Geraniums

Variegated leaves, pink flowers—'Chelsea Gem'.

Cultivars with beautifully marked leaves.

These charming variegated-leaved geraniums, whose colorful foliage results predominantly from chlorophyll deficiencies, come from England. This phenomenon, recognized 250 years ago, has been extensively researched and described since 1853. Since that time, horticulturists and enthusiasts have collected variegated-leaved geraniums ardently. Today there are almost 50 different varieties in England. Unfortunately, these cultivars, which range from small- to large-leaved and from 12 to 20 in. (30–50 cm) in height, are usually available through private collectors or from the British and European Geranium Society. The flowers tend to be rather modest. Here are the popular English cultivars:
• 'Dolly Vardon' (see photo 4, above) has light-red umbels. Growth moderately vigorous.
• 'Freak of Nature' (see photo 3, above) produces no flowers. Growth erect, vigorous.

• 'Madame Salleron' (see photo 1, above) produces no flowers. Growth erect, moderately vigorous.
• 'Masterpiece' has large leaves, slightly sinuate, with a dark-green center: dark, very pronounced leaf rings; and creamy-white margins with a reddish hue. Flowers are small, demidouble, salmon-colored umbels. Growth erect, vigorous.
• 'Miss Burdett Coutts' has small sinuate leaves with a green center, dark-brown leaf rings overlaid with wine-red hue, and narrow white margins. Flowers are single with light-red umbels. Growth is erect and slight.
• 'Pink Golden Harry Hieouver' has large, slightly sinuate leaves, which are hairy, light green to golden green, with wide leaf rings that become lighter toward the margin. Flowers are single, salmon-colored umbels. Growth is erect and vigorous.
• 'The Czar' has moderately large leaves that are slightly sinuate, light

green with dark brown and with extremely broad leaf rings. Flowers are single, crimson umbels.
• 'The Boar' (see photo 2, above) has salmon-colored single flowers. Growth is erect and vigorous.

Blooming Season: April to October.
Family: Geraniaceae (geranium or cranesbill family).
Origin: Original forms, South Africa.
Location: Sunny and airy.
Potting Soil: All-purpose soil mixed with ⅓ sand or loamy, sandy garden soil.
Planting: Set purchased or home-grown (see Propagation) young plants 8 in. (20 cm) apart in container.
Watering, Feeding: Water abundantly during growth period, but avoid standing water. Feed weekly until end of August.
Further Care: Preferably, remove points where flowers have set, so that the plant's energy can be concentrated on the foliage.
Overwintering: Move indoors in as dry a condi-

The variegated-leaved geraniums in the photos:
1 'Madame Salleron'.
2 'The Boar'.
3 'Freak of Nature'.
4 'Dolly Vardon'.

tion as possible. Beforehand, remove wilted and yellowed parts. Put in a bright location at 41°F (5°C), with dry air. Keep almost completely dry. In February, cut back to 3 or 4 nodes on a green stalk and repot.
Pests, Diseases: Aphids, spider mites, whiteflies; geranium rust, geranium wilt, botrytis.
Propagation: By cuttings, from August to mid-March at the latest. The cultivar 'Freak of Nature' is not vigorous enough for reproduction from cuttings because of the small amount of chlorophyll present in the leaves.

Petunias need to be protected from rain.

The large-flowered, white-margined hybrid 'Picotee'.

Petunias—the names derives from the Brazilian term for tobacco, *petún*—have been adapted through breeding for almost 150 years. The famous seedmen Vilmorin (a Frenchman) and van Houtte (a Belgian) along with others from England, participated in the breeding, which began after 1825. In Germany, two breeders in Erfurt, Benary and Heinemann, contributed to the further improvement of the assortment. What many people do not know: double-flowered petunias were being sold as early as 1849. Breeding of intensely double cultivars was successful only some 100 years later, the achievement of the Japanese seedman Sakasa. The parents of the present-day garden petunias are the white-flowering, scented *Petunia axillaris* and *Petunia violacea*, which has violet-pink flowers. Both are annual to subshrubby, somewhat sticky plants.

Today, numerous large-flowered hybrids 10 to 12 in. (25–30 cm) high are on the market. The flower colors range from pure white through various nuances of pink and red to violet. Even yellow and a true sky blue are represented. Yellow flowers were long a coveted goal of breeders and one satisfactorily attained only in recent years. Cultivars such as 'Summer Sun', 'Ruban Jaunes' or 'Magic Jaune', 'California Girl', and 'Yellow Magic' bloom in various shades of yellow and are available with increasing frequency.
In addition, there are small-flowered and many-flowered varieties, as well as cultivars with white-starred or purple-veined flowers and hanging *pendula* forms with 32-in.-long (80 cm) stems. The small-flowered *Petunia* x *multiflora* or *Petunia* x *floribunda* F₁ hybrids are said to be particularly rainproof.

Blooming Season: May to September.
Family: Solanaceae (nightshade family).
Origin: Original forms, South America.
Location: Sunny.
Potting Soil: All-purpose soil, which can be enhanced with slow-release fertilizer.
Planting: Set purchased or home-grown (see Propagation) young plants 8 to 10 in. (20–25 cm) apart.
Watering, Feeding: Water abundantly and feed lightly each week.
Further Care: Deadhead spent flowers daily. Seed formation occurs very rapidly. After the first array of blooms (late July or early August), cut the plants back by one half when their stems grow increasingly long and they start to flop untidily. Petunias will regenerate within 2 weeks, grow bushy again, and flower as luxuriantly as before.
Overwintering: Not applicable.

Pests, Diseases: Chiefly aphids.
Propagation: From seed in February at a ground temperature of 68° to 72°F (20°–22°C).
Decorating Tip: Small-flowered flowers such as marguerite chrysanthemums, blue daisies, lobelia, and Swan River daisies (see photo, page 96) go well with petunias.
Warning: Petunias belong to the poisonous nightshade family.

Phlox drummondii
Annual Phlox, Texas Pride, Drummond Phlox

The range of colors includes tones from white to blue.

☼ 🖈 **1**

English botanist and plant collector James Ramsey Drummond (1851–1921) is the godfather of this annual species of *Phlox*. The fragrant summer flower, 4 to 20 in. (10–50 cm) high, with pale-green lanceolate leaves, has improved enormously since its introduction in 1835. This once exclusively red-flowering species gave rise, through breeding, to plants with various flower colors ranging from white through rose, pink, and violet to blue, as well as to low, compact specimens. You can sow annual phlox yourself (see Propagation) or buy finished plants. The following are sold in bloom from May to July:
• 'Beauty Pracht-mischung', 8 in. (20 cm) high, large-flowered, pure colors.
• 'Sternenzauber', 6 in. (15 cm) high, starred, usually multicolored flowers.
• 'Wagners Fantasie-mischung', 8 in. (20 cm) high, clear, pure colors.
• 'Cäcilienmischung', 8 in. (20 cm) high, all colors with white eye.

Blooming Season: July to September.
Family: Polemoniaceae (phlox family).
Origin: Texas and neighboring states.
Location: Sunny.
Potting Soil: All-purpose mix (can be enriched with slow-release fertilizer) or loamy, sandy garden soil.
Planting: Set purchased or home-grown (see Propagation) young plants 8 to 10 in. (20–25 cm) apart.
Watering, Feeding: Water abundantly, but avoid standing water and feed lightly once a week.
Further Care: Cut off spent flowers regularly.
Overwintering: Not applicable.
Pests, Diseases: On open patios, slugs. Powdery mildew.
Propagation: From seed, February to March, at a ground temperature of 64°F (18°C).

Plectranthus coleoides
Swedish Begonia, Swedish Ivy

Swedish begonia also can be overwintered.

○ 🖈 ⌂

This relative of *Plectranthus fruticosus* is a very popular variegated-leaved plant for flower boxes. It grows subshrubby and low and covers the box with a flood of stems up to 39 in. (1 m) long, bearing attractive foliage. It offers a pleasant means of breaking up any brightly colored planting. The small, oval leaves are green in the pure species, white-margined in the 'Marginatus' cultivar. When rubbed between one's fingers, they exude a bitter, camphorlike scent. The white flowers are inconspicuous and resemble those of *Coleus*.
Blooming Season: Late summer or fall.
Family: Labiatae or Lamiaceae (mint family).
Origin: South Africa, Asia.
Location: Sunny to partially shady.
Potting Soil: All-purpose soil, which can be enhanced with slow-release fertilizer.
Planting: Set purchased or home-grown (see Propagation) young plants 8 to 12 in. (20–30 cm) apart.
Watering, Feeding: Keep moderately damp during the growth period. Feed every 2 weeks from March to August.
Further Care: None.
Overwintering: Bright location at 50°F (10°C). Water little. Repot in spring, although not recommended as old plants become unattractive. Preferably, take cuttings in summer and overwinter them.
Pests, Diseases: Rare.
Propagation: By tip cuttings in March or April or in summer (easy).
Decorating Tip: *Plectranthus coleoides* goes with all balcony flowers. On its own, it is especially attractive in big-bellied terra cotta containers.

Portulaca grandiflora

Portulaca, Moss Rose, Rose Moss, Sun Plant

Portulaca does not need copious amounts of water.

Primula

Primrose

Primula vulgaris hybrids.

Flowers like silk taffeta for expensive evening gowns in dazzling yellow, orange, hot pink, and crimson or pure white are the typical feature of this annual plant. Portulaca has recumbent stems that spread out. On the stems, round, succulent leaves grow on small stalks. The stamens gleam like heaps of gold in the midst of the 3-in. (8 cm) flowers, which open only in sunshine. The portulacas usually available commercially are mixes, for example, 'Gefullte Prachtmischung', 'Einfache Prachtmischung', and 'Calypso-Mischung'.

Blooming Season: June to August.
Family: Portulacaceae (portulaca family).
Origin: Argentina, Brazil, Uruguay.
Location: Sunny and sheltered from rain. Tolerates great heat.
Potting Soil: All-purpose soil with sand added or light, sandy garden soil.
Planting: Set purchased or home-grown (see

Propagation) young plants 6 in. (15 cm) apart.
Watering, Feeding: Water little and feed every 4 weeks, at most.
Further Care: None.
Overwintering: Not applicable.
Propagation: From seed, March to May. May be sown directly in flower boxes.
Decorating Tip: Portulaca goes especially well with gazanias (see page 112) and Livingstone daisies (see page 118), which need the same care.

Gay, bright spring bloomers that also do well in a flower box:
• *Primula denticulata*, globe-shaped primroses 8 to 12 in. (20–30 cm) high that have a rather ornamental effect; the flowers are white or reddish purple.
• *Primula veris*, available only in yellow.
• *Primula vulgaris* (syn. *Primula acaulis*), English primrose, about 4 in. (10 cm) high, large- or small-flowered, in colors of white, yellow, pink, red, violet, lilac, light blue, or dark blue; white-margined or mottled with yellow or pink.
All are started in summer and come onto the market in March or April, with the exception of *Primula vulgaris* hybrids, which are sold from December on. You can keep them in their box for only one season, but you can continue to cultivate them in the garden after the bloom is past.

Blooming Season: Depending on the species

or the cultivar, March, April, May.
Family: Primulaceae (primrose family).
Origin: Original forms, Europe and Asia.
Location: Partially shady.
Potting Soil: Soilless mix or loamy, humus-rich garden soil.
Planting: Set purchased young plants 6 to 8 in. (15–20 cm) apart.
Watering, Feeding: Keep evenly damp. <u>Do not allow to dry out</u>! Feeding can be omitted in annual culture.
Further Care: None.
Overwintering: Not applicable. Plants set in the garden are hardy.
Propagation: From seed (difficult). A matter for horticulturists.
Pests, Diseases: Aphids, ramularia—leaf spot disease.
Decorating Tip: A tone-on-tone combination of pink *Primula denticulata*, *Primula vulgaris* hybrids, daisies, and hyacinths is quite attractive.
Warning: Primroses can induce allergies in susceptible people.

Do you have a garden? Then plant spring primroses—once they have finished blooming—under shrubs, where they will come back repeatedly and, over time, spread themselves as they do in nature.

Rosa
Rose

The dwarf rose 'Sonnenkind', with its deep golden-yellow flowers, has a bushy habit and branches well.

'Daniela' has vivid-green, delicate leaves.

The passion for roses does not stop at the balcony or patio. Of course, container gardeners should not expect that plants with a tiny bit of earth beneath them will live as long as in the garden. Roses are deep-rooted; the more room they have available for their roots, the better they will flourish. Nevertheless, it is worthwhile to try keeping these flowering woody plants in the uncommon surroundings of a box. Numerous slow-growing species now are available; these thrive satisfactorily when planted at least 8 in. (20 cm) deep. Suitable for planting in deep boxes or bowls are all 12- to 16-in.-high (30–40 cm) dwarf roses, such as 'Sonnenkind' (yellow), 'Baby Maskerade' (yellow-orange), 'Guletta' (yellow), 'Orange Meillandina' (orange), 'Daniela' (pale pink), 'Rosmarin 89' (pink), and 'Scarletta' (red). In general, everything that is sold in small pots can also be planted in boxes, including pot roses

and miniature pot roses. New are pot roses that can be reproduced from seed, such as 'Kissy' (dwarf, pale pink, well-branched). Taller ground-cover roses such as 'The Fairy' are also suitable for roomy, deep boxes. This cultivar yields vast quantities of small umbels in very pale pink, forms rather robust leaves, and produces very fine stems that branch extensively. Somewhat lower, at 16 in. (40 cm), is 'Swany'. It forms long stems that are recumbent or curved and erect, and produces swan-white double flowers 1½ to 2⅓ in. (4–6 cm) across. The foliage is dark green and shiny.

Blooming Season: June to fall.
Family: Rosaceae (rose family).
Origin: Cultivated strains.
Location: Full sun, airy.
Potting Soil: All-purpose mix or humus-rich, loose, loamy, sandy garden soil.
Planting: Set purchased or home-grown (see Propagation) young plants 8 to 10 in. (20–25 cm) apart.

Watering, Feeding: Water moderately during growth period. By all means avoid standing water. Feed weekly until late July. If you prefer slow-release fertilizer, sprinkle it on the soil surface twice (in March and June).
Further Care: Deadhead spent flowers to stimulate repeated flowering.
Overwintering: Outdoors with winter protection. Put individual pots in bowls or crates (see pages 28–29), bury boxes in the garden and cover with fir branches. Alternatively, put container indoors in a frost-free, dark, airy place. In spring, replace top layer of soil. Shorten shoots to a handsbreadth. After flush occurs, put outdoors in partial shade.
Pests, Diseases: Aphids, spider mites; powdery mildew, starry sooty mold, rose rust.
Propagation: By cuttings, from mid-August to mid-September. The cultivar 'Sissy', from seed in March at a ground temperature of 68° to 72°F

(20°–22°C).
Decorating Tip: In roomy containers, quite pretty in combination with low lavender (see page 186); in boxes, better planted alone.

Salpiglossis sinuata
Painted Tongue, Velvet Flower

Salvia splendens
Scarlet Sage, Red Salvia

Painted tongue needs wind protection.

Scarlet sage flowers branch singly or in panicles.

Of the eight species of the genus *Salpiglossis*, thus far only *Salpiglossis sinuata* has gained admission to the retail assortment of summer flowers. This annual grows 20 to 39 in. (0.5–1 m) high; it is sticky and covered with soft hair. Painted tongue grows erect and more or less branched. The trumpet-shaped—or, more precisely, funnel-shaped—flowers are white, yellow, purple, red-brown, dark brown, and violet. Bluish, yellow, brownish, or reddish veinings cause them to look especially distinctive, almost like orchids. Seeds and young plants of the 'Grandiflora' mix, which grow 32 in. (80 cm) high, are commercially available. New on the market is the very large-flowered F$_1$ hybrid 'Casino Mix'; it has exceptionally abundant flowers and grows only 24 in. (60 cm) high.

Blooming Season: June to August.
Family: Solanaceae (nightshade family).
Origin: Chile.

Location: Sunny and sheltered from wind.
Potting Soil: All-purpose mix, or humus-, nutrient-rich garden soil. Loves lime.
Planting: Set purchased or home-grown (see Propagation) young plants 10 to 12 in. (25–30 cm) apart.
Watering, Feeding: Keep slightly damp at all times, but avoid standing water and dryness. Feed weekly. High nutrient requirement.
Further Care: Deadhead spent flowers.
Overwintering: Not applicable.
Pests, Diseases: Stem and root rot due to excessive damp.
Propagation: From seed in February in preliminary culture; in March or April, sow directly in the container.
Decorating Tip: Pretty for boxes on the ground that give you a close look at the flowers.
Warning: Painted tongue belongs to the poisonous nightshade family.

Scarlet sage is native to Brazil, where it may reach a height of almost 5 ft (1.5 m). The stems are square; the leaves are ovate and 2 to 4 in. (5–10 cm) long. The scarlet racemes may be single or compound (panicles) and 6 to 8 in. (15–20 cm) long.
Salvia splendens has been cultivated since 1822. The plants we know today are strains treated as annuals; they grow markedly lower than the pure species, flower more prolifically, and display new flower colors. For flower boxes, the low, compact cultivars are preferred, for example:
- 'Johannisfeuer', 10 in. (25 cm) high, blazing scarlet.
- 'Laser Purple', 10 in. (25 cm) high, dark violet.
- 'Melba', 10 in. (25 cm) high, salmon pink with light scarlet.
- 'Carabiniere', 8 in. (20 cm) high, glowing scarlet, thick panicles, dark foliage.

Blooming Season: May to September.

Family: Labiatae or Lamiaceae (mint family).
Origin: Brazil.
Location: Sunny and sheltered from wind and, if at all possible, from rain. The plants will become stunted in the rain.
Potting Soil: All-purpose mix or loamy, humus-rich garden soil.
Planting: Set purchased or home-grown (see Propagation) plants 8 to 12 in. (20–30 cm) apart.
Watering, Feeding: Keep damp, but avoid standing water. Apply low dose of fertilizer weekly.
Further Care: After the first flowering, cut out brown inflorescences so that the plant can put forth new shoots.
Overwintering: Not applicable.
Pests, Diseases: Mites.
Propagation: From seed in March at a ground temperature of 72°F (22°C). Remove shoot tips at a height of 3 in. (8 cm) and root as cuttings.
Decorating Tip: Yellow slipperwort is an excellent partner for red or violet salvia cultivars.

Sanvitalia procumbens
Creeping Zinnia

Scaevola aemula
Blue Fanflower

Blue fanflower does not object to dryness.

Enchanting—creeping zinnia in a hanging basket.

Whether this minisunflower owes its botanical name to the distinguished Sanvitali family of Parma or to an Italian botanist named Sanvitali remains unclear. In any event, the plant reached Europe in 1748 and now enjoys tremendous popularity on both sides of the Atlantic as a bedding and container plant. As the species name—*procumbens* = lying along the ground—tells us, this annual has trailing stems. It reaches a height of only 3 to 6. in. (8–15 cm) and forms branched, outspread stalks on which small, oval-lanceolate leaves grow. The button- or penny-sized blooms consist of outer strap-shaped yellow petals and an almost black disk in the center. In 1987, an orange-flowered cultivar—'Mandarin Orange'—became available.
Blooming Season: June or July to October.

Family: Asteraceae or Compositae (aster or composite family).
Origin: Mexico, Guatemala.
Location: Sunny.
Potting Soil: All-purpose soil mix or loamy garden soil with some sand added.
Planting: Set purchased or home-grown (see Propagation) young plants 6 in. (15 cm) apart.
Watering, Feeding: Water moderately and apply a low dose of fertilizer every 2 weeks. Low nutrient requirement.
Further Care: Deadhead spent flowers regularly.
Overwintering: Not applicable.
Pests, Diseases: Rare.
Propagation: From seed in March at a ground temperature of 59° to 64°F (15°–18°C). In mid-May, set the young plants directly from the propagating bed into the flower boxes.
Decorating Tip: Suitable for shallow containers and as underplanting for yellow-flowered tub plants.

Scaevola aemula is a novelty whose abundance of flowers, repeated blooming, self-cleaning ability, and weather resistance inspire enthusiasm everywhere. This bushy semi-hanging plant is grown as an annual; it produces numerous stems up to about 39 in. (1 m) long. The main and side stems are densely covered at their tips with blue-violet flowers, ¾ to 1 in. (2–2.5 cm) wide that look blue in partial shade and are shaped like small fans. The leaves are slightly succulent, so the plant can recover surprisingly well if its ball occasionally gets dry.
Blooming Season: April to fall.
Family: Goodeniaceae (goodenia family).
Origin: Australia.
Location: Sunny to partially shady.
Potting Soil: All-purpose soil.
Planting: Set purchased young plants 8 in. (20 cm) apart.
Watering, Feeding: Keep sufficiently damp with soft water. By all means avoid standing water. Apply a low dose of fertilizer weekly. The plant comes from the red, sandy soils of Australia and is sensitive to salt and lime.
Further Care: None. Spent flowers drop off by themselves.
Overwintering: A bright location at 59°F (15°C) is possible but not recommended, because the plant usually becomes unsightly.
Pests, Diseases: Leaf miners, whiteflies. Occasionally, *Verticillium* wilt, a fungal disease.
Propagation: A matter for horticulturists. (By cuttings in winter in a mist at 68°F [20°C].)
Decorating Tip: Splendid hanging plant; if well tended, it will reach a diameter of about 39 in. (1 m) without crowding its neighbors in the flower box. Quite attractive in mixed boxes with red and pink geraniums or marguerite chrysanthemums.

Schizanthus x *wisetonensis* Hybrids
Butterfly Flower, Poor Man's Orchid

Scilla siberica
Siberian Squill

The blooms of the butterfly flower should not get wet.

Scilla siberica can be bought in bloom in spring.

Flowers as exotic as orchids and in bouquets to boot—no wonder the butterfly flower has found so many friends. The leaves of the plants are bright green and look almost like ferns. The ground colors of the spotted, striped, or color-washed flowers range from salmon through light rose, pink, red, and burgundy to violet. Well-known cultivars: 'Hitparade' (10 to 12 in. [25–30 cm] high), 'Starparade' (8 in. [20 cm] high, large-flowered), 'Excelsior-Mischung' (16 in. [40 cm] high).

Blooming Season: July to September.
Family: Solanaceae (nightshade family).
Origin: Original forms, Chile.
Location: Sunny.
Potting Soil: All-purpose mix (can be enriched with slow-release fertilizers) or loamy, humus-rich garden soil. Loves lime.
Planting: Set purchased or home-grown (see Propagation) young plants 12 in. (30 cm) apart. Do not plant too close to-

gether; otherwise, the foliage will turn yellow.
Watering, Feeding: Keep damp at all times. Do not pour water over foliage—danger of rot. Feed weekly.
Further Care: Remove yellowed leaves and spent flowers regularly. Cutting back after flowering will make a second array of blooms possible.
Overwintering: Not applicable.
Pests, Diseases: Whiteflies; botrytis.
Propagation: From seed in March or April at a ground temperature of 61° to 64°F (16°–18°C). Set 3 to 5 young plants in each pot in order to obtain bushy specimens.
Decorating Tip: The butterfly flower looks quite attractive in round ornamental bowls or old stone vases.
Warning: The butterfly flower belongs to the poisonous nightshade family.

Of the more than 80 species, *Scilla siberica* is best suited to grow in a box, particularly the cultivar 'Spring Beauty'. The flowers of this cultivar are especially large and vivid blue in color. Moreover, they rise 6 to 8 in. (15–20 cm) above the bulb, whereas the pure species reaches a height of only 3 to 4 in. (8–10 cm). *Scilla siberica* is forced and sold in bloom in spring.
Blooming Season: Depending on the species and the cultivar, March to April.
Family: Liliaceae (lily family).
Origin: Central Russia to the Caucasus and Near East.
Location: Sunny to partially shady. Protect plants in bloom against late spells of frost.
Potting Soil: All-purpose soil (can be enriched with slow-release fertilizer) or loamy, humus-rich garden soil.
Planting: Set the bulbs in groups in the box in September, 4 in. (10 cm) apart and 2 to 3 in.

(5–8 cm) deep. Alternative: Set forced, blooming plants in spring.
Overwintering: Keep planted box in a frost-free, dark place, brighter after flush. Do not let soil dry out. Seldom successful the second year.
Watering, Feeding: Keep planted box slightly damp until flush begins. From then on, water moderately and feed once. Avoid standing water. After the fall of the blossoms, set in the garden with root ball and feed once more.
Further Care: None.
Pests, Diseases: Rare.
Propagation: Not possible in container culture. In the garden, the pure species can be grown from seed, the cultivar 'Spring Beauty', from offset bulbs.
Warning: The bulbs and seeds of some species are poisonous. The juice can cause skin irritations.

Senecio bicolor
Dusty Miller, Sea Ragwort

Dusty Miller—a lovely contrast in plantings.

This plant is usually treated as an annual; it grows 8 to 12 in. (20–30 cm) high. In its native habitat, it grows as a sub-shrub and reaches a height of 16 to 32 in. (40–80 cm). Also sold under its old name, *Senecio cineraria*, this plant is conspicuous by its deeply lobed or laciniate, silvery feltlike foliage. In annual culture, the tiny yellow flowers do not appear. Some well-known cultivars follow:
• 'Silver Dust', 8 in. (20 cm) high, delicate foliage, silvery white.
• 'Diamant', 16 in. (40 cm) high, silvery green.
• 'New Look', 12 in. (30 cm) high, and large, cabbagelike, sinuate leaves with a slightly blu-ish sheen, covered with white, woolly hair.
• 'Cirrus', 8 in. (20 cm) high. Foliage same as 'New Look'.
Blooming Season: In its native habitat, July to September.
Family: Asteraceae or Compositae (aster or com-posite family).

Origin: Mediterranean region.
Location: Sunny and sheltered from rain.
Potting Soil: All-purpose mix or loamy, sandy soil.
Planting: Set purchased or home-grown (see Pro-pagation) young plants 8 to 12 in. (20–30 cm) apart.
Watering, Feeding: Keep only slightly damp and feed every 2 weeks.
Further Care: None.
Overwintering: In a bed in mild regions, without winter protection. Unusual in a box.
Pests, Diseases: Aphids, leaf miners; pow-dery and downy mildew, leaf spot.
Propagation: From seed in March at a ground tem-perature of 64°F (18°C).
Decorating Tip: Prettiest with pastel pink, white, and violet flowers, for example, lobelia, Livingstone daisies, por-tulaca. Alternatively, combine with *Reseda odorata, Helichrysum petiolare* 'Aureum', and some lobelias.
Warning: The plant con-tains poisonous alkaloids.

Tagetes Hybrids
Marigold

Marigolds have warm, sunny colors.

Anyone who is interested in *Tagetes* is confronted with a large number of different strains. Suitable for culture in bowls and boxes are the *Tagetes erecta* hybrids, which grow 12 in. (30 cm) high, and particularly the *Tagetes patula* hybrids, 8 to 10 in. (20–25 cm) high. The graceful *Tagetes tenuifolia* falls in with the trend toward wild flowers. This plant, with its small single flowers, is charac-terized by long, prolific flowering and lack of sen-sitivity to rain. The flow-ers grow over the lush green, pinnate foliage and are single or double, bright yellow and orange or two-toned, orange and gold or orange and brown. Marigolds have a pungent fragrance.
Blooming Season: July to October.
Family: Asteraceae or Compositae (aster or com-posite family).
Origin: Original forms, Mexico and Guatemala.
Location: Sunny to par-tially shady.

Potting Soil: All-purpose mix (can be enriched with slow-release fertilizer) or loamy, humus-rich garden soil.
Planting: Set purchased or home-grown (see Propagation) young plants 6 to 10 in. (15–25 cm) apart.
Watering, Feeding: Keep evenly damp. Feed weekly.
Further Care: Deadhead spent flowers to ensure repeated flowering.
Overwintering: Not applicable.
Pests, Diseases: Aphids, spider mites, slugs.
Propagation: From seed, January to March, at a ground temperature of 64°F (18°C).
Decorating Tip: *Tagetes* are particularly pretty on their own, in a mixture of colors, or in combination with blue flowers. They harmonize well with to-matoes.
Warning: The plants con-tain substances that may induce photodermatitis.

Thunbergia alata
Black-eyed Susan, Thunbergia

☼ 🪣 🌡 **1**

This twining woody plant, grown in its homeland as a perennial, in cool climates as an annual, is easy to raise on your own. The funnel-shaped flowers with the black eye are golden yellow to orange and, in the cultivar 'Alba', white. Flowers without eyes also occur in seed mixes, for example, 'Susie Mix'. The leaves are heart-shaped, long-stemmed, and lush green in color.

Blooming Season: May or June to October.

Family: Acanthaceae (acanthus family).

Origin: Southeastern Africa.

Location: Sunny, warm, and sheltered from wind.

Potting Soil: All-purpose mix or loamy, humus-rich garden soil.

Planting: Set purchased or home-grown (see Propagation) young plants 12 to 16 in. (30–40 cm) apart.

Watering, Feeding: Water abundantly, but avoid standing water. Feed every 2 weeks.

Further Care: Needs a climbing aid with a rough surface.

Overwintering: Not applicable.

Pests, Diseases: Aphids, spider mites, whiteflies.

Propagation: From seed, February on, at a ground temperature of 64°F (18°C). Lay 3 seed grains in each pot. Pinch out young plants once, so that they will branch nicely.

Flowers under Palms

Here, black-eyed Susan vine, with a lush display of flowers, climbs on supporting poles anchored in the tub to the right and left of the Chusan palm.

Thymophylla tenuiloba
Dahlberg Daisy, Golden Fleece

![Dahlberg daisies photograph]

Dahlberg daisies—a dazzle of golden blooms.

☼ 🔧 **1**

This relative of marguerite chrysanthemums and fleabane, with its golden flowers, is very much a part of the standard assortment of container flowers here, although in Europe it is considered a private tip among container gardeners. The Dahlberg daisy grows only 6 in. (15 cm) high and spreads abundantly toward the sides. It has graceful, finely lobed foliage. The flowers, which measure about ⅘ in. (2 cm) across, appear in great numbers throughout the summer.

Blooming Season: July to October.
Family: Asteraceae or Compositae (composite family).
Origin: Southern United States, Mexico.
Location: Sunny.
Potting Soil: All-purpose mix (can be enriched with slow-release fertilizer) or humus-rich garden soil.
Planting: Set purchased or home-grown (see Propagation) young plants 8 in. (20 cm) apart.

Watering, Feeding: Keep moderately damp and apply a low dose of fertilizer weekly.
Further Care: Deadhead spent flowers.
Overwintering: Not applicable.
Pests, Diseases: Aphids; powdery mildew.
Propagation: From seed, February to April, at a ground temperature of 64° to 68°F (18°–20°C).
Decorating Tip: The Dahlberg daisy is particularly attractive as a hanging plant. In a box, it makes a good hanging component in combination with marigolds, yellow-orange lantana, yellow slipperwort, or erect yellow-red geraniums.

Tradescantia x *andersoniana* Hybrids
Spiderwort, Trinity Flower

The purple *Tradescantia* hybrid 'Karin'.

○ 🔧 🪴

Spiderwort is a close relative of such popular indoor plants as *Setcreasea* and *Zebrina*. It grows just as quickly as these plants with beautiful foliage, but it flowers more attractively. This herbaceous plant reaches an average height of 20 in. (50 cm), and its growth is bushy to clusterlike. The light-blue, red-violet, or blue-violet flowers grow in umbels of three or more blooms and contrast nicely with the narrow lanceolate leaves, 6 to 16 in. (15–40 cm) long. Well-known cultivars are: 'C. Weguelin', 'Karminglut', and 'Zwanenburg Blue' (in nurseries that sell herbaceous plants).

Blooming Season: May to September.
Family: Commelinaceae (spiderwort family).
Origin: Original forms, North America.
Location: Sunny to shady, better cool and damp than hot and dry.
Potting Soil: All-purpose mix or loamy, humus-rich garden soil.

Planting: Set purchased or home-grown (see Propagation) young plants 12 to 20 in. (30–50 cm) apart.
Watering, Feeding: During the growth period, keep evenly damp, but avoid standing water. The ball should not dry out. Feed every 4 weeks.
Further Care: None.
Overwintering: Hardy when planted out in the garden. Dies back in the fall and puts forth shoots again in spring. In container, cover with fir brush. If plant becomes dry, water moderately on frost-free days. If necessary, repot in spring.
Pests, Diseases: Aphids.
Propagation: By division before repotting.
Decorating Tip: Makes a good edging or neighboring plant for aquatic plants in a tub.

Tropaeolum peregrinum
Canary-bird Flower

Tropaeolum Hybrids
Nasturtium

Canary-bird flower needs only low doses of fertilizer.

Nasturtium flowers and leaves are edible.

☀ 🔦 ⇗ **1**

☀ 🔦 **1**

This busy annual, high-climbing vine, which reaches a height of almost 13 ft (4 m) in its native habitat, has bare stems and delicate, hand-shaped leaves that have 5 to 7 lobes. Individually, the outline of the lobes resembles the shape of a kidney, a heart, or a circle. The upper surface of the leaf is bright green; the underside, gray-green. The numerous small, feathery flowers are lemon yellow with red spots and have a spur bent in the shape of a hook.

Blooming Season: July to October.
Family: Tropaeolaceae (nasturtium family).
Origin: Peru, probably also Ecuador.
Location: Sunny to partially shady, warm, and sheltered from wind.
Potting Soil: Soilless mix, all-purpose soil with some sand added, or loamy, sandy garden soil.
Planting: Set purchased or home-grown (see Propagation) young plants 12 in. (30 cm) apart.

Watering, Feeding: Water abundantly and apply a low dose of fertilizer every 2 weeks. More leaves than flowers will develop if the plant is given overly rich food.
Further Care: Provide a climbing aid (see pages 50–51).
Overwintering: Not applicable.
Pests, Diseases: Aphids.
Propagation: From seed sown directly in the box from April to May. Alternative: From March on, start indoors; sow 3 to 4 seeds in each 3-in. (8 cm) pot.
Decorating Tip: Canary-bird flower is well suited for use in creating walls of bright-yellow flowers, which can serve as privacy screens or as a background for red or blue flowers.

The most popular nasturtiums are crosses of *Tropaeolum majus* and *Tropaeolum peltophorum*. A distinction is drawn between *majus* cultivars with stems up to 6½ ft (2 m) long and *majus nanum* or 'Tom Thumb' cultivars, which form bushes 10 to 12 in. (25–30 cm) high, with many stems. Both groups include single-flowered and double-flowered plants. The colors range among yellow, orange, salmon pink, red, and scarlet. Frequently the flowers also are speckled or mottled with red-orange. The bright-green leaves are shield-shaped.

Blooming Season: June or July to October.
Family: Tropaeolaceae (nasturtium family).
Origin: Original forms, Peru, Colombia, Ecuador.
Location: Sunny. With less light, many leaves and few flowers develop.
Potting Soil: All-purpose mix or loamy, sandy, nutrient-poor garden soil. If the ground is too rich, excessive leaf formation

and few flowers will result.
Planting: Set purchased or home-grown (see Propagation) low cultivars 12 to 20 in. (30–50 cm) apart, tall cultivars only one per flower box.
Watering, Feeding: Water abundantly. Feed either not at all or every 6 to 8 weeks at most (no heavily nitrogenous fertilizer).
Further Care: If you want tall cultivars to climb, supply a climbing aid (screen wire).
Overwintering: Not applicable.
Pests, Diseases: Aphids, spider mites.
Propagation: From seed sown directly in the box from April to May. Thin out later. Alternative: From March on, start them indoors, putting 3 to 4 seeds in each 3-in. (8 cm) pot.

Low cultivars form dense "flower globes" in big-bellied containers.

Tulipa
Tulip

Tulipa pulchella 'Persian Pearl'.

White, lily-flowered hybrid 'White Triumphator'.

☀ 🗴 🏠 ☠

In the seventeenth century, tulips were so costly that many people had to sell house and home in order to acquire a particular tulip bulb. Today, tulips are affordable for everyone, but the enormous assortment of strains makes the choice difficult for many plant enthusiasts. For planting boxes and bowls, low species and cultivars are used primarily, for example:

• Single early tulips, 6 to 10 in. (15–25 cm) high, flowers up to 5 in. (12 cm) across, petals more or less intensely rounded at the tips, available one-colored or multicolored in many hues, leaves green.

• *Greigii* hybrids, 8 to 10 in. (20–25 cm) high, flowers cup-shaped, orange-red to scarlet red, in the hybrids also yellow-and-red striped or rose-red, leaves brownish green or greenish black striped or spotted.

• *Fosteriana* hybrids, 6 to 16 in. (15–40 cm), flowers cup-shaped with a small black, yellow-bordered spot, orange, bright red, white with yellow central stripe.

• *Kaufmanniana* hybrids, 8 to 10 in. (20–25 cm) high; in the wild form *Tulipa kaufmanniana*, the flowers are broad and bell-shaped, wide open, with pointed yellow petals whose face is flushed with red; flowers of the hybrids in brilliant colors, leaves spotted or striped with purple.

• *Tulipa tarda*, 4 in. (10 cm) high, with 4 to 8 star-shaped, whitish-yellow flowers per stalk, leaves narrow, medium green. Also sold under synonym *Tulipa dasystemon*.

• *Tulipa linifolia*, 8 in. (20 cm) high, signal-light-red flowers, fresh-green leaves.

• *Tulipa clusiana*, 12 in. (30 cm) high, delicate, pointed flowers flamed with white and red that open in the shape of stars, narrow leaves.

• *Tulipa pulchella*, about 5 in. (12 cm) high, flowers egg-shaped, reddish purple, leaves narrow.

Blooming Season: March, April, May, depending on origin.

Family: Liliaceae (lily family).

Origin: Original forms, Asia Minor and Central Asia, Turkestan.

Location: Sunny. Protect plants in bloom against late spells of frost!

Potting Soil: All-purpose mix (can be enriched with slow-release fertilizer) or loamy, humus-rich garden soil.

Planting: Set tulip bulbs in groups during the fall, 2 in. (5 cm) apart and 4 in. (10 cm) deep. Alternative: Some hybrids are available forced (with blooms or buds) in spring and can be planted then.

Overwintering: Keep planted box frost-free and dark, brighter after flush. Do not let soil dry out. Usually not successful the second year.

Watering, Feeding: Keep planted box slightly damp until flush begins. From then on, water moderately and feed once. Avoid standing water. After the blossoms fall, set with root ball in the garden and feed again.

Further Care: After the petals fall off, immediately cut off the rest of the flower. Seed formation exhausts the bulb, which needs its strength for the formation of a new one. As soon as this new bulb is developed, the foliage will turn yellow.

Pests, Diseases: Rarely, fungal diseases.

Decorating Tip: Tulips look particularly beautiful in combination with Siberian squill, hyacinths, and daffodils.

Warning: Tulip bulbs are slightly poisonous and contain substances that can cause allergies in susceptible people.

The lacquer-red 'Salome' grows about 12 in. (30 cm) high and has a small white eye.

Verbenas are among the most popular plants in the container flower assortment. What we have available today in an intoxicating variety of colors is the result of a great many efforts at breeding. The ancestors include *Verbena peruviana*, which supplies the red hues, and *Verbena phlogifolia* and *Verbena incisa*, which contributed the pink and purple nuances. Verbenas owe their fragrance to *Verbena platensis*. Additional cross-connections in breeding produced scarlet colors or white eyes. In the modern hybrids, the flowers appear in dense umbellate spikes. The scale of colors ranges from white through salmon, rose, pink, red, and purple to blue and violet. The oblong-ovate leaves are covered in stiff hairs and serrated at the margin. Although the hybrids carry genes for herbaceous to subshrubby growth, they are treated as annuals. Among the numerous cultivars, those 8 to 10 in. (20–25 cm) high

that grow upright, creeping, or slightly overhanging are most suitable for the balcony, for example:
• 'Blütenmeer Violett' (violet shades), 12 in. (30 cm) high, overhanging.
• 'Novalis' (all color nuances), 8 in. (20 cm) high, grows erect, compact, rounded.
• 'Derby' (all color nuances), 10 in. (25 cm) high, grows erect.
• 'Sparkle', 8 in. (20 cm) high, erect, compact.
• 'Showtime Belle', under 8 in. (20 cm), creeping, purple-red.

Blooming Season: June to October.

Family: Verbenaceae (verbena family).

Origin: Original forms, South America.

Location: Sunny.

Potting Soil: All-purpose soil, which can be enriched with slow-release fertilizer.

Planting: Set purchased or home-grown (see Propagation) young plants 8 in. (20 cm) apart.

Watering, Feeding: Water abundantly, but

avoid standing water. Apply a low dose of fertilizer every 2 weeks. Low nutrient requirement.

Further Care: Deadhead spent flowers regularly.

Overwintering: Not applicable.

Pests, Diseases: Aphids, thrips, spider mites, whiteflies; powdery mildew.

Propagation: From seed, February to April, at a ground temperature of 64° to 68°F (18°–20°C). Caution: The seed often germinates unevenly! The germinating power is not very great.

Decorating Tip: The cool tones of verbenas are a good match for silvery foliage or flowering plants such as dusty miller (*Senecio*) or mealycup sage (*Salvia farinacea* 'Silber').

My Tip: Sometimes you will find hanging verbenas for sale, marketed under the name of Cleopatra verbenas or Italian verbenas. These are hybrids developed from *Verbena tenera*. They reach a height of 6

to 12 in. (15–30 cm), grow herbaceous to subshrubby, and produce 2-in. (5 cm) umbels in purple-pink. The remarkable thing about these plants is their exceptional resistance to rain. They will withstand rainfall that continues for days and will even endure standing water.

The cultivars in the photos:
Left: The pink hybrid 'Delight'.
Above: The purple 'Novalis'.

Viola x *wittrockiana* Hybrids
Pansy

Among the great variety of pansy cultivars, you will surely find your favorite color.

These biennial plants have been cultivated in Germany since 1536. The task of hybridization started in England at the beginning of the nineteenth century. By 1850, French, Belgian, and German breeders were participants in further development. The ancestors of our present-day delicately fragrant cultivars that grow 6 to 10 in. (15–25 cm) high are said to be *Viola tricolor, Viola lutea,* a yellow-flowering wild species, and *Viola altaica.* The principal breeding goals were large, beautifully shaped flowers, an early blooming season, an abundant array of blooms, compact, solid growth, improved hardiness, and robust health. The different strains on the market today are the results of breeders' efforts over a period of two centuries, and the variety is correspondingly wide. There are early and late bloomers, small- and large-flowered plants, self-colored and multicolored cultivars, pansies with eyes and glazed pansies (fine radiating lines in place of eyes). The diversity of the colors seems inexhaustible. Because plants are sold in bloom in September or October and in March or April, you can enjoy a colorful planting of pansies in fall, almost until December if the climate is favorable. Spring, however, is the primary blooming period. Plants set in fall can winter over in their box, but in spring it will take slightly longer for flowering to get under way. Depending on the breed, plants sold in spring are full of buds that will begin to bloom all at the same time, with all their might. From June on, the plants usually become unattractive and are discarded.

Blooming Season: Depending on the strain, in fall and spring.

Family: Violaceae (violet family).

Origin: Original forms, Europe, Siberia, Altai Mountains, North Africa.

Location: Sunny to partially shady.

Potting Soil: All-purpose mix or loamy, humus-rich garden soil.

Planting: Set purchased or home-grown (see Propagation) young plants 4 to 6 in. (10–15 cm) apart.

Watering, Feeding: During the growth period, never allow to dry out, but do not keep too wet. Feed every 2 weeks.

Further Care: Regularly deadhead spent flowers.

Overwintering: Pansies planted in fall can be overwintered outdoors without protection in favorable climate zones, possibly with some fir brush to protect them from the sun. In unfavorable climate zones, keep box in a bright, frost-free place. Important: Do not let the plants dry out in winter. In case of dryness, water moderately on frost-free days.

Pests, Diseases: Aphids; botrytis, powdery and downy mildew.

Propagation: From seed sown in June or July. Do not let propagating container dry out. If you have a garden, sow the seed in a cold frame or in a bed in partial shade. The young plantlets spend the winter in the bed and are set in the containers in spring.

Decorating Tip: Pansies are most effective over a large flat area. Consequently, it is better to plant a group in bowls with a large diameter than to plant them separately in a narrow flower box. The latest thing is F_1 miniature *Viola,* for example, the cultivar 'Alpensommer', with tricolored dark-blue, light-blue, and yellow flowers measuring about 1 in. (2.5 cm) across.

Brown and bronze shades are a favorite goal of breeders.

Viola x *cornuta* Hybrids
Violet, Viola

No one can resist the charm of violets.

☼ ◁ ⊟

Anyone who loves natural, unobtrusive things will delight in these violas. From a creeping rootstock, this herbaceous plant—which grows 8 to 10 in. (20-25 cm) high in its native habitat—forms numerous, usually trigonal stems with oblong-ovate leaves. The violet-colored flowers grow on a curved stalk. Today, nurseries that sell herbaceous plants offer almost exclusively hybrids. These are cultivars of small-flowered types that grow about 4 in. (10 cm) high, as well as cultivars of large-flowered types that reach a height of 8 in. (20 cm).

Blooming Season: Hybrids, May to September. Pure species, June to August.

Family: Violaceae (violet family).

Origin: Pyrenees.

Location: Sunny.

Potting Soil: All-purpose mix or loamy, humus-rich garden soil with some sand added.

Planting: Set purchased or home-grown (see Propagation) young plants 4 to 8 in. (10–20 cm) apart.

Watering, Feeding: During the growth period, keep evenly and slightly damp. Avoid standing water.

Further Care: None.

Overwintering: In favorable climate zones, outdoors (otherwise, put box in a bright, frost-free place). Cover boxes with brush. In case of dryness, water moderately on frost-free days.

Pests, Diseases: Spider mites; powdery and downy mildew, rust, leaf spot diseases.

Propagation: From seed sown in spring at a ground temperature of about 64°F (18°C). Keep young plants cool, at about 54°F (12°C), so that they will stay compact.

Decorating Tip: Small-flowered types are suitable for shallow bowls or as underplanting for taller tulips. Large-flowered cultivars look attractive in a balcony box.

Zinnia elegans
Zinnia, Youth-and-old-age, Cut-and-come-again

Not quite so common—double-flowered zinnias.

☼ ◁ ⇗ **1**

Zinnias, named for German botanist Johann Gottfried Zinn (1727–1759), are among the most rewarding summer annuals. There are a great many cultivars with extremely diverse flower forms and colors. The new low and compact hybrids have proved most reliable in flower boxes and bowls. Some examples:
• 'Peter Pan' series (showered with gold medals), 12 in. (30 cm) high, flowers 3 in. (8 cm) wide in white, golden yellow, orange, salmon pink, crimson, and scarlet.
• 'Dreamland' zinnias, 8 to 10 in. (20–25 cm) high, flowers 3½- to 4-in. (9–10 cm) in creamy white, salmon, pink, light scarlet, golden yellow.
• *Zinnia elegans* 'Thumbelina', 6 in. (15 cm) high, dahlia-shaped flowers in mixed colors.

Blooming Season: July to September.

Family: Asteraceae or Compositae (aster or composite family).

Origin: Mexico.

Location: Sunny, sheltered from wind, and quite warm.

Potting Soil: All-purpose mix or loamy, sandy garden soil.

Planting: Set purchased or home-grown (see Propagation) young plants 6 to 8 in. (15–20 cm) apart. Do not set out any zinnia cultivars before the end of May!

Watering, Feeding: Keep evenly and slightly damp, never wet, and feed every 2 weeks (no highly nitrogenous fertilizer).

Further Care: Regularly deadhead spent flowers.

Overwintering: Not applicable.

Pests, Diseases: Aphids, spider mites, leaf eelworms, slugs.

Propagation: From seed sown February to May, at a ground temperature of 68°F (20°C).

Decorating Tip: The rounded shapes of the zinnia flowers and the pointed, towering flowers of sage and lavender make an exciting combination.

Briza maxima
Greater Quaking Grass

Hordeum jubatum
Squirrel-tail Grass

Greater quaking grass produces cone-shaped flowers.

Squirrel-tail grass is related to brewing barley.

The English common name refers to the conelike panicles that hang on small, hairlike stalks and tremble in the slightest breath of air. Greater quaking grass is an annual plant about 16 in. (40 cm) high, with lanceolate, pointed ligules and cordate to ovate spikelets of five to 12 flowers. Of the 20 better-known species, *Briza maxima* has the largest spikes; the somewhat later-blooming *Briza minima*, lesser quaking grass, has smaller, typically heart-shaped spikes.

Blooming Season: May to June.

Family: Gramineae or Poaceae (grass family).

Origin: Mediterranean region, Canary Islands.

Location: Sunny to partially shady.

Potting Soil: All-purpose mix or loamy, humus-rich garden soil with some sand added.

Planting: Set purchased or home-grown (see Propagation) young plants 8 in. (20 cm) apart in container.

Watering, Feeding: Water moderately, but do not allow to dry out completely. Do not feed.

Further Care: None.

Overwintering: Not applicable.

Pests, Diseases: Rare.

Propagation: From seed sown in April, either in several small pots (advantageous for subsequent plant combinations) or directly in flower boxes.

Decorating Tip: Quaking grass is cut for use in dry arrangements before the seed falls out. It also looks attractive if the flowers are allowed to dry on the plant.

Squirrel-tail grass is an attractive grass whose silvery awn (beard) against the light looks as enchanting as the silky mane of a beautiful horse. This plant, which reaches a height of 16 to 27½ in. (40–70 cm), grows in a box as an annual, in the ground at times as a biennial or triennial. It forms small stands with slender haulms that are leaved up to the top. The spikes, which are 2 to 5 in. (5–12 cm) long, droop elegantly and are especially remarkable for their long awns (bristly fibers), whose silvery sheen often changes to a faint violet toward the tip.

Blooming Season: June to August.

Family: Gramineae or Poaceae (grass family).

Origin: North and South America, Mexico, Siberia.

Location: Sunny to partially shady.

Potting Soil: All-purpose mix or loamy, humus-rich garden soil with some sand added.

Planting: Set purchased or home-grown (see Propagation) young plants 16 in. (40 cm) apart in container.

Watering, Feeding: Water moderately, but do not allow to dry out completely. Do not feed.

Further Care: None.

Overwintering: Not applicable.

Pests, Diseases: Rare.

Propagation: From seed sown in April, either in several small pots (advantageous for subsequent plant combinations) or directly in flower boxes.

Decorating Tip: Quite pretty with low summer flowers with rounded flower forms, for example, marigolds, zinnias, dwarf marigolds.

The awns turn pink in fall.

Lagurus ovatus
Rabbit's-tail Grass

Rabbit's-tail grass invites constant stroking.

☼ 🔔 **1**

The English common name is truly apt. This grass has soft, woolly inflorescences and flat leaves covered with soft hair. This annual to biennial plant forms clusters 8 to 16 in. (20–40 cm) high. It is the only species in the genus.

Blooming Season: June to August; if sown in spring, usually from July on.

Family: Gramineae or Poaceae (grass family).

Origin: Mediterranean region, Canary Islands.

Location: Sunny.

Potting Soil: Loamy, sandy, poor garden soil. In nutrient-rich ground, soft stalks form, and they bend easily.

Planting: Set purchased or home-grown (see Propagation) young plants 8 in. (20 cm) apart in container.

Watering, Feeding: Water moderately, but <u>do not allow to dry out completely. Do not feed</u>.

Further Care: None.

Overwintering: Not applicable.

Pests, Diseases: Rare.

Propagation: From seed sown in April, either in several small pots (advantageous for subsequent plant combinations) or directly in flower boxes.

Decorating Tip: Goes with gazanias or in close-to-nature boxes with camomile, field poppies, or other plants that like poor soil.

Pennisetum alopecuroides
Chinese Pennisetum, Rose Fountain Grass

Fountain grass underplanted with wintergreen.

☼ 🔔 **1**

The botanical name (from Latin *penna* = feather and *seta* = bristles) refers to the feathery, violet-brown-hued spikes which are 6 to 10 in. (15–25 cm) long. *Pennisetum alopecuroides* forms lignifying rhizomes and grows in the garden as a perennial. In nurseries that carry herbaceous plants, it is usually available under the name *Pennisetum compressum*. In a tub, it can winter over outdoors.

Blooming Season: August to October.

Family: Gramineae or Poaceae (grass family).

Origin: Asia to eastern Australia.

Location: Sunny.

Potting Soil: All-purpose mix (can be enriched with slow-release fertilizer) or loamy, humus-rich garden soil.

Planting: Set purchased young plants 16 in. (40 cm) apart in container.

Watering, Feeding: Water abundantly. On hot days, <u>do not allow to dry out</u>. Feed every 2 weeks in summer.

Further Care: None.

Overwintering: In large containers outdoors, cover with brush. Water moderately on frost-free days.

Pests, Diseases: Rare.

Propagation: In large containers, by division in spring.

Decorating Tip: Do not cut off the spikes! They go quite well with fall colors and are simply enchanting in winter when covered with hoarfrost.

Rose fountain grass is extremely thirsty on hot days.

TUB PLANTS

The assortment of plants for large containers has never been greater than it is today. Fascinating exotics from the tropics and subtropics have taken their place alongside the children of the sun from the Mediterranean area with which the boom in tub plants began. In the meantime, familiar and well-loved herbaceous plants from the garden and shallow-rooted or slow-growing woody plants in large containers also have moved onto balconies and patios.

Agapanthus praecox, the African lily, will bloom more magnificently each year if it is overwintered in a cool location.

The English use the term half-hardy plants in referring to exotic species that can endure temperatures a few degrees below the freezing point in their maritime climate. The French, following the historical model of the famous orangery at Versailles, call them *plantes de l'orangerie* ("orangery plants"). In this country, we use the term tub plants, because the first specimens came to us as imports from southern regions, and, owing to their lack of hardiness, had to be cultivated in movable containers. Because these were species that in their native habitats grew as trees, shrubs, or tall herbaceous plants, only a fairly large container—a tub—was suitable. The first tubs probably were wine barrels or other wooden containers.

The Varied Assortment of Tub Plants

The range of tub plants is wider than ever today. On the following 67 pages, you will find—along with all the traditional tub plants from *Abutilon* to *Yucca*, along with palms and giant grasses—exotic newcomers and new hybrids that have proved reliable when grown in large containers. In addition, the most important woody and herbaceous plants from the garden that are of current interest in the context of mobile gardening are included. They all present themselves in different growth forms or configurations, sometimes as a tree, shrub, or climber, sometimes as a standard or hanging plant.

Appropriate Care

Tub plants come from varying regions and naturally have needs that differ greatly from one another. The following plant portraits will better acquaint you with each plant and its individual requirements. Basically, it is important to know what conditions a tub plant is used to in its native habitat. Specific vegetative rhythms and needs for light, water, and nutrients are results of these conditions. Sensitivity to cold, too, is related to the origin of the plant and has a part to play in overwintering. Before buying tub plants, which usually are not exactly inexpensive, consider whether your ward is hardy or whether you will have to provide it with frost-free winter quarters. If overwintering and year-round care meet the specific requirements of our guests, they will not miss their homeland, but will prosper magnificently and spoil us each year with a fresh abundance of flowers.

Popular and Easy to Tend

Angel's trumpet, along with oleander, marguerite chrysanthemums, and citrus, is a favorite tub plant. Here, the red-flowering *Datura sanguinea*.

Abutilon
Flowering Maple, Parlor Maple

Red-flowering *Abutilon* hybrid 'Feuerglocke'.

Flowering maple can grow to 6½ ft (2 m) in a tub.

The botanical name of this plant is derived from the Arab *abu tilun* = Indian mallow. Flowering maple is a free-flowering, rigidly erect shrub with maplelike foliage that is not shed in winter. It can reach a height of about 6½ to 10 ft (2–3 m) in a tub. The plant belongs to a genus that includes 150 species, of which only a few are cultivated as indoor or tub plants. Best-known are probably the cultivars of *Abutilon pictum*, especially 'Thompsonii', which is available predominantly with green and gold variegated leaves. The golden spots are induced by a viral infection, which, however, does not harm the plant and also does not spread to other plants. The red-, orange-, and yellow-flowering hybrids available commercially are descended from crossings of *Abutilon darwinii* with *Abutilon pictum*. Especially popular are standards of *Abutilon megapotamicum*, which often are grafted onto *Abutilon pictum*. Let the main stem grow to a certain height, cut it off, split it, stick a wedge-shaped, tapered scion into the split, and enclose the graft in a plastic bag until it takes.

Blooming Season: Principal flowering period is spring and summer. In a bright location, flowering maple will bloom throughout the year.

Family: Malvaceae (mallow family).

Origin: Central and South America.

Location: Bright, but shelter from blazing sun, rain, and wind. The branches are fragile!

Potting Soil: All-purpose soil, which can be enriched with slow-release fertilizer.

Watering, Feeding: During the vegetative period (March to October), water abundantly, feed weekly until August.

Further Care: Regularly deadhead spent flowers and yellow leaves. If it branches poorly, pinch out shoot tips more frequently.

Overwintering: Bright and cool at 50°F (10°C). Water little. When moving indoors in fall or outdoors in spring, cut back by one half. If necessary, repot from mid-March on and put in a brighter, warmer place.

Pests, Diseases: Whiteflies, aphids, and spider mites. In prolonged rainfall, botrytis will affect the flowers. *Abutilon* reacts to drafty air, extreme fluctuations in temperature, and change of location by shedding its leaves and flowers, but it soon will put forth again.

Propagation: By cuttings in spring. Pinch out young plants frequently.

Decorating Tip: *Abutilon* hybrids easily can be trained into standards (see page 51). They grow so vigorously that they can tolerate training and cutting quite well. If necessary, the cutting back of the finished crown can even extend to the old wood.

Acer palmatum
Japanese Maple

The Japanese maple has enchanting fall colors.

The Japanese maple is a costly, decorative woody plant that grows very slowly. It has fresh-green leaves of 5 to 7 lobes, which—depending on the cultivar—are more or less deeply laciniate and turn reddish-gold in fall. Along with other slow-growing cultivars of *Acer palmatum*, the graceful 'Dissectum' cultivars are particularly suitable for container culture. In tubs, Japanese maples reach a height of about 5 to 6½ ft (1.5–2 m) and a width of up to 6½ ft (2 m). For example:
• 'Ornatum' (syn. 'Dissectum Atropurpureum'), with wine-red, very finely and heavily laciniate leaves.
• 'Dissectum Garnet', with red-brown foliage.
• 'Dissectum Nigrum', with dark red-brown foliage.
Family: Aceraceae (maple family).
Origin: Japan, Korea, China.
Location: Partially shady.
Potting Soil: All-purpose soil with slow-release fertilizer added, slightly acid garden soil, or a mixture of 1 part each.
Watering, Feeding: Keep evenly damp, <u>never allow to dry out, but never let any standing water build up</u>. Feed every 4 weeks until August.
Further Care: Shaping is possible but not necessary.
Overwintering: Outdoors without winter protection. Deciduous. On frost-free days, water dried-out potting soil moderately. Replace top layer of soil in spring.
Pests, Diseases: Damage due to dryness and foliage burn from too much sun.
Propagation: From seed sown in spring.
Decorating Tip: Classic outdoor bonsai.

Aeonium arboreum
Aeonium

With insufficient light, this red cultivar can turn green.

Aeonium, with its juice-filled leaves, can endure periods of low rainfall in its native habitat. The leaves, arranged in the shape of a rosette, grow at the ends of smooth, erect stems up to almost 3 ft (90 cm) high, with little branching. Particularly attractive is the 'Atropurpureum'. It has wine-red leaves, which may turn green in winter from lack of light. The interesting pyramidal inflorescence appears—if at all—only on plants in a location with optimum brightness.
Blooming Season: January to February.
Family: Crassulaceae (orpine family).
Origin: Morocco.
Location: Bright to full sun and sheltered from rain.
Potting Soil: All-purpose soil with loam and sand in a 2:2:1 ratio, or cactus soil.
Watering, Feeding: Water scantily during the growth period. From May to September, add cactus food to the water every 2 weeks.
Further Care: None
Overwintering: Move indoors promptly before frost sets in, and by all means with a dry ball; otherwise, danger of rot. Overwinter in bright place at 50° to 61°F (10°–16°C), water very little. If necessary, repot in spring.
Pests, Diseases: Only with too much water, standing water, or too warm a location in winter. Defoliation from below is typical of the species *Aeonium arborescens*, which forms a trunk.
Propagation: From leaf rosettes or single leaves. Before planting in loamy, sandy potting soil (mixture of ½ loam, ½ sand), let the cut surfaces dry for one or two days.
Decorating Tip: Highly effective in an arrangement with large stones, because the plant grows on rocks in its native habitat.

Agapanthus praecox
African Lily

African lilies will flower only after cool overwintering.

The blue to violet-blue or, more rarely, white umbels on stalks about 39 in. (1 m) long make the African lily one of the most striking tub plants. One umbel may contain as many as 200 individual flowers! The evergreen basal leaves are strap-shaped and grow in a thick bush. Primarily hybrids of *Agapanthus praecox* and its subspecies *minimus orientalis*, and *praecox* are cultivated. The name is derived from the Greek: *agape* = love and *anthos* = flower.

Blooming Season: July to August or September.
Family: Liliaceae (lily family).
Origin: South Africa.
Location: Full sun.
Potting Soil: Blend of loamy garden soil and all-purpose soil.
Watering, Feeding: During the growth period, water abundantly and feed weekly until August. Avoid standing water.
Further Care: None.
Overwintering: Put in a bright, very cool (at most 46°F [8°C]) place. The plant sets its flowers in winter, and for this purpose it needs low temperatures. Slowness to flower in summer is almost always a consequence of excessively warm overwintering. Water little. The foliage must not dry out, however. Repot rarely (not every spring when you move the plant outdoors), because only well-rooted, old plants flower freely.
Pests, Diseases: Rare. Only standing water is dangerous for the fleshy roots.
Propagation: By division in spring. Done at the expense of floriferousness, however.
My Tip: The extremely strong roots of the African lily may burst the container. Do not use exceedingly expensive containers; it is better to choose attractive cachepots.

Agave americana
Agave, Century Plant

Agaves will survive your vacation unaided.

It takes 30 or 40 years for the inflorescence, over 26 ft (8 m) high, to appear. Then the plant dies, but not without having provided ample numbers of offspring. In addition to the solid green species, there are cultivars that have yellow or creamy white stripes or margins. The succulent leaves can grow over 39 in (1 m) long, even in a tub.

Family: Agavaceae (agave family).
Origin: Mexico, naturalized in the tropics, subtropics, and Mediterranean area.
Location: Sunny. Also tolerates partial shade.
Potting Soil: Blend of two parts loamy garden soil, one part all-purpose soil, and one part sand.
Watering, Feeding: Water moderately. During the growth period, apply cactus food no more than once or twice. Overly frequent fertilizing results in immoderate growth.
Further Care: None.
Overwintering: Bright place at 41°F (5°C). Water rarely. If necessary, repot in spring.
Pests, Diseases: Scale and woolly aphids.
Propagation: By offsets, which form in great numbers. Also from seed.
Decorating Tip: Solitary plant.
Warning: The long leaves have sharp-toothed margins and end in hard spines as fine as needles, on which you can seriously injure yourself. For safety, when moving the plant indoors or outdoors, stick corks on the leaf tips (see drawing, page 29). If you have limited space available or if children play nearby, it is better to do without this agave species.

Albizia julibrissin
Silk Tree, Pink Siris Tree (also, mistakenly, Mimosa)

Aloysia triphylla
Lemon Verbena

The flowers are as soft as a kitten's paw.

Lemon verbena is delightfully scented.

Older specimens of this tree will easily withstand a temperature of 14°F (-10°C). The feathery leaves fold up in the evening in a sleeping position; they are shed in winter. The fragrant flowers, arranged in panicles, resemble cosmetic brushes because of their long, protruding, pale-pink stamens. Silk tree reaches a height of about 6½ to 10 ft (2–3 m) in a tub. The cultivar 'Rosea' stays considerably smaller; it is particularly hardy and has crimson filaments.

Blooming Season: July to September.
Family: Fabaceae or Leguminosae (pea or bean family).
Origin: Subtropical Asia from Iran to Japan, Abyssinia, central China.
Location: Sunny and hot. A hot summer and a dry fall promote the maturing of the wood, a prerequisite for the next year's flowering.
Potting Soil: Blend of all-purpose soil with some garden soil.

Watering, Feeding: Keep evenly damp in summer. Feed weekly until late July.
Further Care: Remove side shoots so that an attractive crown will develop.
Overwintering: Does not have to be brought indoors until the temperature drops below 23°F (–5°C). Can be overwintered in a bright or dark place at about 36° to 46°F (2–8°C). Remove old leaves regularly. Water rarely. If necessary, repot from March on.
Pests, Diseases: Scale appear occasionally.
Propagation: From seed.
Decorating Tip: Anyone who has a frost-free conservatory can also keep *Albizia lophantha*. It flowers from March to May. The creamy yellow inflorescences may reach a length of 3 in. (8 cm). The plant will keep its leaves if it stands in a bright location in winter. Both species make good bonsais.

Many people know this shrub by its former name, *Lippia citriodora*, which refers to the wonderful lemon scent of its leaves and flowers. The inconspicuous flowers, pale lilac in color, appear in axillary spikes or terminal (apical) panicles. The fresh-green leaves have glandular dots on their undersides and, when rubbed between two fingers, exude their marvelously refreshing scent. The dried leaves, under the name *Herba verbena odoratae*, are known, particularly in France, as vervain tea. They also are used in the perfume and cosmetic industries. Lemon verbena grows about 39 in. (1 m) high in a tub. Because it becomes somewhat spindly or leggy with increasing age, you will need to arrange for young plants in good time.

Blooming Season: July to September.
Family: Verbenaceae (verbena family).
Origin: South America.
Location: Bright and sunny.

Potting Soil: All-purpose soil.
Watering, Feeding: During the growth period (until August), water abundantly and feed every 2 weeks.
Further Care: None.
Overwintering: Overwinter in a bright or dark place at 37° to 50°F (3°–10°C). Deciduous; therefore, remove old leaves regularly. Water rarely. In March, cut back by one half, shake out the old ball, and pot in new potting soil.
Pests, Diseases: Rare.
Propagation: By cuttings, which take root within 3 to 4 weeks. Pinch out several times so that the plant will be bushy.

In the nineteenth century, *Aloysia*—named after the Princess of Parma—was present in every orangery. Today it is a much-sought-after rarity.

TUB PLANTS

Anisodontea capensis
Cape Mallow

Cape mallow is a tiny flowering miracle.

☀ 🖌 ⌂

This slightly sticky bush about 39 in. (1 m) high is part of the flora of South Africa, as the obsolete botanical names *Malva capensis* and *Malvastrum capensis* (Cape mallow) indicate. *Anisodontea capensis* blooms lavishly. Its single flowers are small and dark pink. They will appear all summer long and in large numbers if the plant is tended properly. The leaves resemble those of *Abutilon*, but at a length of slightly over 1 in. (3 cm), they are somewhat smaller.
Blooming Season: June to September.
Family: Malvaceae (mallow family).
Origin: South Africa.
Location: Sunny.
Potting Soil: All-purpose soil, which can be enriched with slow-release fertilizer.
Watering, Feeding: During the growth phase, keep slightly damp and feed every 2 weeks until August. Temporary dryness (vacation) is tolerated.
Further Care: Cut off stems with withered flowers; this will promote further flowering.
Overwintering: Bright and at 46° to 54°F (8°–12°C). Water only enough to ensure that the plant does not dry out. Cut back in spring and pot in new potting soil.
Pests, Diseases: Whiteflies.
Propagation: From seed or tip cuttings at a ground temperature of 68°F (20°C).
Decorating Tip: *Anisodontea* can be trained to become a bushy pot plant, a pyramid, or a standard.

Arbutus unedo
Killarney Strawberry Tree

Killarney strawberry tree flowers appear in winter.

○ 🖌 ➰ ⌂

The Killarney strawberry tree is a winter-flowering evergreen shrub that remains an attractive tub plant in summer because of its obovate leaves (which are shiny green on the upper surface and matte green underneath).
Blooming Season: November to March; the fruits are also ripe at this time.
Family: Ericaceae (heath family).
Origin: Mediterranean area.
Location: Bright to partially shady and sheltered from wind.
Potting Soil: All-purpose soil, which can be enriched with slow-release fertilizer.
Watering, Feeding: During the growth period, water abundantly. Do not let soil dry out, but avoid standing water! Feed weekly until August.
Further Care: None.
Overwintering: The Killarney strawberry tree will tolerate temperatures as low as 23°F (−5°C) for a short time, so it can be moved indoors late. Put in a bright place at 36° to 46°F (2°–8°C). Do not let ball dry out completely. If necessary, repot in spring. Put in a very bright location in February, because new growth starts early.
Pests, Diseases: Spider mites.
Propagation: By tip cuttings, which even as young plants will flower and fruit.
Warning: It is still unclear whether the Killarney strawberry tree—like many other plants of the heath family—contains poisonous substances.

The fruits resemble strawberries.

Aristolochia macrophylla
Birthwort, Dutchman's Pipe

Car exhaust fumes do not trouble this climber.

You can read the wishes of this high-climbing, counterclockwise-winding plant on its leaves. They grow on greenish stems about 16 to 33 ft (5–10 m) long and are vivid green, up to 12 in. (30 cm) long, and palpably soft. This means: *Aristolochia* does not tolerate blazing sun and, with such huge evaporation surfaces, it needs large amounts of water.

The name Dutchman's pipe is derived from the inconspicuous but extremely interesting single flowers, which are traps for insects. Capsules 4 in. (10 cm) long develop from the flowers.

Blooming Season: June to July.
Family: Aristolochiaceae (birthwort family).
Origin: North America.
Location: Shady to partially shady and sheltered from wind.
Potting Soil: All-purpose mix or loamy, humus-rich garden soil.
Watering, Feeding: Water abundantly during growth period. Feed young plants 2 to 3 times, older ones twice.
Further Care: Provide a climbing aid (taut wires, trellis).
Overwintering: Outdoors without winter protection. Deciduous. In case of dryness, water moderately on frost-free days.
Pests, Diseases: Rare.
Propagation: Matter for horticulturists.
Decorating Tip: The large leaves of *Aristolochia* overlap like roof tiles and provide an impenetrable privacy screen. The plant also will grow in an urban environment without any difficulty.

Aucuba japonica
Aucuba, Spotted Laurel, Gold-dust Plant

Aucuba can be recognized by its gold-dappled foliage.

Undemanding, robust, and extremely decorative—these properties make aucuba a tub plant that can be recommended enthusiastically. The thick, leathery evergreen leaves usually taper gradually, in the form of an ellipse, to a narrow point. In the species, the leaves are green; in many cultivars, they are flecked or dotted with gold. It is to these forms that the last two common names apply. The purplish flowers appear in spring and are inconspicuous. It is primarily the bright-red berries that have great decorative value. The most valuable cultivars are considered to be the bisexual, spotted 'Crotonifolia' and the likewise bisexual, green-leaved 'Rozannie'. Because most aucubas are dioecious, you normally need one male plant and one female plant for fruit to set.

Blooming Season: March to April.
Family: Cornaceae (dogwood family).
Origin: Himalayas to Japan.
Location: Partially shady to shady. Shelter from prolonged rainfall.
Potting Soil: All-purpose mix or loamy garden soil.
Watering, Feeding: During the growth period, water abundantly and feed every 4 weeks until August. Do not let the ball dry out.
Further Care: None.
Overwintering: In a tub, it can tolerate temperature as low as 23°F (–5°C) for a short time; it can be moved indoors late and back outdoors as early as April. Put in a very cool (about 32°F [0°C]) and bright place. The plant retains its foliage. Water sparingly. If necessary, repot in spring.
Pests, Diseases: Watch out for scale! *Ascochyta* caused by prolonged damp, black leaf spots due to overly dark and warm overwintering.
Propagation: By semihardwood cuttings in spring and summer.
My Tip: Aucuba is resistant to car exhaust fumes.
Warning: The berries are slightly poisonous.

Berberis
Barberry

The evergreen cushion barberry, *Berberis candidula*.

The genus includes approximately 190 species of deciduous and evergreen spiny shrubs ranging from dwarfs to large specimens. The following are suitable for tub culture:

• *Berberis buxifolia* 'Nana': shallow-rooted, densely bushy, 16 to 24 in. (40–60 cm) high, evergreen prickly leaves, orange-yellow flowers.
• *Berberis candidula*: shallow-rooted, semispherical, wide and bushy, 20 to 32 in. (50–80 cm) high, evergreen leaves with white undersides, golden-yellow flowers.
• *Berberis thunbergii* 'Atropurpurea Nana', Japanese barberry: shallow-rooted, erect, outstretched, 12 to 24 in. (30–60 cm) high, purplish-brown leaves, bright red in fall, yellowish flowers, coral-red berries.
Blooming Season: Spring.
Family: Berberidaceae (barberry family).
Origin: South America (*Berberis buxifolia*),

China (*Berberis candidula*), Japan (*Berberis thunbergii*).
Location: Sunny to partially shady.
Potting Soil: All types of soils are possible.
Watering, Feeding: Water moderately during the growth period and feed every 2 weeks until August.
Further Care: Cutting back and shaping possible from spring to fall.
Overwintering: Outdoors without protection. In case of dryness, water on frost-free days.
Pests, Diseases: Caterpillars, aphids; some species also mildew.
Propagation: From seed or cuttings.
Decorating Tip: The Japanese barberry is an extremely beautiful background plant for gold and blue flowers. *Berberus buxifolia* can be cut in any shape. Suitable as bonsai.
Warning: The needle-sharp thorns can cause injuries. The berries contain slightly poisonous alkaloids.

Bougainvillea
Bougainvillea

What look like flowers are only bracts.

Bougainvillea's home is the highlands of South America, where French Admiral Louis Antoine de Bougainville (1729–1811) encountered the plant. It was he who introduced it in Europe. Bougainvilleas belong to the Nyctaginaceae, known in German as the "miracle flower family," and one does indeed experience a miracle: What most people take to be brightly colored flowers are not flowers at all, but bracts, which steal the show from the plain, cream-colored blooms.

Of the numerous species and cultivars of this climbing shrub, the ones best for growing as tub plants are the violet-pink *Bougainvillea glabra* and its cultivars 'Sanderiana' and 'Alexandra'. In a tub, they can reach a height of almost 10 ft (3 m). A prerequisite for a splendid array of blooms is a hot, sunny summer. In addition to these two well-known cultivars in the typical bougainvillea lilac hue, this tropical climber

Colorful species and cultivars in the photo:
1 Bougainvillea 'California Gold'.
2 *Bougainvillea glabra*.
3 *Bougainvillea spectabilis*.
4 Bougainvillea 'Jamaica White'.

also surprises us with other colors. In the hybrids, we find cultivars with white, yellow, orange, blood-red, and brick-red shades. At times the colors are also mixed. In India and California, hundreds of breeding forms exist! All were produced by crossing various species and are designated as *Bougainvillea* x *buttiana*.

It is interesting that the red bracts appear as spontaneous changes in the genetic composition of pure-white cultivars. Anyone who grows these incontrovertibly interesting hybrids needs to know that they are less robust than the cultivars of *Bougainvillea glabra*. Horticulturists recommend them mainly for conservatories.

Blooming Season: April to June. But later in areas with unfavorable light and temperature conditions in spring.

Family: Nyctaginaceae (four-o'clock family).

Origin: Brazil.

Location: Full sun, warm, sheltered from wind.

Potting Soil: All-purpose soil.

Watering, Feeding: Water abundantly in the growth period, but avoid standing water! Feed weekly until August. High nutrient requirement.

Further Care: Provide sturdy climbing aid (trellis, frame). Keep overly luxuriant growth in check with gardening shears.

Overwintering: Bright and cool (46°–50°F [8°–10°C]). Move indoors with dry root ball. Cut back overly long shoots. As soon as the foliage falls, stop watering and by all means avoid a cold base; otherwise, the roots may rot. Remove fallen leaves regularly. Pot in new potting soil every 2 to 4 years. To obtain flowers as early as possible, force the plant in March at a sunny window.

Pests, Diseases: Aphids.

Propagation: By semihardwood tip cuttings in spring or summer (difficult).

Greetings from Tuscany
Bougainvilleas can develop as magnificently at your house as in their native Brazilian habitat— given a great deal of sun and an abundance of nutrients.

Buxus sempervirens 'Suffruticosa'
Box, Boxwood, Edging Box

Classic—edging box in a spherical shape.

For topiary artists—a box in the shape of a bird.

The taller variety of box also can be shaped into a spiral.

This small shrub, which reaches a maximum height of about 39 in. (1 m), is thick and bushy; it has evergreen obovate or ovate leaves of shiny dark green. The leaves have a highly pungent smell, especially in warm weather. The tiny, pale-yellow flowers, which grow in tufts, exude a bitter, aromatic scent. The robust *Buxus semper-virens var. arborescens*, which grows considerably higher, can also be kept in a tub. Box, along with yew, is the classic plant for topiary work, which was practiced among the Romans and probably even earlier. In the Middle Ages, the art of topiary was revived, and it was all the rage in the sixteenth century. In the nineteenth century, it won favor once again, and today it is experiencing yet another comeback.

Among the French, the cutting of ornamental edgings for beds has a long tradition, while the English are known for shaping box in all possible configurations. Well-known shapes are spirals, globes, cones, pyramids, mushrooms, standards, and boxtree sculptures such as chickens, swans, and hares. Because box is long-lived, the shaped plants easily can be set in valuable old containers. They should by all means be frostproof, however, because they must spend the winter in the open.

Blooming Season: March or April.
Family: Buxaceae (box family).
Origin: Southwestern Europe, North Africa, western Asia.
Location: Sunny to shady.
Potting Soil: All-purpose mix or neutral to lime-rich garden soil.
Watering, Feeding: Keep evenly damp during the growing period. Box will tolerate short-term dryness, however. Feed monthly from May to August.
Further Care: Cutting back is especially beneficial in late June, also in March. Slight trimming of plants that are already shaped is possible during the entire growth period.
Overwintering: Outdoors without winter protection, but protected from sun. In case of dryness, water with lukewarm water on frost-free days.
Pests, Diseases: Box flea and box gall gnat—usually, however, only when plant is extremely dry. Scale.

Propagation: By division (easy), plant segments deeper than before. Also by cuttings in March or August (tedious).
Decorating Tip: Box is a classic plant for topiary work (see page 50). Suitable as bonsai.
Warning: All parts of these plants, particularly the leaves, contain highly poisonous alkaloids.

Calliandra tweedii
Calliandra, Flame Bush

Callistemon citrinus
Crimson Bottlebrush

Calliandra is occasionally a capricious bloomer.

Crimson bottlebrush will not tolerate hard water.

Of the 120 species which are native primarily to tropical and subtropical America, the evergreen *Calliandra tweedii* has become best known as a tub plant. As the botanical name indicates, this is an extremely handsome shrub (Greek: *kallos* = beauty and *andros* = of the male). The thin, pliant branches droop elegantly. The red flowers, up to 2¾ in. (7 cm) across, consist of a silken-haired floral envelope (perianth) with long, purple-red stamens; they appear from spring to fall.

Blooming Season: April to October.

Family: Fabaceae or Leguminosae (pea or bean family).

Origin: Brazil.

Location: Very bright and warm.

Potting Soil: All-purpose soil.

Watering, Feeding: During the growth period, water moderately, and feed every 2 weeks until the end of July. Avoid standing water!

Further Care: None.

Overwintering: Calliandra does not tolerate cold. Move indoors in late September. The winter quarters should be bright, with temperatures from 54° to 59°F (12°–15°C). Water from time to time. Cut back in March and repot if necessary. Caution: Plants that have been cut back will flower later.

Pests, Diseases: Aphids, if kept in too warm a place with overly dry air in winter.

Propagation: From seed or tip cuttings at a ground temperature of 68° to 77°F (20°–25°C).

My Tip: Attractive alternative for conservatories kept at a moderate temperature: *Calliandra haematocephala*, which bears salmon-colored flowers from October to March and has striking metallic-green foliage. Suitable as bonsai.

Enchanting flowers with long, usually red filaments that are arranged densely around the branches in the shape of bottle brushes make this shrub unmistakable. The stiff evergreen leaves are lanceolate and up to 2¾ in. (7 cm) long. Bottlebrush grows relatively fast, even in a tub, and can reach a height of almost 10 ft (3 m). The types commercially available vary greatly in terms of their growth.

Blooming Season: June to July. Many plants flower twice.

Family: Myrtaceae (myrtle family).

Origin: Southeastern Australia.

Location: Very bright to full sun.

Potting Soil: All-purpose soil, to which 1 part of peat moss can be added.

Watering, Feeding: Water abundantly during the growing period. Avoid standing water and hard water. From May to August, feed weekly with fertilizer for acid-loving plants.

Further Care: Cut back overly long stems after flowering.

Overwintering: Move young plants indoors before the first frost; older ones can tolerate temperatures slightly below the freezing point. Keep in a bright, cool (41°–50°F [5°–10°C]) place. Water approximately every 4 weeks, and do not let the ball dry out. Repot in spring.

Pests, Diseases: Scale, if too warm and dark in winter; in summer, spread by infested plants. Disturbances of growth caused by excessively hard and cold water.

Propagation: From seed or tip cuttings at a ground temperature of 68° to 77°F (20°–25°C). Trim young plants frequently, so that they will branch attractively.

Decorating Tip: *Callistemon* fits well in a collection of Myrtaceae (eucalyptus, common myrtle, ironwood tree, Malabar plum, tea tree) or in a Mediterranean milieu.

The flowers resemble bottle brushes.

Camellia
Camellia

Tea is made from the flowers of the camellia.

○ 🔔 ⌂

Camellia sinensis, which rarely flowers in cold climates, and *Camellia japonica*, which flowers from late fall to early spring, are really conservatory or indoor plants. A summer location outdoors, however, can have a highly positive effect on them: First, the light and atmospheric humidity levels frequently are better outdoors; second, the summer warmth encourages the setting of flower buds, while the coolness of the late summer nights promotes the ripening of the buds.

Blooming Season: Winter and spring.
Family: Theaceae (tea family).
Origin: China, Assam, Burma (*Camellia sinensis*); Japan, Korea, Taiwan, Ryukyu Islands (*Camellia japonica*).
Location: Bright to partially shady.
Potting Soil: All-purpose or soilless mix.
Watering, Feeding: Keep moderately damp year around. Do not use hard water. In *Camellia*

japonica, as soon as the flower buds appear in summer, water less. Use azalea food (or other fertilizer for acid-loving plants) weekly until the end of July.
Further Care: None.
Overwintering: Move indoors before nighttime frost begins. If possible, keep at a temperature not in excess of 54°F (12°C) until the flowers open and no warmer than 59°F (15°C) during flowering. Mist leaves and buds frequently. Water little. If necessary, repot after flowering (by July at the latest).
Pests, Diseases: Lice, sooty mold, leaf drop after overly warm overwintering or with incorrect summer care. Bud drop in *Camellia japonica* may be caused by overly warm temperatures, by turning the plant after the buds are set, and by dry soil, standing water, or excessively hard water.
Propagation: By budless tip cuttings in August.
Decorating Tip: Suitable as bonsai.

Campsis radicans
Trumpet Creeper, Trumpet Vine

Trumpet creeper flowers uninterruptedly.

☀ 🔔 ↬ 🌱

A vigorous, free-flowering climbing vine whose orange flowers grow in bunches of 4 to 12 in terminal clusters and are visible over a long distance. Trumpet creeper, by using its anchoring roots, climbs up walls on its own. When planted in the garden, it reaches a height of about 16½ to 33 ft (5–10 m); in a tub, it grows about 6½ to 10 ft (2–3 m) high. The foliage is light green and feathery (pinnate). These are commercially available:
• *Campsis radicans*.
• The yellow-flowering cultivar 'Flava'.
• *Campsis* x *tagliabuana*, a cross of *Campsis radicans* and *Campsis grandiflora*. It grows shrubbier and somewhat tangled, but flowers quite freely even as a young plant.
• The cultivar 'Madame Galen', with fiery-red flowers, is the best-known form.
Blooming Season: July to September.
Family: Bignoniaceae (bignonia or trumpet creeper family).

Origin: United States.
Location: Sunny and sheltered from wind.
Potting Soil: All-purpose mix or loamy, humus-rich garden soil.
Watering, Feeding: Water abundantly during the growth period, and feed weekly until August.
Further Care: Remove faded "trumpets" regularly.
Overwintering: Outdoors with winter protection (see pages 28–29). Water moderately on frost-free days. In February, cut all the shoots that have flowered back to a few eyes and, if necessary, cut out frozen wood. Trumpet creeper will flower on the new shoots, that is, on this year's wood.
Pests, Diseases: Aphids on the flower buds. Spider mites.
Propagation: By semihardwood cuttings in August.
Decorating Tip: Underplant orange trumpet creeper, which likes a shady base, with dark-blue lobelias.

Canna x indica Hybrids
Canna, Canna Lily, Indian Shot, Flowering Shot

Canna needs large quantities of water.

These exotic- and lush-looking plants have been adapted by breeders since about 1840. Depending on the cultivar, they grow between 1 and 6½ ft (30–200 cm) high. The flower colors range from white through yellow, orange, salmon, and pink to deep red. There are also two-colored varieties. The lush-green leaves—colored reddish brown in some cultivars—contrast beautifully with the intense colors of the flowers. For tub culture, the low cultivars are best, for example, 'Lucifer' and 'Prinz Carneval' (both mottled red and yellow), 'Puck' (yellow), and 'Alberich' (red).

Blooming Season: June to October.
Family: Cannaceae (canna family).
Origin: Original forms, West Indies, Central America, South America, and southern United States.
Location: Full sun.
Potting Soil: All-purpose soil (can be enriched with slow-release fertilizer) or sandy, humus-rich garden soil.
Watering, Feeding: From April or May on, water abundantly; feed weekly until August. Never allow soil to dry out.
Further Care: Deadhead spent flowers, so that blooming will be uninterrupted.
Overwintering: Once the first spells of frost have destroyed the foliage, cut bare stems back to 2 in. (5 cm). Take up knobby rhizomes, let them dry, and store them in dry peat or sand. Overwinter them in a dark place at 46° to 50°F (8–10°C). Take them out in March, pot them, and force them in a warm location. Once flushing starts, put in a brighter place, and water.
Pests, Diseases: Rhizome rot if overwintering is overly damp.
Propagation: By rhizome division in spring. Segments should have 3 to 5 eyes.

Capparis spinosa
Caperbush

Its buds are pickled to produce capers.

Rocks and stone walls are the abode of this shrub. Its slender, hanging branches, which may reach a length of about 39 in. (1 m), bear ovate, plump leaves covered with a blue-green frostlike bloom. The bracts have been converted into thorns. The conspicuous white flowers, equipped with a great many long stamens, appear in the leaf axils. Finished plants are available commercially, but you can raise them yourself.

Blooming Season: Summer.
Family: Capparaceae (caper family).
Origin: Portugal, Mediterranean region, Asia Minor, western Himalayas, peninsular India.
Location: Full sun.
Potting Soil: All-purpose mix with sand added or lime-rich garden soil lightened with perlite or sand.
Watering, Feeding: Water little during the growth period. The roots of the caperbush are extremely vulnerable to damp. Occasional drying out is not harmful. Apply low doses of fertilizer every 4 weeks until August.
Further Care: None.
Overwintering: Move indoors before first frost and possibly cut back. Put in a bright place no warmer than 59°F (15°C). Keep almost dry. If necessary, repot in spring.
Pests, Diseases: Aphids and spider mites if overwintering is too warm. Root rot caused by overwatering.
Propagation: By tip cuttings in a warm propagating bed. Alternatively, from seed, which can be collected through pollination by hand.
My Tip: If you want to pick capers and put them up in jars, remove the unopened flower buds when they are about the size of peas. Let them wilt slightly, so that the spicy methyl mustard oil can develop, then put them, raw, in vinegar or olive oil.

TUB PLANTS

Carissa grandiflora
Natal Plum

The fruits turn scarlet when fully mature.

○   ⬥   ⌂   ☠

Slow-growing evergreen shrub with leathery leaves up to 2¾ in. (7 cm) long and prominent forked thorns over 1 in. (3 cm) long. The white flowers are star-shaped, about 2 in. (5 cm) wide, and fragrant. From them develop the scarlet-red berries.

Blooming Season: Summer. If winter location is bright, also spring.

Family: Apocynaceae (dogbane family).

Origin: Eastern South Africa.

Location: Bright to full sun. Also tolerates shade, but flowers poorly there.

Potting Soil: All-purpose soil, which can be enriched with slow-release fertilizer.

Watering, Feeding: Keep moderately damp during growth period; feed every 2 weeks.

Further Care: None.

Overwintering: Move indoors before frost begins. Does not tolerate cold. Put in a bright, cool (41–50°F [5°–10°C]) place. Water little. If necessary, repot in spring.

Pests, Diseases: If incorrectly overwintered, susceptible to a great variety of pests and fungal diseases.

Propagation: By tip cuttings in a warm propagating bed.

Decorating Tip: Natal plum makes an excellent indoor bonsai.

Warning: With the exception of the berries, all parts of Natal plum are lethally toxic. You can injure yourself on the thorns.

Caryopteris x clandonensis
Blue Mist Shrub, Bluebeards

The blue flowers appear on the new wood.

☀   ◇   ⇗   ⌂   ⌂

The blue of the flowers of this shallow-rooted small shrub is so unusual that the color is mentioned in the names of many cultivars. 'Heavenly Blue' is the best-known hybrid. It grows rigidly upright to a height of about 39 in. (1 m) and has many branches. The lanceolate leaves are deep-green at the tips, while the base of the leaf is gray-green. The leaves have an aromatic scent. The flowers, lush sky blue in color, grow in branched panicles at the ends of new shoots. In the cultivar 'New Blue', which flowers extremely freely, the flowers are dark blue.

Blooming Season: August to September.

Family: Verbenaceae (verbena family).

Origin: Mongolia, northern China. Cultivated form originated in 1930 in England.

Location: Sunny and sheltered from wind.

Potting Soil: All-purpose mix or 2 parts loamy, humus-rich garden soil with 1 part sand.

Watering, Feeding: Water moderately during the growth period. <u>By all means avoid standing water.</u> Feed monthly until August.

Further Care: None.

Overwintering: Move indoors promptly. Overwinter in bright or dark place at 41° to 50°F (5°–10°C). Water moderately. <u>Do not let root ball dry out completely.</u> Cut back in spring to stimulate the formation of many new shoots. Repot if necessary.

Pests, Diseases: Standing water results in disturbances of growth.

Propagation: By semihardwood cuttings in summer.

Decorating Tip: Exceptionally beautiful with red roses in a tub. In addition, in a location near a rock garden (edge of patio) in combination with herbaceous plants, for example, lady's mantle (*Alchemilla mollis*), pink *Aster dumosus*, or Ozark sundrops (*Oenothera missouriensis*).

Cassia, Popcorn Bush

Cassia corymbosa.

☀ 🪣 🏠 🏠 ☠

Cassia didymobotrya, the popcorn bush.

Of the approximately 400 species, the following are most common as tub plants:

• *Cassia corymbosa* grows about 10 ft (3 m) high in a tub. It has usually unpaired pinnate leaves and golden-yellow flowers, which grow at the ends of the shoots in long-stemmed corymbs that rise above the leaves.

• *Cassia corymbosa var. plurijuga* (syn. *Cassia floribunda)*. In this variety, the flowers are larger and the pinnae wider. It easily can be trained as a standard.

• *Cassia didymobotrya* is known as the popcorn bush. The pinnate leaves, up to 14 in. (35 cm) long, have a strong scent of peanut butter. The inflorescence differs from that of other cassias. The numerous flowers, which are up to 1⅗ in. (4 cm) wide, grow in erect candle shapes (thryses), located singly or in groups at the ends of the shoots. These candles continue to grow, while the lower blooms fall off, and they can reach a length of 12 to 20 in. (30–50 cm).

Blooming Season: *Cassia corymbosa*, July to October; with advantageous light and temperature levels (in a conservatory), on into winter. *Cassia didymobotrya*, in a conservatory the year round, with a break in February or March.

Family: Fabaceae or Leguminosae (pea or bean family).

Origin: South America (*Cassia corymbosa*), tropical Africa (*Cassia didymobotrya*).

Location: Full sun.

Potting Soil: All-purpose mix.

Watering, Feeding: Water abundantly during the growth period. Do not let the ball dry out. From September on, water *Cassia didymobotrya* less, so that the shoots can mature. Until end of August, feed weekly.

Further Care: None.

Overwintering: Vulnerability to cold varies greatly among the individual species: *Cassia corymbosa* tolerates light frost and need not be moved indoors so promptly. Before moving plant inside, let ball dry out, and trim the present year's growth by two thirds. Overwinter it in a dark place, with temperature just above the freezing point. Keep the root ball moist. If necessary, repot in spring.

Move *Cassia didymobotrya* indoors before first frost. Overwinter in a bright place at not less than 50°F (10°C). Water moderately. Cut back plant by one half in early March and repot if necessary.

Pests, Diseases: Whiteflies if overwintered at too warm a temperature, aphids on new shoots; botrytis caused by poor ventilation.

Propagation: From seed or semihardwood tip cuttings.

Decorating Tip: Solitary plant. Suitable as bonsai.

My Tip: If you would like to acquire a *Cassia* collection, you can sow over 20 additional species yourself, including the tubular cassia sold as "manna," which has canary-yellow, fragrant flowers, and *Cassia angustifolia*, known as a medicinal plant.

Warning: Many *Cassia* species contain toxic substances.

Don't worry if the new growth of *Cassia* is variegated. Once the temperatures are warmer, the color will change.

Cestrum
Cestrum, Bastard Jasmine, Night Jessamine, Night-blooming Jasmine

Cestrum elegans is extremely decorative, but poisonous.

Of the 200 species in this genus, the yellow-flowering species *Cestrum aurantiacum*, *Cestrum nocturnum*, and *Cestrum parqui*, the red-flowering hybrid *Cestrum* x *newellii*, and the pink cultivar 'Smithii' have attained importance as tub plants. These vigorous shrubs grow over 6½ ft (2 m) high, even in a tub.

Blooming Season:
• *Cestrum aurantiacum*, summer to late fall;
• *Cestrum elegans* and cultivars, April to September;
• *Cestrum parqui* and *Cestrum nocturnum* (night-blooming jasmine), June to July.
Family: Solanaceae (nightshade family).
Origin: Tropical and subtropical America.
Location: Sunny.
Potting Soil: All-purpose mix (can be enriched with slow-release fertilizer). A blend of ½ garden soil and ½ compost.
Watering, Feeding: Water abundantly during the growth period and feed weekly until August.
Further Care: Prop up the crowns of plants in bloom, particularly standards.
Overwintering: Bright location at 41° to 50°F (5°–10°C), without cutting back. Water little. Foliage will be retained; flowering begins in early spring. Alternative: Overwinter in a cool, dark place. Before moving the plant indoors, cut it back almost level with the ground and keep it almost dry. If necessary, repot in spring.
Pests, Diseases: Aphids and whiteflies. Botrytis after periods of inclement weather, blight (*Phytophora*).
Propagation: By herbaceous cuttings in spring.
Decorating Tip: All *Cestrum* species can be trained on a trellis or as standards.
Warning: All parts of *Cestrum* are poisonous.

Cestrum grows rapidly.

Chamaerops humilis
Dwarf Fan Palm

A dwarf fan palm with side shoots.

The only European species of palm, the dwarf fan palm produces several stems and grows bushy. It has bluish-green, deeply laciniate fanleaves up to 24 in. (60 cm) wide. It differs from the Chusan palm (see page 212) in that its leafstalks are heavily covered with thorns. After reaching a height of 8 in. (20 cm), the dwarf fan palm begins to form the first side shoots; then a new tuft of leaves is produced every year. The dwarf fan palm grows slowly, but with good care it can flower fairly early. In a tub it reaches a maximum height of about 10 ft (3 m).
Family: Arecaceae (palm family).
Origin: Mediterranean regions, southern Portugal.
Location: Bright to sunny.
Potting Soil: All-purpose mix.
Watering, Feeding: During the growth period, water abundantly when temperatures are high. Do not allow ball to dry out. Do not pour water into the tuft of leaves, but onto the soil; otherwise, the core may rot! Feed weekly until August.
Further Care: None.
Overwintering: Tolerates temperatures slightly below freezing for a short time and can be moved indoors late. Put in a bright place or, if need be, a completely dark one, at a temperature of 39° to 50°F (4°–10°C). May also be overwintered at somewhat higher temperatures, but the location has to be bright. Water from time to time, less often if location is dark. If necessary, repot in spring.
Pests, Diseases: Aphids and scale if overwintered at overly warm temperature; also spider mites in summer.
Propagation: From seed (year round) and by division.
Decorating Tip: Solitary plant that needs a great deal of room.
Warning: You can injure yourself on the thorny leafstalks. Do without this plant if you have small children or limited space.

Chamelaucium uncinatum
Geraldton Wax Flower

Choisya ternata
Mexican Orange

Chamelaucium creates a pretty effect in summer.

The flowers of *Choisya* have an intense fragrance.

Chamelaucium uncinatum, sold under the name of wax flower, is completely distinct from the climbing wax plant, *Hoya carnosa*. It is an evergreen shrub about 3¼ to 6½ ft (1–2 m) high, with nodding branches. The flat, linear leaves are stiff and needle-fine. The white, pale-pink, or deep-pink flowers grow in groups in cymes, or false umbels.

Blooming Season: March to May.

Family: Myrtaceae (myrtle family).

Origin: Western Australia.

Location: Full sun.

Potting Soil: All-purpose mix.

Watering, Feeding: Water moderately during the growth period, and apply low doses of fertilizer every 2 to 4 weeks until August. The plant is sensitive to overfeeding.

Further Care: After the blooming period, cut back shoots that are growing too lanky and awkward-looking. This will encourage bushy growth.

Overwintering: Bright, cool place at 50°F (10°C). Water little. As soon as the flower buds appear, put plant in a somewhat warmer, much brighter location. Repot if necessary.

Pests, Diseases: Flower drop due to overwatering and too dark a location.

Propagation: From seed or herbaceous cuttings at a ground temperature of 77° to 86°F (25°–30°C). Trim young plants once or twice so that they will branch well.

Decorating Tip: The delicate, silvery foliage is seen to best advantage in front of tub plants with broad leaves of an intense green.

Anyone who loves scented plants but has trouble bringing miniature lemon or orange trees through the winter should try Mexican orange. This evergreen shrub with a round, bushy shape grows up to 39 in. (1 m) high in a tub and not only is far more robust, but also possesses equally beautiful, shiny-green, leathery leaves and white flowers with a delicious fragrance.

Blooming Season: May to June, earlier in a cool conservatory.

Family: Rutaceae (rue family).

Origin: Mexico.

Location: Bright to sunny. Prospers in partial shade, but will lose its compact growth and flower less freely there.

Potting Soil: All-purpose mix.

Watering, Feeding: During the growth period, water abundantly in a sunny location, moderately elsewhere. Feed from April to August. Avoid standing water and do not water with hard water!

Further Care: After the blooming season, remove shoots that spoil the effect. Cutting back is also possible at this time.

Overwintering: Mexican orange is somewhat hardy and can tolerate temperatures as low as 14°F (-10°C), therefore it can be moved indoors late. Put it in a bright place at 41° to 50°F (5°–10°C) or in a dark place at just above freezing temperature. Water sparingly. If necessary, repot in February. Provide good drainage!

Propagation: By tip cuttings in a warm propagating bed.

Decorating Tip: With increasing age, Mexican orange will grow almost round in shape in a suitably bright location; it then will go extremely well with miniature trees shaped to resemble globes.

Chrysanthemum frutescens
Marguerite Chrysanthemum, Shrub Marguerite

Variation of marguerite chrysanthemums in yellow.

A standard tub plant—available commercially are large- and small-headed white, yellow, and pink cultivars, as well as others, such as 'Whity', that grow small and compact, only 20 in. (50 cm) high. Depending on the cultivar, the foliage of this subshrub is coarsely or finely divided, sometimes green, sometimes silvery in color. What many people do not know: The plant can be overwintered successfully and will be more beautiful each year.

Blooming Season: Year round, if spent blossoms are removed routinely and the marguerite stands in a bright location in winter also.

Family: Asteraceae or Compositae (aster or composite family).

Origin: Canary Islands.

Marguerite Chrysanthemum Standard
A mature specimen of *Chrysanthemum frutescens* with beautifully lignified trunk and flower-strewn crown.

Location: Bright to sunny.

Potting Soil: All-purpose soil.

Watering, Feeding: Water abundantly during the growth period. Feed weekly until August.

Further Care: Regularly remove spent flowers and dried-up leaves in the inner portion of the crown.

Overwintering: Move indoors before the first spells of frost. Keep in a very bright place at 41° to 50°F (5°–10°C). Water moderately. If no bright overwintering site is available, move the plant indoors with a dry ball and cut it back by one half. Water scantily; repot in spring. Reduce shoots by one third; if they already have been cut back, cut more to make them neat.

Pests, Diseases: Aphids in May, leaf miners, root fungi if ball is overly wet in winter.

Propagation: Quite easy, by tip cuttings taken in spring from overwintered mother plants or later in August or September. Pinch out young plants several times.

Cistus ladanifer
Rockrose, (Sweet) Cistus

Rockroses—typical of the Mediterranean macchia.

The evergreen shrubs of the Mediterranean macchia grow 3¼ to 6½ ft (1–2 m) high and flower freely in colors of white, pink, or red. The single flowers wilt after eight hours, of course, but new ones are opening all the time. The following cultivars are commonly available:
- *Cistus* x *aguilari*, with deep-green lanceolate leaves and large white flowers.
- *Cistus ladanifer*, which has white flowers with red-brown basal spots.
- *Cistus* x *purpureus*, a pink-flowering, gray-leaved shrub.

The leaves of rockroses exude an aromatic, sticky resinous juice, which at one time had various medicinal uses and played a large role in the perfume industry (gum labdanum or ladanum).

Blooming Season: April to July.

Family: Cistaceae (rockrose family).

Origin: Southwestern Europe, Mediterranean regions, North Africa.

Location: Full sun; otherwise, *Cistus* will not bloom.

Potting Soil: All-purpose mix or loamy, humus-rich garden soil.

Watering, Feeding: During the growth period, water abundantly and feed weekly.

Further Care: Can be cut back by one half after the plant loses its blossoms.

Overwintering: Bright, airy place at 41° to 50°F (5°–10°C). Water moderately and ventilate often—danger of botrytis! Repot young plants every year in early March.

Pests, Diseases: Aphids on freshly emerged leaves; botrytis.

Propagation: In spring, from seed or cuttings. Pinch out young plants several times, so that they will branch nicely.

Decorating Tip: Rockroses fit well in a Mediterranean plant community, in combination with agaves, Livingstone daisies, palms, myrtle, rosemary, and lemon verbena.

Characteristic of *Cistus ladanifer*—the red-brown dots on the petals.

Citrus
Various Citrus Species

The robust Meyer lemon, *Citrus limon* 'Meyerii'.

The four-seasons lemon flowers the year round.

☀ 🜂 ⌂

All *Citrus* species are evergreen woody plants with alternate, somewhat leathery leaves whose leaf-stalks often are broadened like wings. Almost all are equipped with short or fairly long thorns. The flowers, with their white or violet-pink tinge, arise singly or in groups at the leaf axils. This genus, with its great diversity of forms, is difficult to subdivide, because there are many crosses and mutations.
Here are best-known species and varieties:
• *Citrus aurantiifolia* (sour lime, Tahiti lime). It needs more warmth than other citrus species and is often grown in the tropics. It grows shrubby and produces pointed oval leaves, which are small in comparison with those of the lemon tree, and diminutive pear-shaped yellow fruits.
• *Citrus aurantiifolia* x *Fortunella margarita* (limequat): This is a cross that produces tiny yellow fruits and has spindly growth.

• *Citrus aurantium ssp. aurantium* (sour orange, bitter orange, Seville orange, bigarade): Its rind is used to make candied orange peel, popular in baking. The subspecies *ssp. bergamina* (bergamot) is also available, but its intensely scented fruits cannot be eaten.
• *Citrus limon* (lemon tree): This species is characterized by enormously vigorous growth, even in a tub.
• *Citrus limetta* (lime tree): It has thorn-covered branches and yields slightly rounded fruit.
• *Citrus* x *nobilis* (clementine): This hybrid flowers and fruits quite freely.
• *Citrus* x *paradisi* (grapefruit, pomelo): This plant is a cross between *Citrus maxima* and *Citrus sinensis* (the orange tree); in contrast to all its relatives, its fruits are arranged on the stems like grapes. It needs long, hot summers and abundant light, even in winter.
• *Citrus reticulata* (mandarin orange): This is a

slow-growing, bushy, robust species. Its varieties, *var. unshiu* (satsuma) and *var. tangerina* (tangerine), are also frequently available commercially.
• *Citrus sinensis* (orange): Its growth varies, depending on the cultivar. Best-known are Valencia and navel oranges, as well as the blood oranges 'Sanguina' and 'Moro'. Available everywhere are the "small editions" of the *Citrus* clan, which usually are sold as "miniature orange trees": *Citrus microcarpa* (syn. *Citrus mitis*) and the same cultivar crossed with *Citrofortunella mitis*, the calamondin orange.
Blooming Season: In a bright location, almost year around.
Family: Rutaceae (rue family).
Origin: Tropics and subtropics of Asia, West Indies. Today, these plants are grown in groves everywhere the climate permits.
Location: Full sun.

Potting Soil: Blend of ½ all-purpose soil and ½ loamy, humus-rich garden soil.
Watering, Feeding: Water moderately during the growth period. A little is always better than too much. Avoid standing water, but never let the ball dry out completely. Soften the water. Feed weekly until August, ideally with guano fertilizer.
Further Care: Cutting back and pruning are possible at any time, but at the expense of branches capable of flowering.
Overwintering: All *Citrus* species are frost-tender; move them indoors early and with a dry ball. Keep in a bright, airy place at 39° to 46°F (4°–8°C). In a dark location, the leaves will fall, but they will regenerate in spring. Water sparingly. If necessary (older plants, at most every 5 years), repot. Provide good drainage! Do not move outdoors until the end of May.
Pests, Diseases: Aphids in May, scale in summer location, spider mites after

overly dark, warm over-
wintering. Chlorosis (yellow leaves) due to hard,
cold water or overwatering.

Propagation: By cut-
tings (difficult, but often
successful). From seeds of
fruits you have bought.
Unfortunately, you never
know when or whether the
young plant will flower
and fruit. For this reason,
horticulturists graft all
Citrus species.

Decorating Tip: Recommended for anyone who
has limited space is the
small-leaved variety *Citrus aurantium var. myrti-
folia* (myrtle-leaved bitter
orange or 'Chimotto'). It
grows slowly and does not
get too wide, can be kept
in shape easily, flowers
freely, and has a superla-
tive fragrance. Suitable as
a bonsai.

Warning: Many *Citrus*
species have long, sharp
thorns on which you can
injure yourself. When you
move the plants indoors,
tie the stems together
tightly (see drawing 1,
Safety Measures, page
29). In addition, the essential oils contained in the
leaves can induce skin
irritations in sensitive
people, on damp skin, and
under the effect of light.

The Magic of the South
Miniature orange trees
of varying heights. *For-
tunella margarita* (kum-
quat) with green and
variegated foliage and
a calamondin standard
underplanted with
parrot's beak.

Clematis
Clematis

Cobaea scandens
Cup-and-saucer Vine, Cathedral Bells

Also flourishes in a tub—*Clematis montana* 'Rubens'.

Violet flowers of the cup-and-saucer vine.

Clematis flowers, between 2 and 8 in. (5–20 cm) across, are available in white, shades of pink and red, and various nuances of blue and blue-violet. Suitable for tub culture are primarily slow-growing wild forms and their cultivars, such as *Clematis alpina* and *Clematis macropetala*, as well as a great many hybrids. Plants grown in nursery containers can be set from late March to mid-September.

Blooming Season: Depending on the species and the cultivar, from late April to July and later.

Family: Ranunculaceae (crowfoot family).

Origin: China, Himalayas.

Location: Bright to partially shady. Appropriate for the species, likes cool shade for its roots, but sunlight for its blooms.

Potting Soil: All-purpose mix or loamy, humus-rich garden soil. Plant deep; the ball should be at least 4 in. (10 cm) underground.

Clematis flowers look like ornaments.

Watering, Feeding: Water abundantly during the growth period, but avoid standing water. Feed every 4 weeks from April to July.

Further Care: The plants need climbing aids. Cut back or thin out spring-flowering clematis after the blooming period, if at all. Summer-blooming clematis should be cut back to between 16 and 24 in. (40–60 cm) in early spring.

Overwintering: Outdoors with winter protection (see pages 28–29). Water dried-out potting soil moderately on frost-free days. Young plants are frost-tender!

Pests, Diseases: Clematis wilt, a fungal disease.

Propagation: By semihardwood cuttings in June or July in a warm propagating bed.

My Tip: If you want the tendrils to cover something quickly, put 2 or 3 plants in a tub with a diameter of 20 in. (50 cm).

Warning: All the species and cultivars of *Clematis* contain skin irritants.

Cup-and-saucer vine is an inexhaustible bloomer, and even in a tub it may climb to a height of over 13 ft (4 m). Its bell-shaped flowers first are whitish-green; later they turn violet. There are also white, red, and blue cultivars. The fruits, 2 to 2¾ in. (5–7 cm) long and oval in shape, have 3 crenations. In cold climates, however, the fruits rarely are produced. The pinnate leaves are reddish in color when flushing occurs—probably a protection against light—and at their ends are transformed into tendrils. This perennial is usually treated as an annual because it is difficult to bring through the winter.

Blooming Season: From July until the first frost.

Family: Polemonaciae, (phlox family).

Origin: Mexico.

Location: Sunny.

Potting Soil: All-purpose mix or humus-rich garden soil with sand added.

Watering, Feeding: Water abundantly and feed every 2 weeks.

Further Care: Needs wires or poles as a climbing aid. Pinching out the shoot tips will promote branching and ensure a long blooming period.

Overwintering: Usually not applicable. Possible in a frost-free conservatory, where the bloom, which starts late and outdoors is brought to an end by frost, can be enjoyed over its entire duration.

Pests, Diseases: Aphids.

Propagation: From seed sown in February or March at a ground temperature of about 64°F (18°C) (easy).

Decorating Tip: Very fast growing and enchantingly beautiful for a privacy screen. Also good as a wall cover.

Cordyline australis
New Zealand Cabbage Tree, Giant Dracaena, Grass Palm

The red-leaved cultivar of the Dracena.

This plant, which resembles yucca, sometimes is incorrectly sold under the name *Dracaena indivisa*. A look at the roots, however, will reveal the difference: Dracaenas have slender, orange-yellow roots; those of the New Zealand cabbage tree are thickened and club-shaped (claviform). In its native habitat, *Cordyline* develops into a "tree" up to 39 ft (12 m) high. Its sword-shaped leaves, which reach a length of about 39 in. (1 m), form a tuft and droop elegantly. In a tub, this plant does not bloom.

Family: Agavaceae (agave family).
Origin: New Zealand.
Location: Sunny.
Potting Soil: All-purpose mix or loamy, humus-rich garden soil.
Watering, Feeding: Water moderately during the growth period. Do not allow ball to dry out. Feed every 4 weeks until August.
Further Care: None.
Overwintering: Allow ball to dry before moving indoors. Keep in a bright location at about 36° to 50°F (2°–10°C). Remove frozen tufts after they have dried up. The plant then usually will shoot up again from its base in spring and produce more than one stem. The result will be extremely attractive. If necessary, repot in March.
Pests, Diseases: Rare.
Propagation: From seed or tip and stem cuttings.
Decorating Tip: The rare cultivar 'Atropurpurea', with bronze-red foliage, makes a beautiful solitary plant. It grows somewhat more slowly and is more vulnerable to cold than the green cultivar.

Cotoneaster
Cotoneaster

Cotoneaster standard with autumn crocuses.

Because cotoneaster is so undemanding, this shrub is frequently planted in public green areas. Moreover, this woody plant with its showy adornment of berries makes a welcome spot of color in fall. The following species and cultivars have proved particularly reliable for container culture:

• *Cotoneaster adpressus* (deciduous, 10 in. [25 cm] high; flowers pink, lightly scented; berries red).
• *Cotoneaster dammeri* and cultivars (evergreen 20 to 39 in. [0.5–1 m] high; flowers small, white; berries red).
• *Cotoneaster microphyllus* 'Cochleatus' (evergreen, 12 to 16 in. [30–40 cm] high; flowers small, white; berries red).
• *Cotoneaster* x *watereri* hybrid 'Pendulus' (partly evergreen, up to 6½ ft [2 m] high in a tub; flowers in large, white corymbs; berries light red).

Blooming Season: June.
Family: Rosaceae (rose family).
Origin: China.
Location: Bright to partially shady.
Potting Soil: All-purpose mix or any garden soil.
Watering, Feeding: Water moderately during the growth period, but do not allow to dry out. Feed every 4 weeks.
Further Care: If necessary, light shaping is possible during the growth period. In late June (possibly also in March), you can cut back harder.
Overwintering: Outdoors with winter protection (see pages 28–29). Water moderately on frost-free days.
Pests, Diseases: *Cotoneaster* x *watereri* hybrid 'Pendulus' is susceptible to fire blight.
Propagation: By semihardwood cuttings in summer.
Decorating Tip: Suitable as bonsai.
Warning: The berries are slightly poisonous.

Cupressus macrocarpa
Monterey Cypress

○ ⚘ ⌂

This evergreen needle-leaved woody plant usually is sold as an indoor cypress, but it does not grow particularly well at room temperature. A cool overwintering and a summer spent outdoors are preferable. The gold-needled cultivar 'Goldcrest' is especially attractive.

Family: Cupressaceae (cypress family).

Origin: Southern California.

Location: Bright to partially shady. The needles will parch in blazing sun.

Potting Soil: All-purpose mix.

Watering, Feeding: Keep evenly damp throughout the summer. Avoid dry ball and standing water! Until September, feed every 4 weeks. If you want faster growth, feed weekly.

Further Care: Shaping possible during the entire growth period.

Overwintering: In a bright place at 41° to 50°F (5°–10°C).

Pests, Diseases: Spider mites if overwintering is too warm.

Propagation: By tip cuttings in summer (difficult).

Decorating Tip: Symmetrically arranged pairs of standards are particularly striking, and you easily can shape them yourself.

Standard
Cupressus macrocarpa is often sold as an indoor plant, but it will not prosper without an abundance of fresh air.

Cycas revoluta
Cycas, Sago Palm

Cycas revoluta grows extremely slowly.

The slow-growing cycas is one of the most beautiful, but also most expensive tub plants. Only young plants—including some bonsais—are usually available commercially. Cycas existed millions of years ago, before flowering plants. Like the needle-leaved woody plants, it belongs to the gymnosperms, in which the ovules lie exposed on the megasporophylls. These, covered with thick hair, are the golden-yellow parts that emerge in the center of the thick tufts of leathery fronds after the plant reaches a certain age. The stamens of the dioecious plant are arranged in closed cones. The thick, short trunk is developed only at an advanced age.

Family: Cycadaceae (cycad family).
Origin: Japan.
Location: Partially shady to shady and sheltered from rain.
Potting Soil: All-purpose soil mixed with sand.
Watering, Feeding: Water moderately during the growth period. Always let the soil dry out between times. By all means avoid standing water. Apply low doses of fertilizer weekly until August. Experts swear by guano or dried cattle manure dissolved in water.
Further Care: None.
Overwintering: In a bright place at about 54° to 59°F (12°–15°C), no colder if at all possible. Give it fresh air on frost-free days! Water scantily. Repot young plants every 2 years in spring, old ones, rarely.
Pests, Diseases: Woolly aphids if winter location is too warm and poorly ventilated, scale in summer.
Propagation: From seed sown at high ground temperatures (difficult).
Decorating Tip: Ornamental plant for shady locations.
Warning: Do not eat any part of this plant—there is a danger of poisoning! Watch out for children and pets!

Cytisus
Broom

Broom exudes its scent into the spring air.

This small shrub is a spring bloomer. With its fresh colors, it creates a cheerful atmosphere. It flowers on year-old shoots or on shoots from the preceding year or years. Here are some appropriate species and cultivars:
• *Cytisus* x *beanii*, a scented broom (creeping, about 16 to 32 in. [40–80 cm] high, sun-yellow).
• *Cytisus* x *kewensis* (loosely overhanging, 12 to 20 in. [30–50 cm] high, creamy yellow).
• *Cytisus decumbens* (bushy, 8 in. [20 cm] high, brilliant yellow).
• *Cytisus purpureus* (shrubby and erect, about 16 to 24 in. [40–60 cm] high, pinkish-purple).
Blooming Season: May or June; *Cytisus purpureus*, June or July.
Family: Fabaceae or Leguminosae (pea or bean family).
Origin: Central and southern Europe. Those available commercially usually are cultivated.
Location: Sunny.
Potting Soil: All-purpose mix or loamy, sandy garden soil. Broom does not take root well if the ball is not already permeated with roots when the plant is set.
Watering, Feeding: Water and feed sparingly during the growth period. Avoid standing water.
Further Care: Plants that bloom in spring can be cut back to one third directly after the flowering period. Summer-flowering species should be thinned out only slightly. They too can be cut after flowering.
Overwintering: Outdoors with winter protection (see pages 28–29). Water dried-out potting soil moderately on frost-free days.
Pests, Diseases: Rare.
Propagation: Usually by cuttings taken after the blooming period is over. Sowing and grafting also possible.
Decorating Tip: In a trough at least 39 in. (1 m) long, plant one *Cytisus* x *kewensis* and one *Cytisus purpureus* together.
Warning: All parts of broom are poisonous.

Datura (recently became *Brugmansia*)
Angel's Trumpet

Brugmansia x *candida* 'Plena' with double flowers.

Datura meteloides—the blue thorn apple.

Cyphomandra betacea, a close relative of *Datura*, needs the same care.

Angel's trumpets are among the most attractive tub plants that we have. Their nodding, at times hanging, flowers—shaped like funnels, trumpets, or tubes—can grow as long as 20 in. (50 cm). In the evening, they exude an intoxicating scent. The fruits—egg-shaped or spindle-shaped, depending on the species—do not appear in cold areas. The leaves of the shrublike or treelike plants are, as a rule, large, lush green, and ovate, but they may show extraordinary diversity, even on a single plant. The botanical name *Datura* is—as many people are unaware—not Latin, but is derived from the Old Indic *dhattura*, the popular name for the thorn apple, *Datura metel*. Recent research in the United States has shown that the name no longer is correct for the shrubby species. They now are to be reassigned to the genus *Brugmansia*, where they had been placed in 1805. Although the name *Datura* is still quite popular, the best-liked species and cultivars will be given their correct names in the following list. Next to them you will find other names, if any are known, under which the species in question is available on the market.

- *Brugmansia aurea* (*Datura affinis*, *Datura pittieri*), white to apricot in color, gigantic leaves.
- *Brugmansia suaveolens* (*Datura gardneri*), white; cultivars 'Rosa Glocke', 'Rosa Traum', both pink.
- *Brugmansia arborea* (*Datura speciosa*, *Datura knightii*, *Datura frutescens*), white.
- *Brugmansia sanguinea* (*Datura bicolor*, *Datura lutea*, *Datura chlorantha*, *Datura rosei*), red-yellow, unscented.

- *Brugmansia* x *candida*, white; cultivar 'Grand Marnier', yellow.
- *Brugmansia* x *insignis*, creamy white.
- *Brugmansia versicolor* (*Datura mollis*), white, pink, salmon.
- *Datura meteloides* (blue thorn apple), an annual plant with white flowers edged in pale violet, has the spiny fruits typical of *Datura*.

Blooming Season: July to September. *Brugmansia sanguinea*, fall, winter, or spring.

Family: Solanaceae (nightshade family).

Origin: South America.

Location: Sunny to partially sunny and sheltered from wind.

Potting Soil: All-purpose mix enriched with slow-release fertilizer or nutrient-rich garden soil with peat added.

Watering, Feeding: During the growth period, water abundantly and feed weekly until August. High nutrient requirement!

Further Care: Remove faded trumpets.

Overwintering: In a bright place at about 39° to 54°F (4°–12°C), or in a dark location. If overwintered in a dark place, cut back hard in fall. Put *Brugmansia sanguinea* in a bright location; otherwise, it may not flower in winter. Water little. In spring, remove overly long, thin, and dead stems and repot in roomy containers.

Pests, Diseases: Aphids, leaf bugs, spider mites, whiteflies, weevils.

Propagation: By cuttings taken from spring to fall (easy).

Note: Give the same care to the closely related *Cyphomandra betacea*. It grows as a shrub or a small tree, forms highly decorative, large, heart-shaped leaves, and produces "potato flowers" tinged with white to pink, from which red, egg-

shaped fruits up to 3 in. (8 cm) long develop.

Decorating Tip:
Brugmansia is decidedly a solitary plant. If you would like to show it off and want an even more abundant display of flowers, you also can plant it outdoors in your garden and lift it in the fall for overwintering.

Warning: All parts of *Datura* and *Brugmansia* species are poisonous. Their intoxicating fragrance can cause headaches in susceptible people. The flowers contain roughly twice as much toxin as the leaves. Even more dangerous is *Datura meteloides*, the blue thorn apple. This species is closely related to the infamous *Datura stramonium*, the common thorn apple, known as a poisonous and medicinal plant. It also yields fruits that resemble spiny green chestnuts. With the exception of the fruits, *Cyphomandra* also is poisonous.

Trumpets on Trees
Because all *Brugmansia/ Datura* species are vigorous and fast-growing they need heavy, stable tubs. Shown here is *Brugmansia aurea* (*Datura affinis*). The treelike, gnarled growth is the result of cutting back.

Ensete ventricosum
Abyssinian Banana

Bananas are tub plants that need a great deal of room.

In its native habitat, where it still is found in thin mountain woodlands over 6,560 ft (2,000 m) high, the ornamental banana may grow almost 43 ft (13 m) high. The leaves, up to about 20 ft (6 m) long and 39 in. (1 m) wide, are impressive. In a tub, seedlings attain a height of 39 in. (1 m) during the first year, and with increasing age, heights of 6½ to almost 10 ft (2–3 m) and leaves of corresponding lengths are not uncommon.

Family: Musaceae (banana family).

Origin: South Africa, central Africa, and northeastern Africa.

Location: Sunny to partially shady and sheltered, because strong wind will tatter the beautiful leaves.

Potting Soil: Loamy garden soil with an equal part of all-purpose soil.

Watering, Feeding: During the growth period, water abundantly and feed weekly until September. High nutrient requirement.

Further Care: None.

Overwintering: Move indoors promptly. In a heated conservatory, leave leaf tufts as they are and keep soil slightly damp; otherwise, cut the plant back to the leaves of the central core and overwinter in a bright place at 50°F (10°C). If the location is too cold, there is a danger of soil fungi; if too warm, of premature flushing that will sap the plant's strength. <u>Water sparingly, and do not pour water into the central core</u>; otherwise, the plant will decay. Repot young plants in spring, old ones only if necessary.

Pests, Diseases: Spider mites in summer. Soil fungi due to cold base.

Propagation: Year round from seed, propitious in January or February. Fresh seed is best.

Decorating Tip: Needs more space than any other tub plant!

Note: Give the same care to *Musa basjoo* and *Musa x paradisiaca*. They tolerate freezing temperatures as low as 23°F (–5°C) and can be overwintered at about 36 to 41°F (2–5°C).

Eriobotrya japonica
Loquat

Loquat adorns itself with feltlike leaves.

The loquat is a small evergreen tree that easily can grow over 6½ ft (2 m) high in tub culture. Its most beautiful adornments are the leaves, up to 12 in. (30 cm) long, with a dark-green upper surface and a silvery or reddish, tomentose underside. It is grown in almost all subtropical countries for its fruits (loquats), which taste like apricots or plums. In cold climates, it flowers and fruits only when kept under glass year around.

Blooming Season: September to October; fruit ripens in May.

Family: Rosaceae (rose family).

Origin: Japan, China.

Location: Sunny to partially shady. Sheltered from rain if at all possible. In overly wet summers, danger of *Eriobotrya* scab on the leaves.

Potting Soil: Loamy garden soil with equal parts of sand and all-purpose soil.

Watering, Feeding: During the growth period, water moderately. Always let the top layer of soil become dry before watering again. Feed every 2 weeks until August.

Further Care: None.

Overwintering: Tolerates freezing temperatures as low as 23°F (–5°C); do not move indoors too early! Cutting back (for reasons of space) is tolerated, but usually is superfluous. Put in a bright place at 50°F (10°C) or if necessary, a dark place at 41°F (5°C). Water sparingly. Repot in spring if needed.

Pests, Diseases: *Eriobotrya* scab caused by prolonged wetness of leaves.

Propagation: From seed or tip cuttings in warm propagating bed.

Decorating Tip: The loquat is an attractive solitary plant for conservatories.

Erythrina crista-galli
Coral Tree

Eucalyptus
Eucalyptus, Gum Tree, Cider Gum

The coral tree—an exotic, extremely effective plant.

Eucalyptus citriodora is lemon scented.

Are you looking for a striking tub plant that needs little care? Then coral tree is the right plant for you. This shrub, which in its native habitat grows over 26 ft (8 m) high, in a tub attains a height of almost 6 ft (1.8 m). It usually forms only one short, thick trunk, on which great numbers of new, often thorny stems develop each year. In summer they are topped by long racemes that appear in batches, with brilliant, deep-red single flowers that are conspicuous over a long distance.

Blooming Season: July or August to October.
Family: Fabaceae or Leguminosae (pea or bean family).
Origin: Brazil.
Location: Full sun, hot.
Potting Soil: All-purpose mix or blend of loamy garden soil, peat, and sand in equal parts.
Watering, Feeding: From the beginning of the growth period until August, water abundantly and feed weekly. Thereafter, do not fertilize any more and water less. Avoid standing water!
Further Care: Do not trim during the growth period, because the racemes develop at the ends of the youngest stems.
Overwintering: Move indoors with dry ball. Cut main stem back to about 4 in. (10 cm). Keep dark and dry at 46°F (8°C). Repot in late February. As soon as the new growth appears, put plant in a brighter, warmer spot.
Pests, Diseases: Whiteflies and spider mites in summer.
Propagation: By tip cuttings taken after the flush. Alternatively, from seed (easy), sown year round (early spring is best). Plants reproduced from seed, however, will flower only after 3 to 4 years.
Decorating Tip: The showy, bright-red flowers are seen to best advantage when the coral tree stands alone.

Of the over 500 species of this genus, the following have achieved importance as evergreen tub plants:
• *Eucalyptus ficifolia*, has slightly thicker lanceolate leaves. Its flowers are various shades of red.
• *Eucalyptus globulus*, the blue gum tree. One of the most beautiful species. Grows very rapidly.
• *Eucalyptus gunnii*, cider gum, has gray-green leaves and creamy white flowers, which appear on relatively young plants. Characteristic of the genus are the silvery blue primordial leaves, which are shaped differently from those of older plants.

Blooming Season: Summer, but in cold climates it rarely flowers.
Family: Myrtaceae (myrtle family).
Origin: Australia, Tasmania.
Location: Sunny to partially shady.
Potting Soil: All-purpose mix.
Watering, Feeding: During the growth phase, water abundantly. Use soft water. Avoid standing water, but do not let the ball dry out, because the foliage will not recover from dryness. Feed little or not at all, in order to keep from stimulating growth—which is vigorous anyway—unnecessarily.
Further Care: Do not cut! Exception: *Eucalyptus gunnii*.
Overwintering: In bright, airy place at about 36° to 50°F (2°–10°C). Water little. If necessary, repot in spring.
Pests, Diseases: Rarely, because of the strong essential oils.
Propagation: From seed (easy), year round (propitious in early spring). Alternatively, by cuttings (difficult).
Decorating Tip: The blue-gray foliage is particularly lovely near pale-yellow or pale-pink summer flowers.

Euonymus
Spindle Tree

The spindle tree, *Euonymus fortunei*.

Euonymus fortunei 'Emerald 'n Gold' is hardy.

Of the more than 170 species, the following are best known because they are undemanding.

• *Euonymus fortunei*, a hardy shrub 8 in. to almost 10 ft (20–300 cm) high that climbs by means of anchoring roots or creeps on the ground. The evergreen leaves are ovate or roundish, coarsely leathery, green, yellow-variegated, or white-margined; the flowers are inconspicuous. Cultivars: 'Emerald Gaiety' (8 to 39 in. [20–100 cm]), 'Emerald 'n Gold' (8 in. to 5 ft [20–150 cm]), 'Minimus' (5 ft [150 cm], tolerates shade), 'Vegetus' (2 to 10 ft [60–300 cm], abundant yellow fruit in fall).

• *Euonymus japonica*, of which there are also many varieties with variegated leaves, is rarely hardy in a tub in the cold areas.

Blooming Season: June or July.

Family: Celastraceae (stafftree family).

Origin: China, Japan.

Location: Sunny to partially shady.

Potting Soil: All-purpose soil, (enriched with slow-release fertilizer) or loamy, humus-rich garden soil.

Watering, Feeding: Keep moderately damp. Feed every 2 weeks in summer.

Further Care: Shaping and cutting back are possible at any time. Usually, you will only need to cut awkward stems.

Overwintering: *Euonymus fortunei*, outdoors without protection. In case of dryness, water moderately on frost-free days. *Euonymus japonica*, in a bright place just above the freezing point. Water sparingly.

Pests, Diseases: Rare, in *Euonymus fortunei*; in *Euonymus japonica*, mildew.

Propagation: By cuttings, from August to October.

Decorating Tip: *Euonymus fortunei* and its cultivars—for example, 'Coloratus'—have colored foliage in fall ranging from pale pink through red and purple-red to brown-red. They look wonderful with chrysanthemums.

Ficus carica
Fig

The fig tree has unusual flowers.

Its large, palmate-lobed, lush-green leaves make this relative of the Indian rubber tree one of the most magnificent deciduous trees grown in tubs. The flowers are curiosities in themselves. They are concealed inside the urceolate (jug-shaped) inflorescence axis, which has only one small opening for pollination by gall wasps. In some of the strains grown today, (seedless) fruits develop (see photo, page 38) even without pollination. In a tub, they form roughly pea-sized flowers in the leaf axils in late summer and fall. With some luck, they will make it through the winter and mature the following spring or summer.

Blooming Season: In its native subtropical habitat, 3 times a year; in the cold regions, in spring and fall.

Family: Moraceae (mulberry family).

Origin: Mediterranean area, Near East, northwestern India.

Location: Until the new leaves have attained full growth, bright but not sunny; later, sunny and warm.

Potting Soil: All-purpose mix and loamy garden soil in equal parts.

Watering, Feeding: During the growth period, water abundantly, and feed weekly until August.

Further Care: None.

Overwintering: The fig tree tolerates temperatures a few degrees below freezing point and need not be moved indoors immediately. Put in a bright place at about 36° to 46°F (2–8°C) (or a dark place, if need be). Water little. If necessary, repot in spring. Move outdoors as early as possible.

Pests, Diseases: Scale, aphids, spider mites; diseases of the bark and wood.

Propagation: In spring, by cuttings or runners, at a ground temperature of 77°F (25°C).

My Tip: The fig needs a great deal of space. Suitable as bonsai.

Fuchsia
Fuchsia

Single plants of erect-growing *Fuchsia* hybrids are suitable for tub culture, as are cultivars with pendulous growth, which are particularly popular as standards. In addition, there are pyramids and bushy shrubs that seldom grow higher than about 5 ft (1.5 m), as well as conditionally hardy fuchsias, such as the varieties of *Fuchsia magellanica* or the cultivar 'Vielliebchen'.

Blooming Season: Summer to late fall.

Family: Onagraceae (evening-primrose family).

Origin: Original forms, Caribbean, Mexico, Central and South America, New Zealand.

Location: Bright to partially shady and sheltered from wind.

Potting Soil: All-purpose mix.

Watering, Feeding: During the growth period, water abundantly and feed weekly until August.

Further Care: Prune plants regularly and trim frequently at the start of the vegetative period. Standards need a support (see page 51).

Overwintering: In a bright or dark place at about 43° to 46°F (6–8°C). Water little and give fresh air on frost-free days. In spring, remove feeble shoots and crossing shoots; cut present year's shoots back leaving 1 to 3 eyes. When new growth occurs, repot and put in brighter position.

Pests, Diseases: Aphids, whiteflies, spider mites; botrytis, fuchsia rust.

Propagation: By herbaceous cuttings in spring, by semihardwood cuttings in summer (easy).

Fuchsia Collection with Many Forms
Fuchsias are so diverse that they will tempt you to start a collection.

Gaultheria procumbens
Wintergreen

Hebe x *andersonii* Hybrids
Hebe

The spherical checkerberries appear from September on.

The racemes of *Hebe* are violet, red, or white.

Wintergreen is an evergreen dwarf shrub that grows up to 8 in. (20 cm) high. It produces long, shiny, ovate leaves from ⅖ to 1 in. (1–3 cm) long and pale-pink flowers that grow singly or in racemes, from which thick, globular, red checkerberries 8 to 15 mm in size develop from September on. Wintergreen, which puts forth underground runners, grows so as to form a carpet and is therefore an ideal ground cover in larger plantings. In fall, its foliage turns wine-red. Wintergreen once was an established household remedy for cystitis and kidney ailments. The major active substances are a glycoside, a bitter constituent, various tannins, and methyl salicylate.

Blooming Season: July to August.
Family: Ericaceae (heath family).
Origin: North America.
Location: Partially shady to shady.
Potting Soil: Blend of ½ all-purpose soil, ½ peat moss, and some sand.

Watering, Feeding: Keep slightly damp during the growth period. Do not water with hard water; wintergreen is sensitive to lime. Until August, add rhododendron food or another lime-free fertilizer to the sprinkling water.
Further Care: Shaping possible at any time.
Overwintering: Outdoors without winter protection. Water dried-out potting soil moderately on frost-free days.
Pests, Diseases: Rare.
Propagation: By stolons (easy) or from seed.
Decorating Tip: Ideal ground cover; goes well with *Erica*.

Of the 140-odd species of hebe, only the *Hebe* x *andersonii* hybrids are suitable for container culture. These pretty little shrubs arose from crosses between *Hebe salicifolia*, *Hebe speciosa*, and other species. The racemes vary among white, crimson, and blue-violet, depending on the cultivar. The evergreen leaves have a leathery feel; in the form 'Variegata', they are variegated.

Blooming Season: Varies according to cultivar, usually late summer.
Family: Scrophulariaceae (figwort family).
Origin: Original forms, New Zealand.
Location: Bright and sheltered.
Potting Soil: All-purpose soil, to which slow-release fertilizer and sand can be added.
Watering, Feeding: During the growth period, water regularly, but avoid standing water. Until August, feed every 2 weeks.
Further Care: None.
Overwintering: In a bright place at 46° to 50°F (8°–10°C). Water sparingly, but do not allow to dry out. Repot in spring.
Pests, Diseases: Disturbances of growth caused by standing water.
Propagation: By tip cuttings in summer at a ground temperature between 68° and 72°F (20°–22°C) (easy). Repot young plants several times, and clip often, so that they will branch attractively.
Decorating Tip: A pretty late-summer bloomer that is attractive in combination with *Erica* and dusty miller. Also can be planted in flower boxes.

Hedera helix

English Ivy, Canary Island or Algerian Ivy

In a tub, ivy produces shoots about 5 to 6½ ft (1.5–2 m) long and can spread to a width of 3⅓ to 6½ ft (1–2 m). The evergreen leaves, depending on the species and the cultivar, have 3 to 5 lobes (in old age, also lozenge-shaped) with a leathery sheen, green or variegated. Only older plants flower and fruit. Ivy is resistant to automobile fumes.

Family: Araliaceae (aralia or ginseng family).

Origin: Original forms, southern, eastern, and central Europe, North Africa, Near East, Azores, Canary Islands, Madeira, Ireland.

Location: Partially shady to shady.

Potting Soil: All-purpose mix or sandy, humus-rich garden soil.

Watering, Feeding: During the growth period, keep thoroughly damp, but avoid standing water. From May to August, feed every 8 to 10 weeks.

Further Care: Train young plants to grow up a pole; otherwise, they will creep. Light shaping is tolerated at any time. Cutting back is best done in late July.

Overwintering: Outdoors with winter protection (see pages 28–29). Using lukewarm water, water dried-out potting soil on frost-free days.

Pests, Diseases: Rare.

Propagation: By cuttings taken from spring to fall or from seed.

Warning: The berries are quite poisonous.

Ivy: Variations on a Theme

In addition to variegated and green cultivars with leaves of different shapes, there are delicate standards grafted on ivy aralia.

TUB PLANTS

Hedychium gardnerianum
Ginger Lily

The spikes have a bewitching scent.

A magnificent herbaceous plant that grows over 39 in. (1 m) high and renews itself each year from a tuberous rootstock. Notable characteristic: The wonderfully fragrant spikes, which are about 20 in. (.5 m) long, made up of creamy-yellow to golden-yellow single flowers with protruding, reddish filaments. The almost equally long leaves, up to 6 in. (15 cm) wide, are the perfect finishing touch to the exotic, luxuriant effect.

Blooming Season: August to September. Forced plants, from July on.
Family: Zingiberaceae (ginger family).
Origin: Eastern Himalayas, Nepal, Sikkim.
Location: Sunny, bright, or partially shady.
Potting Soil: Blend of ½ all-purpose soil and ½ loamy garden soil.
Watering, Feeding: During the growth period, water abundantly and feed weekly.
Overwintering: Move plant indoors before first frost, let it finish blooming indoors, cut it back even with the soil, then keep it dark and almost dry, at 39° to 50°F (4°–10°C). In February, set rhizome, preferably in wide containers, with new soil. Force in a bright, warm location.
Pests, Diseases: Rare.
Propagation: By division when transplanting or from seed.
Decorating Tip: The large leaves and the unusual inflorescence are most effective when ginger lily is on its own.

Hibiscus rosa-sinensis
Chinese Hibiscus

Hibiscus comes in many flower colors and shapes.

The blooms of the widely scattered Chinese hibiscus are the embodiment of the exuberant blaze of colors seen in the tropics. No wonder the hibiscus was chosen as the state flower of Hawaii, where there are said to be over 2,000 cultivars! The plants we buy today—with single or double, self-colored or two-colored flowers of normal size or as big as dinner plates, in colors of white, yellow, orange, pink, or red—are hybrids from a great many mates. Growth regulators are used to treat them so that they will fit on a window sill as indoor plants, but over time the effect diminishes, and after about a year the tropical shrubs resume the growth characteristic of their species and reach heights of 3⅓ to 5 ft (1–1.5 m) in a tub.

The hibiscus flowers in the photos above:
1 *Hibiscus rosa-sinensis* 'Vollmond'.
2 White flowers with pink veins.
3 Demidouble variety.
4 Demidouble salmon-colored cultivar.

Blooming Season: March to October.
Family: Malvaceae (mallow family).
Origin: Tropical Asia, probably southern China.
Location: Bright, sunny, sheltered from wind and rain. Do not change location because the buds may fall off.
Potting Soil: All-purpose soil.
Watering, Feeding: During the growth period, water abundantly, but do not let the ball become dry or permit standing water to form. Leaves drop if ball becomes dry. Until August, feed twice a week.

Hydrangea macrophylla
Common or French Hydrangea, Hortensia

Hydrangeas need partial shade and soft water.

Hydrangea also looks attractive in a tub. Its gigantic white, pink, red, or blue ('Adria', 'Nachtigall') paniculate inflorescences consist of stunted, sterile single florets whose actual beauty lies in the colored sepals.

Blooming Season: June and July. Plants that bloom from March to May are forced by horticulturists.

Family: Saxifragaceae (saxifrage family).

Origin: Japan.

Location: Partially shady.

Potting Soil: Blend of ½ all-purpose soil and ½ peat moss.

Watering, Feeding: From March to late August, water abundantly, then somewhat less. Soften the water; hydrangeas have low tolerance for lime. Until August, add rhododendron food or other acid-loving plant fertilizer to the water every 2 weeks.

Further Care: Deadhead spent flowers. After the flowering period, cutting back is possible.

Overwintering: In a bright or dark place at 39° to 46°F (4°–8°C). The hydrangea sheds its foliage. Remove dried leaves so that no seats of disease can develop. Water little, but do not let ball become completely dry. In spring, repot and put in a brighter location.

Pests, Diseases: Aphids, spider mites. Chlorosis due to overly hard water.

Propagation: By herbaceous cuttings in May or June (difficult).

Decorating Tip: Hydrangeas are extremely versatile. They give an English aristocratic effect in weathered gray stone containers, but in an oak tub they have a country air.

Plate-shaped hydrangea.

Iochroma cyaneum
Iochroma, Violet Bush

The lilac color varies from one location to another.

The name (from Greek: *ion* = violet and *chroma* = color) refers to the violet flower color of this genus. *Cyaneum*, or "dark blue" places added emphasis on the reference to the highly individual color that makes this shrub, which grows 3⅓ to 5 ft (1–1.5 m) high, unmistakable. Unfortunately, the brilliance of the color is often disappointing in cold regions. The tube-shaped flowers, however, are still quite decorative. They hang in bunches and in great numbers from the shoot tips. The elliptical leaves, like the branches, are covered with gray hair. The long stems are fragile.

Blooming Season: July to August.

Family: Solanaceae (nightshade family).

Origin: Colombia.

Location: Bright to partially shady and sheltered from wind.

Potting Soil: All-purpose mix or rich garden soil, with peat added.

Watering, Feeding: During the growth period, water abundantly and feed weekly until late August (high nutrient requirement).

Further Care: Tie up shoots constantly.

Overwintering: Can be cut back to height of about 39 in. (1 m) in fall, then overwintered in dark (or bright) place at about 43° to 54°F (6°–12°C). Water little. Repot in spring.

Pests, Diseases: Spider mites, whiteflies, occasionally aphids.

Propagation: By herbaceous cuttings in summer, preferably taken only from plants that flower freely.

Decorating Tip: What about a violet-colored arrangement of *Iochroma*, passionflower, nightshade, and heliotrope? *Iochroma* makes an enchanting color contrast for orange flowers or *Citrus* plants.

Warning: All parts of *Iochroma* are poisonous.

TUB PLANTS

Ipomoea
Morning-Glory

Ipomoea purpurea has multicolored flowers.

☼ 🚿 ↝ 1 ☠

The sisters of bindweed are just as vigorous as the dreaded weed. The morning-glory, grown mostly as an annual, quickly twines upward to a height of about 10 ft (3 m) and flowers lavishly. Its funnel-shaped single flowers are approximately 4 in. (10 cm) wide and open one after another. The leaves are cordate and slender-pointed. Available are the following:
- *Ipomoea tricolor* (syn. *Pharbitis rubrocaerulea*), with flowers in the characteristic sky blue and in various pastel shades.
- *Pharbitis purpurea* (syn. *Ipomoea purpurea*), with forms whose flowers may be white, pink, red, violet, blue, striped, three-colored, or double.
- The red-flowering *Quamoclit vulgaris* (syn. *Quamoclit pennata*) also is known by the synonym *Ipomoea quamoclit*. The brown, papery fruits contain brown seeds.

Blooming Season: July to September.
Family: Convolvulaceae (morning-glory family).

Origin: Tropical America.
Location: Sunny and sheltered from wind.
Potting Soil: All-purpose soil mix or loose garden soil.
Watering, Feeding: During the growth period, water abundantly. Do not allow to dry out. Feed once or twice weekly.
Further Care: Provide climbing aid.
Overwintering: Not applicable.
Pests, Diseases: Sensitive to cold, wet weather and susceptible to spider mites.
Propagation: From seed in March or April at a ground temperature of 64°F (18°C).
Decorating Tip: In a short time, morning-glories will overrun trellises, pyramids, railings, and frames.
Warning: *Ipomoea* species may contain an amide of lysergic acid, a narcotic akin to LSD.

Ipomoea tricolor—in a particularly beautiful blue.

Jasminum nudiflorum
Winter Jasmine

A sunny-yellow spring greeting—winter jasmine.

○ 🚿 🪴

Before anything else is blooming, winter jasmine will create a springlike mood. The loosely structured, wide-spreading, and extremely pendulous shrub is—as many people are unaware—a climbing woody plant that can reach a height of about 10 ft (3 m) when provided with a climbing aid.
In a tub, it usually is grown as a "golden fountain of flowers." The leaves, ⅖ to 1 in. (1–3 cm) long, are lanceolate and deep green; because they are shed just before spring, they are termed partly evergreen. The yellow flowers, which measure about 1 in. (3 cm) across, appear on the previous year's wood. In the cold regions, the black fruits rarely are produced.
Blooming Season: February to April.
Family: Oleaceae (olive family).
Origin: Western China.
Location: Sunny to partially shady, sheltered.
Potting Soil: All-purpose mix or loamy, humus-rich garden soil. Loves lime.

Watering, Feeding: Water moderately; after the bloom, feed monthly until August.
Further Care: Periodically thin out stems that have finished blossoming, if the plant is getting too thick.
Overwintering: Outdoors, with winter protection (see pages 28–29) only in extremely cold locations. On frost-free days, water dried-out potting soil moderately.
Pests, Diseases: Rare.
Propagation: By pieces of stems that strike root upon touching the soil; in June or July, by cuttings.
Decorating Tip: A solitary plant unsuited for underplanting and combination planting by virtue of its tousled growth. Flows attractively over walls and can be used for plant troughs that stand along patio boundaries. Suitable as bonsai.

Juanulloa

Juanulloa aurantiaca

New fascinating beauty—*Juanulloa aurantiaca*.

This evergreen shrub 1⅓ to 6½ ft (1–3 m) high, with its orange-red flowers and oval-lanceolate, leathery, dark matte-green leaves, is still a rarity on the market. Experience in its care is correspondingly scant. Its inclusion in the family of the extremely vigorous nightshades suggests that *Juanulloa* can be grown without difficulty, but we have yet to learn whether it will flower reliably year after year. It will depend primarily on the amount of light we can offer it throughout the year.

Blooming Season: June to October.

Family: Solanaceae (nightshade family).

Origin: Peru, Mexico.

Location: Sunny, warm, sheltered from wind, preferably with humid air. In its native habitat, also grows epiphytically.

Potting Soil: All-purpose soil, which can be enriched with slow-release fertilizer.

Watering, Feeding: During the growth period, do not allow to dry out.

From April to August, feed every 2 weeks.

Further Care: None.

Overwintering: Bright and warm (at least 59°F [15°C]), ideally in conservatory or greenhouse. Keep slightly damp, repot in March.

Pests, Diseases: Thus far, no typical ones are known. Nevertheless, the possibility of scale and aphid infestations should not be ruled out.

Propagation: Probably by cuttings in spring or summer. No experience is yet available.

Warning: *Juanulloa*, like all other members of the nightshade family, is poisonous.

Crape Myrtle

Lagerstroemia indica

Crape myrtles reach tree height even in a tub.

A deciduous large shrub or small tree that needs warm, sunny summers and golden fall days to reveal the beauty of its flowers. In cold regions, you will probably wait in vain for it to bloom. The attractively crinkled flowers may be white, pink, red, or violet, depending on the cultivar. They appear only at the tips of thick, year-old stems. The dark-green leaves are elliptical or elongate; the branches are tetragonal; the trunk has a silky sheen.

Blooming Season: August to October; in cool areas, unfortunately, usually quite late. Even forcing will scarcely accelerate the bloom.

Family: Lythraceae (loosestrife family).

Origin: China, Korea.

Location: Sunny and, in the beginning, sheltered from wind. Best against a white house wall that will reflect light and heat.

Potting Soil: All-purpose soil with sand added.

Watering, Feeding: During the growth period, keep evenly damp and feed every 2 to 4 weeks until August. Avoid standing water and dryness of the ball; otherwise, buds will drop!

Further Care: None.

Overwintering: Because crape myrtles that have attained full growth tolerate short periods of freezing temperatures even as low as 5°F (–15°C), the plants can be left outdoors relatively long. Before moving them indoors, cut back single-trunked plants as you wood common white willows, to stumps; with multiple trunks, remove all the thin stems and shorten the thick ones. Keep dark and almost dry at 39° to 46°F (4°–8°C). In spring, repot if necessary and put the plant in a bright location to force it. Be careful of the new shoots when you move it outdoors; they break easily and are sensitive to light.

Pests, Diseases: Aphids on the young shoots. Powdery mildew.

Propagation: From seed or by tip cuttings in August.

Lantana Hybrids
Lantana

A favorite standard—yellow lantana.

Several lantanas quickly form a bush.

☀ ⟋ ⌂ ☠

The great Swedish botanist Linnaeus transferred the name *Lantana*, said to be an old name for *Viburnum*, to this genus, to which over 150 species—most of them tropical to subtropical—belong. Only two, however, have been cultivated by horticulturists: *Lantana camara*, brought to England in 1819, and *Lantana montevidensis*, which reached Germany in 1820. Both species are essentially the ancestors of the *Lantana* x *camara* hybrids. They arose from multiple crossings around the turn of the century in France. During the *Belle Epoque*, this shrub, 12 to 39 in. (30–100 cm) high, played a significant role. Lantana then fell somewhat into obscurity, but some years ago, it again became a commonly used pot and bedding plant. Its numerous flowers cover the ovate leaves, which have a network of wrinkles, and attract many butterflies. The umbellate inflorescences, which are tightly packed in tiny, semirounded heads, have a peculiar property: They change constantly. Flowers that upon opening are orange change to yellow or dark crimson; pink ones suddenly turn fiery red or lilac. Only a few cultivars have stable colors. Lantana is particularly pretty as a standard.

Colored flowers change constantly; white ones remain relatively stable.

Blooming Season: June to October.
Family: Verbenaceae (verbena family).
Origin: Original forms, tropical America.
Location: Sunny.
Potting Soil: All-purpose soil, which can be enriched with slow-release fertilizer.
Watering, Feeding: During the growth period, keep moderately damp; feed every 2 weeks until August. Avoid standing water.
Further Care: Frequent pinching out until June will encourage branching and flowering. Remove the berrylike drupes (stone fruits) promptly in order to stimulate further abundant flowering.
Overwintering: Bright at about 43° to 50°F (6°–10°C). Keep almost dry. Regularly remove fallen leaves. Every spring, repot and cut back stems by one half.
Pests, Diseases: Whiteflies, spider mites.
Propagation: By herbaceous tip cuttings in spring, after the flush.

Decorating Tip: Appropriate underplanting for Lantana standards: Low, small-flowered marguerites in yellow (*Chrysanthemum multicaule* 'Kobold'), lobelias in blue (*Lobelia erinus*), or sweet alyssum (*Lobularia maritima*) in white. Lantana is suitable as bonsai.
Warning: All parts of the plant are poisonous.

Laurus nobilis

Laurel, Bay, Bay Laurel, Sweet Bay

Evergreen woody plant with dark-green, leathery leaves that are used as a seasoning. The greenish-yellow male and female flowers grow on two different plants. They appear only on uncut plants that grow outdoors in the ground. Deep-black berries develop from the female flowers.

Blooming Season: April to May.

Family: Lauraceae (laurel family).

Origin: Mediterranean regions.

Location: Sunny to shady.

Potting Soil: All-purpose mix or loamy garden soil with some peat and sand added.

Watering, Feeding: During the growing period, keep moderately damp. The ball should never dry out, especially not during the flush. Feed weekly until August.

Further Care: In summer, occasionally hose off with a strong jet of water.

Overwintering: Tolerates freezing temperatures as low as 14°F (–10°C) for a short time. Keep in a bright, airy place at 32° to 43°F (0°–6°C); if need be, can also be overwintered in dark, cool quarters. Water little. If necessary, cut back in March, but avoid harming the leaves! Repot infrequently.

Pests, Diseases: Scale.

Propagation: By semihardwood cuttings in August or September.

Proud Doorman
Spherical laurel trees are particularly popular at entrances.

Lavandula angustifolia
True Lavender

Blue lavender is well known. White lavender, such as the cultivar 'Nana Alba', however, is a much-sought-after rarity.

Lavender—small flowers, big scent.

Lavender will bring the scent and atmosphere of Provence to your balcony or patio and let you imagine the incomparable blue of the lavender fields of southern France shimmering in the sunlight. Did you know that these blue hedgehog-shaped plants arranged neatly in rows are not true lavender (*Lavandula angustifolia*) at all, but a cross with *Lavandula latifolia*? This variety, called lavandin, unlike its relative from the mountains, yields copious amounts of oil for the perfume industry even when grown on lower ground. The two species are as different in their aromas, however, as a wild strawberry and a supermarket breed: Lavandin oil smells somewhat more acrid than the oil of *lavande fine*, three times more expensive, which is distilled from the flowers of *Lavandula angustifolia*.
True lavender (*Lavandula angustifolia*), cultivated in Europe since 1500, is an old medicinal plant. The dried flowers contain soothing, deodorizing, and digestant substances; they are used as tea and in bath additives and personal grooming products. Because lavender has such a fresh scent, its branches traditionally are put with linen or lingerie, hence the name (from Latin: *lavare* = to wash). *Lavandula angustifolia* is an evergreen branching subshrub with linear leaves that are covered with silver-gray hair changing to a green color toward the top. It grows no more than 24 in. (60 cm) high. The flowers, which grow in terminal false spikes, in the pure species are violet-blue. In addition, there are a great many cultivars. The largest assortment is found in nurseries that sell herbaceous plants. The best-known cultivars are: 'Hidcote Blue' (dark violet, 16 in. [40 cm]), 'Hidcote Giant' (violet, 24 to 32 in. [60–80 cm]), 'Dwarf Blue' (dark blue, 12 in. [30 cm]), 'Grappenhall' (clear blue, 24 to 36 in. [60–90 cm]),

'Munstead' (light blue, 16 in. [40 cm]), 'Rosea' (light pink, 16 in. [40 cm]), and 'Nana Alba' (white, 8 in. [20 cm]).
Blooming Season: June to July, often to September.
Family: Labiatae or Lamiaceae (mint family).
Origin: Western Mediterranean region to Greece.
Location: Sunny.
Potting Soil: All-purpose mix or loamy, humus-rich garden soil. Likes lime.
Watering, Feeding: Water little and <u>do not feed</u>.
Further Care: Can be cut back after blooming in order to renew.
Overwintering: In sheltered situations without winter protection, in the open with winter protection of fir brush (see drawing, page 29). In case of dryness, water moderately on frost-free days. In spring, remove brush and cut plant back to one third. Alternative: Overwinter in a bright, frost-free place!
Pests, Diseases: Rare, owing to the protective essential oils.

Propagation: The pure species, from seed (spreads itself in the garden); the cultivars, by summer cuttings, which easily strike root in a blend of garden soil and sand.
Decorating Tip: Underplant a rose standard with low lavender. Alternatively, surround the tub with a ring of pots containing lavender. Lavender will keep aphids away from roses.

Leonotis leonurus
Lion's Ear

Lion's ear blooms in the fall.

☼ 🪣 ⟿ 🏠 🏠

Bizarre subshrub that from afar resembles a giant dead nettle. Depending on the location, it reaches a height of 3⅓ to 6½ ft (1–2 m). The tubular orange flowers, almost 2 in. (5 cm) across, are tomentose. They grow in dense axillary false whorls and account for almost half of the plant's height. The lanceolate leaves are about 4 in. (10 cm) long.

Blooming Season: September to November.
Family: Labiatae or Lamiaceae (mint family).
Origin: South Africa.
Location: Full sun and sheltered from wind. The stems snap easily.
Potting Soil: All-purpose soil, which can be enriched with slow-release fertilizer.
Watering, Feeding: During the growth period, water abundantly; from May to August, feed every 4 weeks.
Further Care: None.
Overwintering: Move indoors after the first spells of frost, always with a dry root ball to preclude decay. Cut off flowers (for use in a vase), cut stems back to 4 to 8 in. (10–20 cm). Put plant in bright or dark place at 41° to 50°F (5°–10°C) and keep almost dry. Regularly remove fallen leaves. In February, repot if necessary, dampen slightly, put in a brighter, warmer location.
Pests, Diseases: Aphids and whiteflies. Rare.
Propagation: From seed or cuttings in spring. Pinch out often at the beginning.
Decorating Tip: In a winter garden, lion's ear will retain its foliage, grow higher, and flower longer.

Leptospermum scoparium
Tea Tree, New Zealand Tea Tree, Manuka

The tea tree "drops its needles" when the ball is dry.

☼ 🪣 🏠

Tea tree is a novelty that is becoming increasingly popular in this country as an indoor plant and tub plant. It is sold in May or June as a bushy pot plant or graceful standard. The growth, flower colors, and leaf forms are quite variable. The plant may present itself as anything from a shrub 12 in. (30 cm) high to a tree almost 33 ft (10 m) tall. The evergreen leaves are green or bronze-red and usually have a narrow, sharp tip. The flowers are white, pink, or red, and some are double.

Blooming Season: May to June.
Family: Myrtaceae (myrtle family).
Origin: New Zealand, Australia.
Location: Full sun.
Potting Soil: Blend of ½ all-purpose soil and ½ peat moss with some sand or soilless mix.
Watering, Feeding: During the growth period, water abundantly with soft water. If the ball is dry, the plant will shed its leaflets. <u>Do not use hard water</u>! Until August, add rhododendron food or another acid-loving-plant fertilizer to the water every 2 weeks.
Further Care: Cut back after flowering.
Overwintering: Bright, cool (39°–50°F [4°–10°C]), and dry location. Ventilate on frost-free days! Water just enough to keep the ball from drying out. Repot in March.
Pests, Diseases: Rare.
Propagation: From seed in spring or by herbaceous tip cuttings in March, April, or August. Pinch out frequently.
Decorating Tip: The fine-leaved, graceful tea tree is most effective against a quiet background, for example, a hedge or a white house wall. Suitable as bonsai.

187

Lilium Hybrids
Lilies

Lonicera henryi
Honeysuckle

Lilium regale grows about 39 in.(1 m) high.

The scent of the flowers develops in the evening.

Plant them in February or March in a tub with a diameter of at least 8 in. (20 cm). Important: Under the potting soil, a 1-in.-deep (3 cm) drainage bed of coarse sand, gravel, or perlite is needed. Set the bulbs (three or more per pot) on this layer 2 in. (5 cm) apart and cover with at least 6 in. (15 cm) of soil. Pour a little water on the pots and stand them outdoors in the sun.

Blooming Season: Summer.

Family: Liliaceae (lily family).

Origin: The northern hemisphere; commercially available forms improved by breeding.

Location: Sunny and sheltered from wind.

Potting Soil: All-purpose soil or loamy, humus-rich

Want to Try This?
Highly suitable for pot culture are Turk's cap lilies, *Lilium martagon* (with strongly revolute perianth segments) and *Lilium* x *auratum* hybrids.

garden soil with Styrofoam chips, perlite, or sand added.

Watering, Feeding: From May to September, water abundantly. <u>Avoid standing water at all costs</u>! In April or May, sprinkle a handful of slow-release fertilizer on the surface of the pot.

Further Care: Hold in place with supporting stakes or a ring for holding herbaceous plants. Cut off spent flowers and let plants die back slowly.

Overwintering: In October or November, cut off yellowed stalks. In December, move indoors and overwinter there, in a dark place, at 32° to 41°F (0°–5°C). <u>Do not allow to dry out completely</u>. Repot every 2 years, in February or March.

Pests, Diseases: Botrytis and bulb base rot caused by standing water. Viral diseases.

Propagation: By seed, division, axillary tubers, or bulb scales, depending on the species or cultivar.

Warning: Lily bulbs are poisonous.

Honeysuckle, when planted in the open, can reach a height of about 10 to 13 ft (3–4 m). Experts consider this twining plant especially well suited to tub culture because of its evergreen, beautifully formed lanceolate leaves, its dense growth, and its scented, yellow-red flowers, from which decorative fruits develop in fall. Moreover, this species is said to be less troubled by aphids than its deciduous relatives.

Blooming Season: June to July.

Family: Caprifoliaceae (honeysuckle family).

Origin: Western China.

Location: Sunny to partially shady.

Potting Soil: All-purpose soil or any garden soil.

Watering, Feeding: During the growth period, water abundantly. <u>Do not let the ball dry out</u>! Until August, feed every 4 weeks.

Further Care: Provide a climbing aid (lattice, trellis, wire). Cutting back possible after flowering.

Overwintering: Outdoors with winter protection (see pages 28–29). In case of dryness, water moderately on frost-free days. If necessary, repot in spring.

Pests, Diseases: Rarely, aphids.

Propagation: By cuttings in early summer.

Decorating Tip: Because *Lonicera* is extremely fast-growing and dense, it makes an excellent privacy screen and windbreak. Underplanting—ivy, for example—is advisable. It will keep *Lonicera*'s base damp.

Warning: The berries are poisonous.

The fruit of the honeysuckle.

Mandevilla laxa
Mandevilla, Chilean Jasmine

The scent of Mandevilla is intoxicating.

Mandevilla, a twining plant with enchantingly fragrant flowers, quickly reaches a height of about 16½ ft (5 m). The snow-white, funnel-shaped flowers appear on the new shoots, open in succession, and grow in loose racemes of up to 20 blossoms. The fresh-green, oval-lanceolate leaves are shed in winter.

Blooming Season: June to August.

Family: Apocynaceae (dogbane family).

Origin: Argentina, Bolivia.

Location: Full sun.

Potting Soil: All-purpose soil, which can be enriched with slow-release fertilizer.

Watering, Feeding: During the growth period, water abundantly, and feed weekly until August. Thereafter, keep only slightly damp.

Further Care: Mandevilla needs a sturdy trellis. Be on the alert for infestations of pests, mainly aphids.

Overwintering: Move indoors with a dry ball, cut back almost to the bottom. Keep in a dark, cool (39°–46°F [4°–8°C]), dry place. Water very seldom. In March, repot and put in a brighter, warmer location so flushing can begin.

Pests, Diseases: Quite often, aphids and spider mites.

Propagation: From seed or cuttings in a warm propagating bed.

Warning: All parts of *Mandevilla* are poisonous. The fragrance can cause headaches in susceptible people.

Metrosideros excelsa
Ironwood Tree

The undersides of the leaves are covered with fuzz.

Flowers or leaves—both are charming in the ironwood tree. The flowers, which have scarlet-red filaments 1⅖ in. (3.5 cm) long, grow in terminal cymes (false umbels). They develop from snow-white, woolly buds. The branches and the undersides of the shiny, dark-green leaves also are covered with white fuzz. In its native habitat, the ironwood tree can grow over 65½ ft (20 m) high. It usually is bought as a branching bush that keeps its tub-sized dimensions even with increasing age. The botanical name (*metros* = marrow and *sideros* = iron) refers to the hard wood. The wood of the species *Metrosideros umbellata*, for example, is used in shipbuilding.

Blooming Season: In the northern latitudes, early summer; in its native habitat, late winter.

Family: Myrtaceae (myrtle family).

Origin: New Zealand.

Location: Very bright to full sun.

Potting Soil: Blend of ½ all-purpose soil and ½ peat moss.

Watering, Feeding: During the growth period, water abundantly. Avoid standing water and hard, cold water. Ironwood tree tolerates only very little lime! Until August, use rhododendron food or other fertilizer for acid-loving plants weekly.

Further Care: Can be trimmed after flowering.

Overwintering: Bright and cool (41°–50°F [5°–10°C]). Water approximately every 4 weeks. Do not let the ball dry out. In spring, repot young plants—older ones, only every 3 to 4 years.

Pests, Diseases: Scale in overly warm, dark wintering site; in summer location, can be transmitted by other scale-infested plants. Disturbances of growth due to use of overly hard, cold water.

Propagation: From seed or tip cuttings at a ground temperature of 68° to 77°F (20°–25°C) (difficult).

Myrtus communis
Common Myrtle

Myrtles are long-lived in tubs.

☀ 🪣 🏠

Berries may develop from the flowers.

Like laurel, myrtle is a tub plant with centuries of tradition. In antiquity, it was used for cultic purposes and as a cosmetic and medicinal plant. Egyptian women embellished their hair and clothing with flowering branches of myrtle. Among the Greeks and Romans, the myrtle was sacred, devoted to Aphrodite, or Venus. Ancient coins show the goddess adorned with a myrtle wreath. Pliny recommends roasted wild boar with myrtle sauce as a special culinary experience. Myrtle oil once was used as a remedy for many kinds of diseases and as a cosmetic. From ancient times, the myrtle has been a symbol of virginity, and this tradition is reflected in the still-current custom, in Germany, of wearing a bridal wreath made of myrtle branches. The evergreen shrub, which can grow extremely old if well tended, reaches a height of about 39 in. (1 m) in a tub. All summer long, it bears white flowers, from which protrude the frothy filaments typical of the myrtle family. They are followed by blue-black, edible berries sometimes as large as peas. The ovate or lanceolate leaves have a leatherlike luster and a strong, aromatic smell when bruised. The pure species is seldom available for sale. The plants we buy today are well-proven cultivars such as 'Hamburger Brautmyrte' or 'Königsberger Brautmyrte'.

Blooming Season: June to October.
Family: Myrtaceae (myrtle family).
Origin: Mediterranean regions.
Location: Full sun.
Potting Soil: All-purpose soil, which can be enriched with slow-release fertilizer.
Watering, Feeding: During the growth period, keep evenly damp. Avoid standing water and dryness of the ball. Soften water if at all possible. Until August, feed weekly.
Further Care: Regularly trim shoot tips of young plants to make them bushy.
Overwintering: Bright, cool (41°–50°F [5°–10°C]) location. Keep only slightly damp. Repot in March—young myrtles every year, older ones when necessary. Cutting back in spring is possible, but it will mean fewer flowers.

Pests, Diseases: Scale and aphids after excessively warm overwintering. Whiteflies.
Propagation: By tip cuttings in spring and summer. Pinch out several times.
Decorating Tip: Myrtles can be trained to form enchantingly beautiful standards (see page 51). Suitable as bonsai.

Nerium oleander
Oleander, Rose Bay

Nicotiana x sanderae
Tobacco Plant

Double- and single-flowered oleanders.

The tobacco plant's entire range of color.

Oleanders may have single or double (some of them scented) flowers in white, ivory, yellow, salmon, orange, pink, or red. The single-flowered cultivars are less sensitive to rain.

Blooming Season: June to October.

Family: Apocynaceae (dogbane family).

Origin: Mediterranean regions, Asia.

Location: Sunny, bright, sheltered from rain.

Potting Soil: All-purpose mix or loamy, humus-rich garden soil.

Watering, Feeding: Water abundantly in summer. Oleanders love water in the saucer. Until late August, feed well weekly.

Further Care: Do not remove peduncles (main flower stalks), which continue to develop even in fall.

Blooms in the Sun... Roots in the Water

That's how oleanders like it. In rainy summers, you will wait in vain for flowering to begin.

The cultivars in the photos above:
1 'Mont Blanc'.
2 'Pink Beauty'.
3 Dark-pink double cultivar.
4 'Professor Grandel'.

Overwintering: Before moving plant indoors, cut out bare and overly long stems. Put in a bright, cool (39°–46°F [4°–8°C]) place. Water little. More warmth from March on will promote early development of flowers. Repot younger plants every spring, older ones less frequently.

Pests, Diseases: Aphids, scale, spider mites; *Ascochyta* (fungal disease), oleander cancer (bacterial disease).

Propagation: By cuttings from June to September, in water.

Decorating Tip: Oleander can be trained as a standard (see page 51).

Warning: All parts of the plant are highly poisonous.

The botanical name can be traced back to a French envoy, Jacques Nicot (1530–1600). He is said to have been the first to introduce tobacco to the royal courts of France and Portugal.

Nicotiana alata, *Nicotiana sylvestris*, and most of all *Nicotiana x sanderae* became known as ornamental plants. Today there are numerous hybrids of this annual plant, which range from 24 to 39 in. (60–100 cm) in height. The hybrids have sweet-smelling flowers in white, yellow, pink, or red. The lower leaves are large, spatulate, and slightly undate (wavy); the upper ones are lanceolate.

Blooming Season: July to September.

Family: Solanaceae (nightshade family).

Origin: Original forms, South America.

Location: Sunny.

Potting Soil: All-purpose soil (can be enriched with slow-release fertilizer) or loamy, humus-rich garden soil.

Watering, Feeding: Water abundantly and feed weekly. High nutrient requirement.

Further Care: Regularly deadhead spent flowers.

Overwintering: Not applicable.

Pests, Diseases: Aphids, slugs.

Propagation: From seed (light germinator) in February or March.

Decorating Tip: A single plant in a large tub with nutrient-rich potting soil will grow into a tall, slender "shrub" covered with flowers. Quite pretty as underplanting: lobelias (*Lobelia erinus*).

Warning: All parts of tobacco plants are poisonous. The scent may cause headaches in susceptible people.

Olea europaea
Olive

The Mediterranean olive tree.

Olive trees leave their stamp on the Mediterranean landscape. The shimmering luster of their leaves—with their blue-green upper surfaces and silvery, willowlike undersides—is something no vacationer will ever forget. The evergreen olive tree quickly reaches a height of up to 6½ ft (2 m) in a tub, but initially it branches slowly. The small, creamy-white flowers appear in axillary racemes. Outside their natural range, olive trees seldom form fruits, because a different cultivar is needed for this purpose as a pollen contributor. Moreover, the fruits require warm temperatures in fall to ripen. Formerly, olive trees were rarely available commercially, but today they are frequently for sale—usually the thornless variety, *var. europaea*.

Blooming Season: July to August.
Family: Oleaceae (olive family).
Origin: Mediterranean countries.

Location: Full sun.
Potting Soil: All-purpose mix or loamy garden soil.
Watering, Feeding: During the growth period, keep evenly damp. Until August, feed every 2 weeks.
Further Care: Cutting back and shaping are possible at any time.
Overwintering: Tolerates temperatures a few degrees below freezing point. Keep bright and cool (36°–50°F [2°–10°C]). (Can also stand in a dark place, but will lose its foliage.) Air on frost-free days! In March, repot if necessary; in April, put plant outdoors in a sheltered location to prevent premature flushing.
Pests, Diseases: Rare. Fungal infections on the leaves are possible in August.
Propagation: By scarified olive pits in spring or tip cuttings in summer, at a ground temperature over 86°F (30°C).
Decorating Tip: Suitable as bonsai.

Pandorea jasminoides
Pandorea

With abundant light, Pandorea is long-flowering.

In Italy, the jasminelike climber pandorea is known as *Bignonia semperflorens*, ever-blooming bignonia. In optimal light conditions—for example, if kept year-round in a very bright conservatory—its 2-in.-wide (5 cm), funnel-shaped, pink-and-white flowers will begin to open as early as March, and flowering will continue until it abates slowly in fall. The pinnate, glossy green leaves are evergreen. When grown in a tub, pandorea needs a trellis, anchored in the container, to support its long shoots. On the market you will find, in addition to the species, cultivars such as the pure-white 'Alba' and the pink 'Rosea'.

Blooming Season: July to September.
Family: Bignoniaceae (bignonia or trumpet creeper family).
Origin: Australia.
Location: Bright to sunny.
Potting Soil: All-purpose soil, which can be enriched with slow-release fertilizer.

Watering, Feeding: During the growth period, keep evenly damp. Feed weekly until August.
Further Care: Although pandorea can twine itself, arrange the shoots on the trellis and tie them securely.
Overwintering: Move pandorea indoors early; it is sensitive to cold. Keep bright at 59°F (15°C) and water moderately. In spring, replace top layer of soil. If necessary, repot: The plant will have to be removed from the trellis, and cutting back the shoots usually is unavoidable.
Pests, Diseases: Aphids.
Propagation: By cuttings in spring or summer.
Decorating Tip: Pandorea is a long-blooming privacy screen with Mediterranean charm.

Parthenocissus quinquefolia
Virginia Creeper

Fiery autumn colors of Virginia creeper.

Favorite food for birds—blue berries on red stalks.

☼ 🔨 🔓

With its brilliant scarlet autumn foliage, this twiner will bring color to your balcony or patio in fall. Planted in the garden, it reaches a height of more than 39 ft (12 m). It climbs by means of tendrils that are morphologically stems, which occasionally terminate in adhesive disks. In the botanical standard work *Illustrierte Flora von Mitteleuropa* (*Illustrated Flora of Central Europe*), the origin of the adhesive disks is described quite graphically: "In their early stage, the ramifications of the lucifugous tendrils do not yet produce adhesive disks; they are involuted in the shape of hooks and only insignificantly thickened. Once in proximity to a solid object, the ramifications spread apart and attach themselves to its sides. Within two days, the curved tips thicken, turn bright red, and change into disklike structures that are inseparably bonded to the underlying surface by means of an adhesive—viscous ini-

tially, then solidifying—exuded by the cells of each disk." The deciduous, finger-shaped leaves, up to about 5 in. (12 cm) long, are shed gradually in fall. The unobtrusive, greenish-white flowers grow in panicles beneath the foliage. They are fragrant and are frequently visited by bees, while the pea-sized blue berries on red stalks are a favorite food for birds. In contrast to its relative *Parthenocissus tricuspidata* (Boston ivy), which was cultivated in Europe as early as 1862, Virginia creeper has been known there only since 1929. Even today, it still is often confused with the other species. Some varieties have arisen in the meantime:
• *Parthenocissus quinquefolia var. engelmanii*. This variety differs from the pure species in that it has more graceful leaves, which turn dark red in fall, and better-developed adhesive disks, which permit the plant to climb almost 33 ft (10 m) high

when planted out in the garden. Moreover, improved ability to adhere helps this plant climb even smooth walls.
• *Parthenocissus quinquefolia var. hirsuta*. In this variety, the leaves and shoots are covered with soft hair (*hirsuta*). Autumn coloring is light red.

Blooming Season: June to August.

Family: Vitaceae (grape family).

Origin: North America to Mexico.

Location: Sunny to partially shady. In a sunnier position, autumn coloring is more intense.

Potting Soil: All-purpose soil or loamy, humus-rich garden soil.

Watering, Feeding: During the growth period, water abundantly. Until August, feed every 8 weeks.

Further Care: The plant needs a sturdy taut wire or a frame for climbing.

Overwintering: Outdoors with winter protection (see pages 28–29). In case of dryness, water moderately on frost-free days.

Pests, Diseases: Fungal infection that causes the shoots to become limp (rare).

Propagation: From hardwood cuttings (matter for horticulturists).

Decorating Tip: In fall, you can set the young plant in a pot that fits exactly into the mouth of a big-bellied container. The fiery red foliage will make it appear to have lava running over it. Suitable as bonsai.

TUB PLANTS

Passiflora
Passionflower

The robust *Passiflora caerulea* 'Constance Elliot'.

☀ 🪣 🏠

All the species are magnificent evergreen climbers with 3- to 7-lobed leaves up to 5 in. (12 cm) long and spiral tendrils that are morphologically stems, arising from the leaf axils.

• *Passiflora edulis* decks itself in white-and-purple flowers, from which develop—given sunny, warm fall days—red-brown or (in the form *Passiflora flavicarpa*) yellow fruits (passion-fruits, such as maypops) about 2 to 3 in. (5–8 cm) long.

• *Passiflora caerulea* yields even more splendid violet-blue or white ('Constance Elliot') flowers.

• *Passiflora violacea* is similarly free-flowering, with violet-colored blooms.

Blooming Season: Depending on the species, June to September.
Family: Passifloraceae (passionflower family).
Origin: Tropical and subtropical South America.
Location: Sunny.
Potting Soil: All-purpose soil, which can be enriched with slow-release fertilizer.
Watering, Feeding: During the growing period, water abundantly, and feed weekly until August. Avoid standing water.
Further Care: Provide a climbing aid (see page 51).
Overwintering: Move indoors with a dry ball before frost begins. Keep bright at 50°F (10°C). Water rarely. Regularly remove fallen leaves. When moving plant indoors or in March, cut side shoots back leaving 3 to 5 eyes. Repot every 2 years.
Pests, Diseases: Spider mites, scale, and woolly aphids. Yellow leaves caused by lack of nutrients and by standing water.
Propagation: By tip cuttings in a warm propagating bed or from seed (easy).
My Tip: The specimens trained on hoops and sold as indoor plants often will not survive the stay outdoors.

Passiflora flavicarpa with fruits (passion-fruits).

Phoenix canariensis
Canary Island Date Palm

In time, the fronds become increasingly outspreading.

☀ 🪣 🏠

In the words of an Arab poet, the date palm bathes its feet in water and its head in the fire of heaven, which refers to the fact that it is a classic oasis plant. In warm regions popular among vacationers, *Phoenix canariensis* regularly produces its lush, golden-yellow inflorescences, which in cool areas—where the plant is grown in a tub and with inadequate levels of light—appear extremely rarely or not at all.

Blooming Season: August or September.
Family: Arecaceae (palm family).
Origin: Canary Islands.
Location: Full sun. Acclimate for 2 weeks beforehand in a shady location to prevent the leaves from getting burned.
Potting Soil: All-purpose mix or loamy, sandy garden soil.
Watering, Feeding: Water abundantly during the growing period, and feed every 2 weeks until August.
Further Care: Spray plant occasionally with the water hose, so that no pests can settle in. Cut withered fronds off neatly.
Overwintering: Bright place at 41° to 50°F (5°–10°C). Keep ball only slightly damp. In spring, repot young plants every 2 to 3 years, older ones when necessary. In repotting, you can cut the root ball below and on the sides with a sharp knife.
Pests, Diseases: Scales and spider mites after overly warm overwintering. Phoenix smut (rare). Overwatering in winter can lead to root or core rot and to the death of the plant.
Propagation: Year-round, from seed.
Decorating Tip: This palm grows quite rapidly into an outspreading plant; consequently, it needs ample space.
Note: The true date palm, *Phoenix dactylifera*, requires the same care.

Phormium tenax
New Zealand Flax

Phyllostachys
Phyllostachys

The striped cultivars of *Phormium tenax* 'Variegatum'.

Phyllostachys nigra and *Phyllostachys aurea*.

Interesting evergreen rosette plant with sword-shaped leaves that grow almost 10 ft (3 m) high in the plant's native habitat, 5 to 6½ ft (1.5–2 m) high in a tub, and arise from a rootstock. The fibers extracted from them are among the most elastic in the plant kingdom. The fiber bundles extend almost the length of the leaves, so that even the strongest man cannot tear a leaf counter to the direction of the fibers. Old specimens form a shaft with a matte-red panicle that towers far above the leaves. In addition to the green species, the yellow-and-white-striped cultivar 'Variegatum' is also well known.

Blooming Season: Late summer.

Family: Liliaceae (lily family).

Origin: New Zealand.

Location: From sunny to shady.

Potting Soil: All-purpose mix or loamy garden soil with peat moss added.

Watering, Feeding: During the growth period, water abundantly, and feed weekly until August. The plant can endure less-ideal care for some time.

Further Care: None.

Overwintering: New Zealand flax tolerates light frost. Overwinter in a bright location at 39° to 50°F (4°–10°C), or in a dark place if need be. Water little. Regularly remove withered leaves. In spring, repot if necessary.

Pests, Diseases: Thrips with exceedingly warm overwintering.

Propagation: By division of older plants in spring or from seed (tedious).

My Tip: If you lack room, it is better to choose the less-vigorous cultivars. Quite pretty are the copper-red 'Atropurpureum', the creamy white-striped 'Cream Delight', or the yellow-and-white-striped 'Yellow Waves'.

This stoloniferous bamboo genus with light-green, graceful leaves and colored, striped, or spotted stems conquered our gardens long ago. These are suitable for tub culture:

• *Phyllostachys aurea* (golden bamboo) and its cultivar 'Holochrysa', with stems in yellow-orange hues.

• *Phyllostachys aureosulcata* 'Spectabilis', which experts consider one of the most beautiful bamboos of all.

• *Phyllostachys nigra* (black bamboo), which produces few stolons. All grow over 6½ ft (2 m) high in a tub.

Family: Gramineae or Poaceae (grass family).

Origin: China, Japan.

Location: Sunny.

Potting soil: All-purpose soil, which can be enhanced with loamy garden soil and slow-release fertilizer. The container has to be 3 to 4 times the size of the root ball, with at least a 13-gal (50 L) capacity.

Watering, Feeding: During the growth period, water abundantly, but avoid standing water. Bamboo is not a swamp plant! Until late August, fertilize lightly every 3 weeks.

Further Care: To keep the plant from drying out, you can use fallen bamboo leaves to mulch it (mulch = cover the surface of the soil with plant matter).

Overwintering: Outdoors with winter protection (see pages 28–29) or in a bright room just above freezing point. In case of dryness, water with warm water on frost-free days. In spring, thin out older stems.

Pests, Diseases: Rare, because of the high silicic acid content.

Propagation: By division.

Decorating Tip: Beautiful companion plants: maple, aucuba, azalea, hydrangea, pine, clematis, spindle tree.

TUB PLANTS

Pittosporum tobira
Pittosporum

A stately tub plant—*Pittosporum*.

☀ 🔍 ⌂

Flowering *Pittosporum tobira* 'Variegatum'.

The unique capsular fruits of *Pittosporum*.

Pittosporum is an undemanding, healthy, and thoroughly decorative plant that reaches quite a stately height in a tub. In the Mediterranean countries, this evergreen shrub is used everywhere for hedging along the streets. Automobile exhaust fumes apparently do not affect the glossy, obovate leaves. The creamy white, lemon-scented flowers appear in clusters between March and early summer, depending on the overwintering. The fruit is a capsule inside which the seeds are imbedded in a resinous, sticky mass—hence the name (*pitta* = resin and *spora* = seed). Additional species that are sometimes available commercially:

• *Pittosporum tenuifolium* is natural in New Zealand. When fully mature, this large shrub or tree may reach a height of 29½ ft (9 m). In comparison with *Pittosporum tobira*, it has small leaves, at most about 3 in. (7 cm) long. Attractive features are the almost black leaf-stalks, the black bark of the young branches, and the dark-red flowers, which appear in the leaf axils in spring. *Pittosporum tenuifolium* makes wonderful pyramids or standards. If you are lucky, you will find one of the numerous cultivars with silvery, red, or variegated leaves.

• *Pittosporum undulatum* comes from eastern Australia, where it forms a beautiful, dome-shaped crown. This species grows fairly slowly and is conspicuous for its dark-green, shiny leaves that are 6 in. (15 cm) long and have wavy (*undulatum*) margins. The flowers appear in late spring. Experts consider it one of the most beautiful trees for cool, frost-free greenhouses.

Blooming Season: March to May.
Family: Pittosporaceae (pittosporum family).
Origin: Subtropical China, Japan, South Korea.
Location: Sunny to partially shady.
Potting Soil: All-purpose mix or loamy garden soil with peat moss and sand added.
Watering, Feeding: During the growth period, water abundantly in a sunny location. Until August, feed every 2 weeks.
Further Care: Cutting back and shaping possible at any time.
Overwintering: The plant tolerates some frost. Overwinter in a bright location at 32° to 50°F (0°–10°C), or in the house. If need be, also in a dark place, which must be cool because leaf drop will occur in an overly dark, warm situation. If overwintered cool, water little. Repot young plants in spring, older ones when necessary.
Pests, Diseases: Aphids, fungal infections.

Propagation: From seed or semihardwood cuttings (easy).
Decorating Tip: The uniformly deep green of the foliage and the formal growth make pittosporum a tub plant that can be used to create visual points of rest or accents.

Pleioblastus fortunei 'Variegatus'
Pleioblastus

The new growth is particularly beautiful.

☼ 🔎 🏠

Of the 20-odd species of the highly stoloniferous bamboo genus, this white-striped cultivar is one of the best known. Introduced in Belgium in 1863, it now is praised by international bamboo experts as an optimal cultivar for tub culture. The stems, 12 to 16 in. (30–40 cm) long, are green; the leaves, relatively wide for bamboo, are striped with white.
Family: Gramineae or Poaceae (grass family).
Origin: Japan.
Location: Sunny.
Potting Soil: All-purpose mix or loamy, humus-rich garden soil. Plant container must be 3 to 4 times larger than the root ball.
Watering, Feeding: During the growth period, water abundantly, and feed weekly until August.
Further Care: None.
Overwintering: Outdoors with winter protection (see pages 28–29). Alternatively, sink tub in a hole dug in the ground and cover plant with foliage or brush. In case of dryness, water with warm water on frost-free days.

In March, cut off just above the ground. The colors of the new growth will be particularly intense.
Pests, Diseases: Rare, owing to the salicic acid content.
Propagation: By division.
Decorating Tip: This bamboo will also fit on a small balcony. Planted outdoors in beds, it is a favorite ground cover, which has unusual charm because of its striped foliage.

Plumbago auriculata
Plumbago, Leadwort

Plumbago should be sheltered from wind and rain.

☼ 🔎 💧 ➶ 🏠 🏠

Plumbago is a dependable long-bloomer. The phloxlike flowers appear at the ends of new shoots in rich, short, almost one-sided spikes. In the pure species, they are sky-blue, in the cultivar 'Alba', snow-white. In a tub, plumbago can grow over 6½ ft (2 m) high and equally wide. It produces long, wind-sensitive, fragile stems that later are overhanging. The undersides of the small leaves are covered with a light-colored powder.
Blooming Season: June to October.
Family: Plumbaginaceae (leadwort family).
Origin: South Africa.
Location: Sunny, sheltered from wind and preferably also from rain.
Potting Soil: All-purpose mix or loamy, humus-rich garden soil.
Watering, Feeding: During the growth period, water abundantly, and feed weekly until August.
Further Care: Regularly pinch off spent flowers. Because of their sticky-haired calyxes, the flowers do not fall on their own. Shaped plants (standards, pyramids) need frequent cutting.
Overwintering: Move indoors with a dry root ball. Shorten stems by one half. Keep in a bright place at 41° to 46°F (5°–8°C), almost dry. If need be, overwinter in a dark, cool location, where the plant will lose much of its foliage. Consequently, in this case, cut the stems almost even with the ground. In spring, repot and put in a warmer location to force.
Pests, Diseases: Rarely, aphids.
Propagation: From July on, by semihardwood cuttings (easy).
Decorating Tip: Plumbago also can be grown on a trellis or as a standard, a hanging plant, or a pyramid.

The phloxlike flowers of plumbago flowers.

Podranea ricasoliana
Podranea

Polygonum (Fallopia) aubertii
Knotweed

Podranea—beautiful as a cascading standard.

Knotweed in bloom looks as delicate as a veil of tulle.

Podranea—a sister of the trumpet creeper (*Campsis*)—is still a relative newcomer. *Podranea ricasoliana* (sometimes also *Podranea brycei*) is now available from specialized mail-order firms. This vigorous evergreen climber produces annual shoots up to about 10 ft (3 m), also long and bell-shaped or funnel-shaped flowers as wide as 2 in. (5 cm). The latter, pink with red markings, grow at the ends of the shoots, in panicles up to 12 in. (30 cm) long. The foliage is pinnate.

Blooming Season: July until fall, in a winter garden until December.

Family: Bignoniaceae (bignonia or trumpet creeper family).

Origin: Tropical South Africa.

Location: Sunny and sheltered from rain, if possible.

Potting Soil: All-purpose mix (can be enriched with slow-release fertilizer) or loamy, humus- and nutrient-rich garden soil.

Watering, Feeding: During the growth period, water abundantly, and feed weekly until August. High nutrient requirement.

Further Care: Podranea needs a climbing aid, to which it has to be tied.

Overwintering: Before moving indoors, cut stems back to a basic structure about 32 in. (80 cm) high. Keep bright and cool (43°–50°F [6°–10°C]) or, if need be, dark and almost dry. With cool overwintering, the plant will lose almost all its foliage. Remove the fallen leaves regularly. Repot in spring.

Pests, Diseases: Aphids on the soft shoot tips and flower buds.

Propagation: By tip cuttings in spring.

Decorating Tip: Experts consider podranea the most beautiful of all the Bignoniaceae. It still is a rarity that not everyone has.

Because of its extremely fast-growing shoots, in a short time knotweed will form a green cover on everything to which the plant can hold. Planted in the garden, it easily will add several yards (m) in a year and can reach a height of almost 50 ft (15 m). In a tub, it still can grow as high as 16⅖ to 23 ft (5–7 m). Its deciduous leaves are a vivid green, reddish during flushing, but not overly attractive. The plant's beauty lies in the creamy-white panicles, which create a frothy effect and are 8 to 16 in. (20–40 cm) long. They are honey-yielding flora, and the tiny nuts provide food for birds.

Blooming Season: July to October.

Family: Polygonaceae (buckwheat or knotweed family).

Origin: Western China, Tibet.

Location: Sunny to partially shady.

Potting Soil: All-purpose mix (can be enriched with slow-release fertilizer) or loamy, humus-rich garden soil.

Watering, Feeding: During the growth period, water abundantly, and feed weekly until August. High nutrient requirement.

Further Care: Needs a climbing aid (taut wires, lattice for twining). Can be kept in shape with shears at all times.

Overwintering: In a tub, outdoors with winter protection (see pages 28–29). In case of dryness, water on frost-free days. In spring, replace top layer of soil and, if necessary, cut plant back.

Pests, Diseases: Aphids and whiteflies if dryness occurs.

Propagation: By cuttings in late June or hardwood cuttings from October on.

Decorating Tip: Knotweed is good for quickly covering walls, posts, balcony railings, and arbors with green. It can be grown as a climber or as a hanging plant. The flowers are quite lovely in a vase.

Campanulate—the funnel-shaped flowers of *Podranea*.

Potentilla fruticosa
Cinquefoil

Pseudosasa japonica (syn. *Arundinaria japonica*)
Pseudosasa, Arrow Bamboo

Cinquefoil blooms for months.

Pseudosasa does well in the shade.

Densely branching, broad, and bushy cinquefoil is a deciduous small shrub that grows no higher than 3⅓ ft (1 m). The threefold to sevenfold leaves are ⅖ to 1 in. (1–3 cm) long and green to bluish-green in color. The flowers, ⅘ to 1 in. (2–3 cm) across, grow singly or in groups on new wood and are bright yellow or, in some cultivars, white, light pink, or dark pink. Suitable for tub culture are various yellow-flowering cultivars such as 'Gold Star' or 'Goldteppich'. 'Goldfinger', with lemon-yellow flowers, 'Hachmanns Gigant', with brilliant-yellow flowers, and the white 'Abbotswood' are not susceptible to powdery mildew. Pink flowers are found in 'Princess' or 'Royal Flush'. All the cultivars listed grow 26 to 39 in. (65–100 cm) high.

Blooming Season: Depending on the cultivar, May or June to September or October.

Family: Rosaceae (rose family).

Origin: Northern temperate zone.

Location: Sunny.

Potting Soil: All-purpose soil or loamy, humus-rich garden soil.

Watering, Feeding: During the growth period, water moderately. The plants will tolerate short-term dryness. Until August, feed every 4 weeks.

Further Care: Can be shaped at any time.

Overwintering: Outdoors with winter protection (see pages 28–29) of fir brush. In case of dryness, water moderately on frost-free days. In spring, cut back and thin out.

Pests, Diseases: Mildew.

Propagation: From June to August, from semihardwood cuttings.

My Tip: Recommended for smaller containers or alpine gardens in troughs is *Potentilla aurea*, an herbaceous plant 6 to 8 in. (15–20 cm) high, whose golden-yellow flowers appear in June or July.

This bamboo species reached Europe in 1850, and at first it was cultivated only in France. It produces green stems. When planted out in the ground, it reaches a height of about 10 ft (3 m), in a tub, about 6½ ft (2 m). The Japanese, who call this plant "metake," use the ramrod-straight stems to make arrows. The leaves are 12 in. (30 cm) long, over 1 in. (3 cm) wide, and have a leathery sheen. The flowers are a curiosity: With bamboo, no one is glad to see flowers appear, because the plant usually dies soon thereafter. Of course, the plants flower—depending on the species—simultaneously throughout the world, only once every 10 to 12 years. In the past few years, *Pseudosasa* did bloom worldwide, so plants bought now will not be blooming soon.

Origin: Japan, South Korea.

Family: Gramineae or Poaceae (grass family).

Location: Partially shady to shady.

Potting Soil: All-purpose mix or loamy, humus-rich garden soil. Container has to be 3 to 4 times the size of the root ball. Provide good drainage (see page 26).

Watering, Feeding: During the growth period, water abundantly. From May to August, fertilize lightly.

Further Care: None.

Overwintering: Outdoors with winter protection (see pages 28–29). Alternatively, sink tub in a hole dug in the ground and cover with brush. In case of dryness, water with warm water on frost-free days. Protect from sun.

Pests, Diseases: Rare.

Propagation: By division.

Decorating Tip: Bamboo is the "shadow counterpart" of the sun-loving *Phyllostachys* (see page 197). Like *Phyllostachys*, it is partly evergreen.

Pomegranate

Pyracantha, Firethorn

Was the pomegranate Eve's apple?

Pyracantha x *coccinea* hybrid 'Golden Charmer'.

The pomegranate is a very old useful plant that was holy in many civilizations. Its seeds were a symbol of fertility. The only pomegranates suitable for tub culture are single- or double-flowered ornamental cultivars with red or, less frequently, white or yellow flowers, which appear only on new wood. The pomegranate tree grows 2 to 6½ ft (0.6–2 m) high and fruits occasionally. Dwarf cultivars, which grow no higher than 3⅓ to 5 ft (1–1.5 m)—'Nana', for example—flower especially freely and early. The small, glossy-green, oval leaves turn bronze when flushing occurs and brilliant yellow in fall. They are shed during overwintering.

Blooming Season: July to August.

Family: Punicaceae (pomegranate family).

Duo with Tradition
Pomegranate tree with underplanted variegated ivy, two plants with a long history.

Origin: Near East.

Location: Sunny.

Potting Soil: All-purpose mix or loamy, humus-rich garden soil.

Watering, Feeding: From March to the middle or end of July, water abundantly and feed every 4 weeks. Thereafter, keep drier.

Further Care: None.

Overwintering: When moving plant indoors, remove weak branches and shorten main stems by one third. Keep in a bright place at 36° to 43°F (2°–6°C) or, if need be, put it in a dark place and keep it almost dry. Regularly remove fallen leaves. Repot young plants every 2 years, older ones only when necessary.

Pests, Diseases: Aphids.

Propagation: By leafless parts of branches, 4 in. (10 cm) long, in February or March.

Decorating Tip: The long-lived pomegranate is a magnificent plant for use in flanking entries, staircases, and terraces. Suitable as bonsai.

Among the woody plants that bear decorative fruits, pyracantha is one of the most attractive. Because of its susceptibility to fire blight and pyracantha scab, however, it almost disappeared from the retail assortment of woody plants. In the meantime, new strains have become available that are believed to be resistant. For tub culture, the suitable plants from this assortment are the erect, bushy hybrids of *Pyracantha coccinea* that grow up to 6½ ft (2 m) high, for example, 'Golden Charmer' (bright orange fruits) or 'Soleil d'Or' (golden-yellow fruits).

Blooming Season: May; fruits, August to September.

Family: Rosaceae (rose family).

Origin: Southern Europe, southwestern Asia.

Location: Sunny to partially shady.

Potting Soil: Blend of 2 parts all-purpose mix and 1 part loamy, sandy garden soil.

Watering, Feeding: Water moderately, do not allow to dry out completely. From May to August, feed every 2 weeks.

Further Care: In late fall, reshape by cutting back stems that jut out.

Overwintering: Outdoors with winter protection (see pages 28–29). With young plants, also protect the branches with fir brush. Important: In case of dryness, water moderately on frost-free days.

Pests, Diseases: The susceptibility of the above-named cultivars to pyracantha scab is rated as very low.

Propagation: Matter for horticulturists.

Decorating Tip: This evergreen woody plant with decorative fruit will underscore the red-gold atmosphere created by Virginia creeper and maple.

Warning: Pyracantha has thorny stems on which you can injure yourself.

Quamoclit lobata
Spanish Flag, Crimson Star Glory

Rhodochiton atrosanguineus
Red Cloak

The flowers change color three times.

☼ 🖐 1 ☠

Equally unusual as a climber or a hanging plant.

☼ 🖐 ⇗ 1

Spanish flag, like its sister the morning-glory (see page 182), produces lush masses of flowers. This plant in its native habitat is a climbing herbaceous plant that is treated in the cool regions as an annual, where it winds to a height of 16½ to 19⅔ ft (5–6 m) and forms 3-lobed leaves, heart-shaped at the base, where they join the petiole. The inflorescence differs considerably from that of other Convolvulaceae. The flowers grow in forked, secund (bending to one side) bundles up to 16 in. (40 cm) long. The buds are bright red, but turn orange before blooming and white after opening. The yellow filaments, over twice as long as the corolla, protrude and are slightly bent. Some confusion exists in the nomenclature of this genus; Spanish flag is thus often sold under its other names, *Ipomoea lobata*, or *Mina lobata*.
Also suitable for tubs: *Quamoclit coccinea* (syn. *Ipomoea coccinea, Mina sanguinea*), which grows only about 6½ ft (2 m) high.

Blooming Season: July to September.
Family: Convolvulaceae (morning-glory family).
Origin: Southern Mexico.
Location: Sunny.
Potting Soil: All-purpose mix or sandy, humus-rich garden soil.
Watering, Feeding: During the growth period, water moderately and feed weekly until August. Avoid standing water.
Further Care: Spanish flag needs a twining aid (see page 51).
Overwintering: Not applicable.
Pests, Diseases: Spider mites.
Propagation: In March, from seed, in a warm propagating bed.
Decorating Tip: Spanish flag will twine all over trellises within a short time and quickly create a beautiful privacy screen.
Warning: Spanish flag, like its relative the morning-glory, may contain an amide of lysergic acid, a narcotic akin to LSD (*ly-sergic acid diethylamide*).

The English common name is a translation of the botanical name, which is composed of the Greek *rhodon* = rose and *chiton* = dress. It refers to the rose-red calyxes. *Rhodochiton atrosanguineus* only recently was "dug up" again by commercial gardeners, tested for its usefulness as an ornamental plant, and found to be satisfactory. Treated as an annual in the cool zones, it is a climbing subshrub with cordate leaves. Using its petioles and peduncles, it winds its way up to a height of about 10 to 23 ft (3–7 m) and flowers extremely freely. The corolla of the dark blood-red flowers is covered with glandular hair. After pollination, the rose-red calyx remains on the plant. Well-known cultivar: 'Purple Bells'.

Blooming Season: August to October.
Family: Scrophulariaceae (figwort family).
Origin: Mexico.
Location: Sunny and sheltered.
Potting Soil: All-purpose mix.
Watering, Feeding: During the growth period, water moderately and feed weekly.
Further Care: Twining aid necessary.
Overwintering: Not applicable.
Pests, Diseases: White-flies, spider mites.
Propagation: From seed between November and July. The plants start to flower only 5 months after the seeds are sown. Preferably, buy finished plants.
Decorating Tip: *Rhodochiton* is also quite an enchanting hanging plant.

Rhododendron x *repens* Hybrids
(Dwarf) Rhododendron

Rhododendrons are elegant spring bloomers.

With these strains, the blooming season on your balcony or patio can begin as early as mid-April, if the weather conditions are advantageous. These evergreen shrubs grow 24 to 39 in. (60–100 cm) high and about 3⅓ to 5 ft (1–1.5 m) wide. They grow quite slowly and almost cushion-shaped. The umbels, composed of 2 to 7 overhanging, bell-shaped flowers, are light or dark red in color, with a very few being pink. Many cultivars—'Scarlet Wonder', for example—have glossy red buds.

Blooming Season: April or May.

Family: Ericaceae (heath family).

Origin: Original form *Rhododendron forrestii* (syn. *Rhododendron repens*), Tibet and China.

Location: Partially shady and sheltered from wind.

Potting Soil: Blend of ½ all-purpose mix and ⅓ peat moss.

Watering, Feeding: During the growth period, water abundantly with soft water; in April, sprinkle a handful of slow-release fertilizer on the surface of the soil.

Further Care: Protect early blooms against late spells of frost by using bubble wrap or fir brush. Break off spent flowers.

Overwintering: Outdoors without winter protection. Protect from sun! The soil should not be allowed to dry out completely, nor should standing water be permitted.

Pests, Diseases: Chlorosis, leaf spot disease, soot, spider mites, weevils.

Propagation: By cuttings (difficult), by layers (easy, but scarcely feasible in a tub), or grafting.

Decorating Tip: Solitary plant. Suitable as bonsai.

Warning: Rhododendrons contain poisonous substances.

Rhus typhina
Staghorn Sumac

Staghorn sumac displays beautiful autumn colors.

Graphically beautiful leaves that turn yellow and orange-red in fall and panicles up to 8 in. (20 cm) long, from which club-shaped, 6-in. (15 cm) fruits develop, are the hallmarks of this undemanding woody plant. Staghorn sumac, a shallow-rooted plant, grows about 13 to 19⅘ ft (4–6 m) high in a garden, about 6½ ft (2 m) high in a tub. It has multiple stems and bushy growth. If it is trained, through cutting, as a one-stemmed plant, its roof-shaped crown will be more effective. The cultivar 'Dissecta' is most suitable for container culture. It grows more slowly, stays smaller, and has particularly decorative, finely laciniate (deeply segmented) leaves.

Blooming Season: June to July.

Family: Anacardiaceae (cashew family).

Origin: North America.

Location: Sunny to partially shady.

Potting Soil: All-purpose mix or any garden soil.

Watering, Feeding: During the growth period, keep evenly and slightly damp. Until August, feed every 2 weeks.

Further Care: Cut in fall or spring to desired shape.

Overwintering: Without winter protection. In roof-covered locations, do not allow ball to dry out completely. In spring, replace top layer of soil.

Pests, Diseases: Rare.

Propagation: From runners, should any appear in the container.

Decorating Tip: Typical solitary plant.

Warning: Staghorn sumac exudes a corrosive fluid when injured. Wear gloves when cutting the plant, and do not rub your eyes!

Robinia pseudoacacia
Black Locust, False Acacia

For container culture, it is best to use the slow-growing cultivar 'Frisia', also known as golden acacia on account of its foliage, which is golden-yellow the year round. Planted in the garden, it reaches a height of 29½ ft (9 m); in a container at least 24 in. (60 cm) deep, it grows up to 6½ ft (2 m) high. The globe-shaped cultivar 'Umbraculifera' grows somewhat lower.

Blooming Season: June.
Family: Fabaceae or Leguminosae (pea or bean family).
Origin: Eastern and central North America.
Location: Sunny.
Potting Soil: Blend of 2 parts all-purpose mix and 1 part loamy, sandy garden soil.
Watering, Feeding: During the growth period, water moderately and do not feed. Nitrogen producer!
Further Care: None.
Overwintering: Without winter protection. In roof-covered locations, do not let ball dry out completely.
Pests, Diseases: Rare.
Propagation: From stolons, should any appear in the container.
Decorating Tip: Pairs of globe-shaped locusts are decorative on either side of a doorway. Sometimes an underplanting simply will not flourish. The problem may be caused by substances that the locust secretes in the root zone.
Warning: The seeds and bark of the locust are poisonous.

Splendid Autumn Appearance
The foliage, which is golden the year round, is particularly effective in fall with ornamental fruit-bearing woody plants as an underplanting.

The bedding rose 'Bonica 82'—a pink dream in a tub.

Rose standard with marguerite underplanting.

Can you put the queen of flowers, which we know to have deep roots, in a container? Yes, if you choose slower-growing and shallower-rooted cultivars. Rose breeders long ago provided us with a great many cultivars for container culture. For tubs, they recommend dwarf or ground-cover roses—such as 'Zwerg-königin', 'Sonnenkind', 'The Fairy', or 'Swany'—grafted onto standards. If you have extremely roomy, deep tubs, you can indulge in a charming climbing rose such as 'Super Dorothy', grafted onto a standard.

Low bedding roses, however, are most suitable for tubs:

• 'Marlena', 14 in. (35 cm) high. Bright dark-red, double flowers, which fade nicely and are rainproof.
• 'Heinzelmännchen', 14 in. (35 cm) high, compact growth. Blood-red, large double flowers in umbels that have an abundant second bloom.
• 'Mariandl', 20 to 24 in. (50–60 cm) high. Blood-red double flowers.
• 'Champagner', 24 in. (60 cm) high. Finely formed cream-colored flowers with pale pink tinge.
• 'Bonica 82', 24 in. (60 cm) high. Heavily double light-pink flowers. Very frost hardy.
• 'Goldmarie', 24 in. (60 cm) high. Double, golden-yellow flowers with a slightly reddish hue when fading. Lightly scented.
• 'Rosamunde', 20 in. (50 cm) high. Medium-sized flowers in vibrant pink, lightly scented. Very winter hardy.
• 'Orange Triumph', 24 in. (60 cm) high. Flowers orange and scarlet. Very frost hardy. Roses grown in nursery containers can be planted at any time of year except winter. Bare-root plants bought should be set in tubs in spring. Provide good drainage.

Blooming Season: June to fall.
Family: Rosaceae (rose family).
Origin: The origin no longer can be reconstructed. Only cultivated forms are available commercially.
Location: Full sun and airy.
Potting Soil: All-purpose mix or humus-rich, loose, loamy, sandy garden soil.
Watering, Feeding: During the growth period, water moderately. Avoid standing water. Until late July, feed weekly. Alternatively, in March and June, sprinkle slow-release fertilizer on the surface of the soil and work it in slightly.
Further Care: Cut spent flowers off neatly to spur reblooming.
Overwintering: Outdoors with protection (see pages 28–29) or in dark rooms just above freezing point. Water moderately and remove fallen leaves regularly. Replace top layer of soil in spring. Shorten stems of bedding roses by a handbreadth; if you want to renew the plant, cut back harder. Cut stems of standards to a length of 6 to 8 in. (15–20 cm); remove dead wood, weak stems, and stems turning inward. Later, pinch out the new leaf growth, leaving 3 leaves.
Pests, Diseases: Aphids, spider mites; mildew, star-shaped sooty mold, rose rust.
Propagation: By cuttings from mid-August to mid-September, or by grafting.
Decorating Tip: Roses need deep plant containers. They should be at least 14 in. (35 cm) tall, preferably 20 in. (50 cm) or more.

Salix
Willow

Sesbania tripetii
Scarlet Wisteria Tree

Pussy-willow standard—a delight for the bees.

Flowers from spring to fall—scarlet wisteria.

A standard with pendulous pussy willows surrounded by a gay, colorful group of daffodils, tulips, bluebells, and perhaps also primroses in pots—this is springtime on a patio or a balcony. If you want the beautiful improved hanging form, you will have to go to the nursery in spring and ask for the weeping sallow or goat willow (*Salix caprea* 'Pendula') or for the rosemary willow (*Salix* x *repens ssp. rosmarinifolia*). In addition to these two popular standards, there are other slow-growing willows that often are planted in tubs—for example, the creeping *Salix* x *grahamii* (8 to 12 in. [20–30 cm] high, vivid green, long-lasting leaves) and *Salix* x *simulatrix* (creeping, fairly thick-stemmed, roundish leaves, large winter buds).

Blooming Season: March to May, depending on the species or the cultivar.

Family: Salicaceae (willow family).

Origin: Europe, Asia.

Location: Sunny.

Potting Soil: All-purpose mix or loamy, humus-rich garden soil.

Watering, Feeding: During the growth period, water abundantly, and feed until August.

Further Care: Willows can, if necessary, be shaped with shears at any time. Cut out old wood every 2 to 3 years. Tie standards.

Overwintering: Without winter protection. In case of dryness, water on frost-free days.

Pests, Diseases: Rare.

Propagation: Nongrafted willows, by hardwood cuttings 10 to 12 in. (25–30 cm) long, from mid-July to late September.

Decorating Tip: The creeping willows look quite handsome in troughs with alpine plantings.

In English-speaking countries, this plant is known as scarlet wisteria because of its flowers, which grow next to one another in groups of 10 in hanging panicles. Experts still argue that *Sesbania punicea* may be a more correct name for this attractive long-flowering plant. In any event, the bush, with the fine paired leaflets of its "mimosa foliage," enriches the assortment. *Sesbania* develops few branches and can grow up to 10 ft (3 m) high and 6½ ft (2 m) wide.

Blooming Season: Spring to fall.

Family: Fabaceae or Leguminosae (pea or bean family).

Origin: Argentina.

Location: Sunny and warm.

Potting Soil: All-purpose mix or loamy, humus-rich garden soil.

Watering, Feeding: During the growth period, water moderately, and avoid standing water. Until August, feed weekly. Thereafter, the wood has to mature fully, so that it does not rot in winter.

Further Care: If you break off the fruits at once, scarlet wisteria will bloom repeatedly.

Overwintering: Move plant indoors with dry ball and possibly cut back slightly. The stems tend to dry back greatly in winter. Overwinter in a dark place at 39° to 50°F (4°–10°C), and keep almost dry. Scarlet wisteria sheds its leaves, so they have to be removed regularly. If the plant grows unsightly and spindly, with wide-spreading branches, it can be cut back almost even with the ground.

Pests, Diseases: Mildew.

Propagation: By semi-hardwood stem cuttings in summer.

Decorating Tip: Scarlet wisteria also can be trained as a miniature tree by trimming 3 or 4 times.

Nightshade climbs and flowers like jasmine.

Solanum rantonnetii has proved reliable in a tub.

Of the exotic *Solanum* species that have conquered the tub-plant market in recent years, *Solanum rantonnetii* has gained the greatest acceptance. This is not surprising, in view of the mass of blossoms that almost cover the small, oval, soft-haired leaves. The blue-violet "potato flowers" with the deep-yellow eyes appear well into fall. The shrub, which grows as high as 6½ ft (2 m) in a tub, has pliant stems that develop an urge to climb if given the opportunity.

Other well-known species:
• *Solanum jasminoides* (jasmine nightshade) is from Brazil. This evergreen shrub is reputedly one of the fastest-growing climbers. It branches extensively, and with sufficient fertilizer and a bright location the year round, it produces stems up to almost 33 ft (10 m) long. *Solanum jasminoides* yields clusters of white to pale-blue flowers from spring until fall. This very robust plant should be overwintered in a frost-free, bright location.
• *Solanum wendlandii* (Costa Rica nightshade, giant potato vine) is said to be the most beautiful species of the *Solanum* clan. It climbs about 39 in. (1 m) high with hook-like spines. The leaves are rather large (up to 10 in. [25 cm] long), and the lilac-colored flowers reach a width of 2⅓ in. (6 cm). They grow in lush clusters and appear in summer. Before overwintering, cut this vigorous

plant back. It would shed its leaves anyway.
• *Solanum muricatum* is a perennial creeping plant that produces stems up to about 39 in. (1 m) long. The new breed 'Pepino Gold' grows especially well in hanging baskets. The golden-yellow, tennis-ball-sized fruits develop from the violet flowers. In the temperate region, they begin to ripen from August on. The juicy, firm fruit is eaten (when fully ripe) raw. The taste is reminiscent of melon and pear, with a hint of slight bitterness.

Blooming Season: July to October.
Family: Solanaceae (nightshade family).
Origin: Argentina, Paraguay.
Location: Sunny to partially shady.
Potting Soil: All-purpose soil.
Watering, Feeding: During the growth period, water abundantly, and feed weekly until August.
Overwintering: Before moving indoors, cut back by about one half. Over-

winter cool, at 39° to 50°F (4°–10°C), and almost dry. Repot in early March and put in a brighter, warmer place to force. Alternative: Put in a bright spot in a conservatory that is not overly warm; keep slightly damp.
Pests, Diseases: Aphids, whiteflies, spider mites.
Propagation: By semihardwood cuttings in summer.
Decorating Tip: This plant also can be grown on a trellis to create a "blue wall."
Warning: All parts of *Solanum rantonnetii*, *Solanum jasminoides*, and *Solanum wendlandii* are poisonous. With the exception of the fruit, *Solanum muricatum* is also poisonous.

Solanum muricatum yields edible fruits.

209

Strelitzia reginae
Bird-of-paradise Flower, Bird's-tongue Flower, Strelitzia

Bird-of-paradise—the floral emblem of Los Angeles.

Charlotte von Mecklen-burg-Strelitz (1744–1818), later the wife of George III of England, gave this banana plant its botanical name. It is the floral emblem of Los Angeles. The English common names refer to the flowers, which resemble birds' heads. Bird-of-paradise flower is a multistemmed, trunkless herbaceous plant 3⅓ to 6½ ft (1–2 m) high, with evergreen, oval-lanceolate, leathery leaves on long stalks. The inflorescence emerges from the base and is located on a strong peduncle. The imposing flowers in colors of orange and sky blue arise from a boat-shaped, red-margined bract. They are among the costliest cut flowers.

Blooming Season: February to August.
Family: Musaceae (banana family).
Origin: Cape Province of South Africa.
Location: Sunny and sheltered from wind.
Potting Soil: All-purpose soil with sand or Styrofoam flakes added. Loamy, humus-rich, sandy garden soil.
Watering, Feeding: During the growth period, water moderately and feed every 2 weeks until August. Avoid standing water.
Further Care: After the bloom, repot in large containers with good drainage. Do not injure roots!
Overwintering: Move indoors before first frost. Keep in a bright place at about 46° to 54°F (8°–12°C) and water little.
Pests, Diseases: Scale.
Propagation: In spring, by division of older plants or from seed. Seedlings will flower for the first time 3 to 4 years later.

Syringa microphylla
Autumn Lilac

The flowers exude the typical lilac perfume.

Among the large number of magnificent lilac species and hybrids available for the garden, nurseries recommend primarily *Syringa microphylla* for large containers. This erect small shrub grows 3⅓ to 6½ ft (1–2 m) high and forms wide bushes with elegantly overhanging, soft-haired stems. The elliptical, roundish leaves are 1½ in. (4 cm) long, with dark-green upper surfaces and gray-green undersides. The violet-pink flowers grow in large, fine-haired panicles up to 2⅘ in. (7 cm) across; they exude the typical lilac perfume. When fading, they turn somewhat lighter in color. The pure species flowers only in June. The cultivar *Syringa microphylla* 'Superba', the one usually available commercially, is more attractive and flowers more freely. It also can be purchased as a very pretty standard grafted on *Ligustrum*.

Blooming Season: The pure species: June. Cultivar 'Superba', in June, with a second bloom from August to September.
Family: Oleaceae (olive family).
Origin: Original form, northern China.
Location: Sunny.
Potting Soil: All-purpose mix or loamy, humus-rich, permeable garden soil. Provide good drainage.
Watering, Feeding: During the growth period, keep evenly damp. Avoid standing water. Until August, feed every 4 weeks.
Further Care: None.
Overwintering: Outdoors with winter protection (see pages 28–29). In case of dryness, water on frost-free days. In early spring, remove dried-up wood and overly dense growths of wood.
Pests, Diseases: Rare.
Propagation: Matter for horticulturists.
Decorating Tip: Autumn lilac, because of its slightly overhanging form, is a very pretty choice for large containers that are used to border a patio.

Tibouchina urvilleana
Brazilian Glorybush, Spider Flower

Trachelospermum jasminoides
Chinese Star Jasmine

Brazilian glorybush—its flowers are deep violet.

Intensely fragrant cultivars usually flower less freely.

"This lilac color is unique," says everyone who sees the flowers of *Tibouchina* for the first time. They grow in groups at the ends of the branches, measure about 5 in. (12 cm) across, and display a blue-violet color that can be seen from afar. The copiousness of the flowers and their long blooming period—which, however, can be enjoyed in its entirety only by owners of conservatories—compensate for the short life of the individual flowers. The leaves, which have a velvety look, also are attractive. They are about 6 in. (15 cm) long, oval-lanceolate, deep-green, longitudinally veined, and covered with fine hair on their upper surfaces. In fall, the older leaves turn a beautiful red. Brazilian glorybush grows rigidly upright, with little branching. Without cutting, its lower parts become leafless. In its native habitat, it grows about 10 to 20 ft (3–6 m) high, in a tub, about 6½ ft (2 m).

Blooming Season: August to May.
Family: Melastomaceae (meadowbeauty family).
Origin: Brazil.
Location: Sunny.
Potting Soil: All-purpose soil.
Watering, Feeding: During the growth period, keep moderately damp, and feed every 2 weeks until August. Avoid standing water.
Further Care: Pinch out young plants often, so that they will be bushier.
Overwintering: Bright and cool (41° to 50°F [5°–10°C]) location. Water little. In late winter, cut shoots back into the thin new wood. If necessary, repot in May.
Pests, Diseases: Rare. With standing water, danger of root fungi.
Propagation: By soft cuttings in spring in a warm propagating bed.
Decorating Tip: Put 2 or 3 plants together in a large tub to achieve a bushier effect overall.

This marvelously beautiful evergreen climbing shrub is related to *Mandevilla* and oleander. You can let it climb or use it as a ground cover. Its elliptical-lanceolate leaves, about 3 to 5½ in. (7–14 cm) long, are deep green and leathery. The jasmine-scented white flowers grow 1 in. (2.5 cm) long in loose cymes in the upper leaf axils. Heavily scented cultivars generally flower less freely than less-fragrant ones. Chinese star jasmine grows slowly in the early years, but in sufficiently large containers, it later can speed up the pace of its growth and produce stems 6½ to 16½ ft (2–5 m) long.
Blooming Season: Summer.
Family: Apocynaceae (dogbane family).
Origin: Japan, Korea, China.
Location: Sunny to partially shady.
Potting Soil: All-purpose mix or loamy, humus-rich garden soil.

Watering, Feeding: During the growth period, water moderately and feed weekly until August.
Further Care: Overflowing growth can be kept in shape with shears at any time.
Overwintering: Bright and cool (41° to 50°F [5°–10°C]) location. If the plant is moved indoors late, you also can keep it in a dark place if need be, but not too warm; otherwise, leaf drop will occur. Water little. If necessary, repot in spring.
Pests, Diseases: Scale, aphids, whiteflies, spider mites.
Propagation: By tip cuttings taken in summer from specimens that bloom well (difficult).
Decorating Tip: Chinese star jasmine can be grown on a trellis and as a pyramid. It also is useful for covering pillars and posts. Suitable as bonsai.
Warning: The plant holds a milky juice. All parts of star jasmine are poisonous. The heavy scent can cause headaches.

Reach for your shears when Chinese star jasmine starts to grow too tall.

Trachycarpus fortunei
Chusan Palm

Washingtonia
Petticoat Palm, Washington Palm

Robust solitary palm for large patios.

Caution—the leafstalks of the petticoat palm are thorny!

Of all the palms grown in pots and tubs, the Chusan palm is the most resistant. It will tolerate temperatures as low as 3°F (-16°C) for a short time: In Germany, older specimens that flower and fruit are found growing outdoors in sheltered locations. In southern England and southern Switzerland, on the northern Italian lakes, along the southern Atlantic Coast, and on the French Riviera, the Chusan palm is part of the landscape. It can also be found in Oregon and North Carolina. In a tub, it grows 6½ to 13 ft (2–4 m) high and forms a hairy trunk with almost circular, shiny-green fronds on stalks 16 to 35 in. (40–90 cm) long. The trunk grows only a few inches per year in a tub.

Blooming Season: Summer.

Family: Arecaceae (palm family).

Origin: Burma, central and eastern China, Japan.

Location: Old plants, sunny; younger ones, partially shady.

Potting Soil: All-purpose soil or loamy, sandy garden soil.

Watering, Feeding: During the growth period, keep moderately damp and apply low doses of fertilizer weekly until August.

Further Care: None.

Overwintering: Move indoors late and remove brown fronds. Put in a dark place at 32° to 41°F (0°–5°C) (or in a bright location in a room). Water little, so that the core will not rot. Air on frost-free days! Repot in spring, but only if the ball is being squeezed out of the pot. Put in partial shade to adjust gradually to the increase in light intensity; otherwise, it may well be scorched.

Pests, Diseases: Rare. Spider mites, scale, fungal disease.

Propagation: Year round from seed.

Decorating Tip: Solitary plant; allow 8 ft (2.5 m) for the diameter of its crown.

The petticoat palm forms almost circular fans, which unlike those of many other palm species do not drop off once they have reached a certain age, but turn down and surround the trunk like petticoats worn one over another—hence the first, apt American name. Available commercially are the following:
• *Washingtonia robusta*, from Mexico, with shiny green fans.
• *Washingtonia filifera*, from California, with gray-green leaves, from the segments of which hang down great numbers of light-colored to brown filaments (*filifera* = filiferous, thread-forming). The petioles are thorny. Both plants, by virtue of the leafstalks' pattern of attachment, produce picturesque trunks. Petticoat palms grow fairly quickly and can reach a width of over 6½ ft (2 m) and a height of almost 10 ft (3 m), even in a tub.

Family: Arecaceae (palm family).

Origin: Arizona, California, Mexico.

Location: Old plants, sunny; younger ones, bright to partially shady.

Potting Soil: All-purpose mix or loamy, sandy garden soil.

Watering, Feeding: During the growth period, water abundantly and apply low doses of fertilizer weekly until August. Important: Do not wet the core of the plant, because it might rot.

Further Care: None.

Overwintering: Bright at 41° to 46°F (5°–8°C). Water little. Repot young plants in spring, older ones only if the ball is being pushed out of the pot. Provide good drainage!

Pests, Diseases: Scale, aphids.

Propagation: Year round from seed.

Decorating Tip: The petticoat palm is a solitary plant that grows quite rapidly and needs a great deal of space.

Warning: You can injure yourself on the thorny leafstalks.

Yucca

Of the 40-odd known species of *Yucca*, these are most commonly used as tub plants:
• *Yucca aloifolia*, with hard, daggerlike leaves.
• *Yucca elephantipes*, the giant yucca, with relatively soft leaves.
Old specimens produce imposing creamy-white inflorescences that tower above the plant.

Blooming Season: August or September.

Family: Agavaceae (agave family).

Origin: Mexico, Central America, southern United States.

Location: Sunny.

Potting Soil: All-purpose mix or loamy, humus-rich garden soil with sand added.

Watering, Feeding: During the growth period, water abundantly, and feed every 2 to 3 weeks until August. Avoid standing water.

Further Care: In spring or summer, shorten plants that have grown too large, cutting them anywhere you choose. Use the "scraps" from cutting to reproduce the plant.

Overwintering: Move indoors with dry ball. Keep bright and cool (41° to 50°F [5°–10°C]), water little. If necessary, repot in spring.

Pests, Diseases: Rare.

Propagation: By tip cuttings or stem cuttings in summer.

Warning: You can injure yourself on the daggerlike leaves of *Yucca aloifolia*.

Die-hard Yucca
Yucca aloifolia (center) in easy-care company: *Dracaena draco* (left) and *Cordyline australis* (right).

Dwarf conifers retain their small size for years and thus are ideal for a long-lasting planting.

Dwarf conifers are slow-growing needle-leaved woody plants that either remain small naturally or result from mutations that were selected and further reproduced vegetatively. Following are the most important pointers on care for the species and cultivars shown in the photo (from left to right):

Dwarf Sawara False Cypress

The dwarf form of the Sawara false cypress, *Chamaecyparis pisifera* 'Filifera Nana', grows as a bushy shrub with thin branches whose tips overhang with a fountainlike effect. It will grow no higher than 3⅓ ft (1 m) in 10 to 15 years, but when fully mature (planted out in the ground) it can be 10 ft (3 m) high and wide.
Location: Sunny to partially shady. Resistant to automobile exhaust fumes.
Potting Soil: All-purpose mix or sandy, humus-rich, and loamy garden soil.
Watering, Feeding: Keep evenly and slightly damp. Tolerates limy water. From the second year on, occasionally apply weak doses of fertilizer from the start of the growth period to August.

Blue Dwarf Juniper

Juniperus squamata 'Blue Star' first grows compact, then spreads out with increasing age. It produces an unevenly shaped cushion, and in 10 to 15 years it will grow 12 to 16 in. (30–40 cm) high and about twice as wide. The silver-blue needles are pointed and sharp.
Location: Bright to sunny. Resistant to automobile exhaust fumes.
Potting Soil: All-purpose mix or sandy, humus-rich garden soil.
Watering, Feeding: Keep evenly and slightly damp. Avoid standing water. From the second year on, apply fertilizer every 4 weeks.

Dwarf Juniper

Juniperus communis 'Meyer' is a pillar-shaped shrub with loosely shaped limbs and rather blunt tips. It grows no higher than 5 ft (1.5 m).
Location: Bright to sunny. Resistant to automobile exhaust fumes.
Potting Soil: All-purpose mix or any garden soil.
Watering, Feeding: From March to April, use fertilizer every 4 weeks.
Further Care: Shake off snow in winter.

Norway Spruce

The Norway spruce, here *Picea abies* 'Nidiformis', as a young plant forms a nest-shaped depression instead of a peaked top. It is a dwarf form with slightly ascending green-needled branches and slightly nodding tips. In 10 to 15 years, it reaches a height of only 20 in. (50 cm).
Location: Bright to sunny. Does not flourish well in large cities because of polluted air.
Potting Soil: All-purpose mix or damp, cool, rich garden soil.
Watering, Feeding: During the growth period, apply fertilizer every 4 weeks until August.

Overwintering: All the cultivars listed above are overwintered outdoors. Important: Do not forget to water on frost-free days. Wrap up frost-sensitive containers!

Pinus mugo Cultivars
Dwarf Pine

Thuja occidentalis Cultivars
Dwarf Arborvitae, White Cedar

Dwarf pine with phlox and houseleek.

This golden-yellow *Thuja* creates a sunny effect.

The dwarf pine, *Pinus mugo*, is the chief parent of the numerous dwarf cultivars that are offered for sale today. Its native habitat is the mixed coniferous forests of central and southern Europe, and it grows as a trunk-forming shrub up to 16½ ft (5 m) high. Here are the best known dwarf forms:
• *Pinus mugo* 'Gnom' has dense, spherical growth, 20 to 24 in. (50–60 cm) high, needles dark green.
• *Pinus mugo* 'Mops', with growth that is spherical and flat-bottomed to cushion-shaped is 12 to 16 in. (30–40 cm) high, and 20 to 24 in. (50-60 cm) wide. Needles are dark green with silvery needle sheaths.
• *Pinus mugo* 'Jacobsen', with its flat growth, is almost like a ground cover. Needles are thick and dark green, terminal shoots like foxtails.
Family: Pinaceae (pine family).
Origin: Original form, central and southern Europe.

Location: Sunny.
Potting Soil: All-purpose soil mixed with some peat moss. Loamy, humus-rich, slightly acid garden soil.
Watering, Feeding: Water moderately, but do not allow to dry out. Tolerates hard water. From the second year on, apply fertilizer every 4 weeks from May to August.
Overwintering: Outdoors without winter protection. Water on frost-free days.
Pests, Diseases: Woolly aphids that attack pines.
Propagation: Matter for horticulturists.
Decorating Tip: Dwarf pine makes an excellent miniature tree (see photo, above). Ask a bonsai expert how to shape it.

The sufficiently well known arborvitae, a representative of cool spruce and fir forests, commonly grows in cold, swampy soils. About 1,000 forms of this extremely variable species are known, including highly diverse dwarf forms. Following are the best known:
• *Thuja occidentalis* 'Little Gem' has erect growth, up to 3⅓ ft (1 m) high. Stems are horizontal in some instances, with dark-gray needles.
• *Thuja occidentalis* 'Recurva Nana' with growth that is spherical to wide and cone-shaped, is 20 to 24 in. (50–60 cm) high and wide. Branches are unevenly erect and spreading, with bent over and twisted branch tips. Needles are matte green and scaly; they turn brown in winter.
• *Thuja occidentalis* 'Sunkist' has erect growth habit and is cone-shaped. In a tub is rarely higher than about 5 ft (1.5 m). Needles are golden yellow, light yellow during flushing, and green-yellow in winter.
Family: Cupressaceae (cypress family).
Origin: Original forms, North America, Canada.
Location: Bright to sunny.
Potting Soil: All-purpose soil with some peat moss added. Loamy, sandy, slightly acid garden soil.
Watering, Feeding: Keep evenly damp. Sensitive to dry soil and air. From May to August, apply fertilizer every 4 weeks.
Further Care: None.
Overwintering: Outdoors without winter protection. Water on frost-free days.
Pests, Diseases: Thuja shoot death.
Propagation: Matter for horticulturists.
Decorating Tip: The golden-colored forms are most effective against dark backgrounds (walls, hedges) or in combination with plants that have dark-green leaves.

Conifers will not tolerate standing water; provide good drainage.

215

HERBS · VEGETABLES

Freshly picked basil and chives, and tomatoes right off the bush—that is a healthful kind of luxury. Not surprisingly, the culinary pot garden brimming with herbs, fine vegetables, and fruits is becoming increasingly popular. Many of these plants flourish splendidly in boxes and other vessels. There are even custom-tailored breeds of some vegetable and herb species, designed especially for container culture.

Monkey flowers (left) are a welcome spot of color against the green of basil (center) and parsley (right).

The small kitchen balcony for drying laundry has had its day—long live the kitchen balcony for gourmets, hobby cooks, and herb fans! Since the news has spread that a useful garden high in the air can be quite beautiful, many container gardeners have switched from masses of flowers to colorful, aromatic green plants. The choice of vegetables and herbs to tend in planter boxes or pots on your balcony or patio depends on the area required and on your personal needs. These same factors determine whether you should add small fruit trees to the other plants. Climbers such as scarlet runner beans and peas can be grown on a wall, as can tomatoes, which will profit from the summer heat pooled at the wall of a building. Strawberries or tiny cocktail tomatoes make splendid hanging plants. The boxes on outer balustrades should be reserved for leaf lettuce, spinach, and herbs that do not grow overly high. Vigorously growing herbs or vegetables such as rosemary, tomatoes, or lovage, as well as small fruit trees, need a large container and a place where they can stand alone, sheltered from wind.

Plants for the Kitchen Balcony

The most popular annual and perennial herbs and vegetables are sold in spring at some weekly markets, in garden supply stores, and through mail-order garden suppliers. An even greater diversity of species is available to you if you want to raise the plants yourself from seed. With many cultivars bred especially for container culture, the seeds also are more readily obtainable than the young plants. Slow-growing small fruit trees for container culture are sold by good nurseries and mail-order suppliers. When you buy or place an order, ask whether the cultivar is self-pollinating or whether you need a second cultivar for pollination.

Appropriate Care

It is as true for herbs and vegetables as for container flowers and tub plants: Care and overwintering depend to the greatest extent on the specific plant's native habitat, growth, and vegetative rhythm. Because most of them have an aroma and generally need sun and warmth to develop their scents and tastes, the ideal kitchen balcony faces south. Preventive measures and organic agents (see page 30) are quite important in the protection of plants that are to be eaten. Standing the containers where air can circulate and providing appropriate care for each species (see Plant Portraits, pages 218–227) will prevent diseases and infestations of pests and help keep vegetables and herbs attractive enough to eat.

Bright-blue Flowers

The flowers decorate the rosemary plant from May to June. After that, nasturtium, chives, borage, basil, and sage will flower, in addition to cucumbers, peas, and beans. Who can claim that an herb and vegetable balcony is nothing but green-on-green!

Allium schoenoprasum
Chive

If you let the flowers grow, your harvest will decrease.

Chives are perennial plants that grow about 12 in. (30 cm) high. The tubular leaves—thin or thick, depending on the cultivar—grow from small bulbs, whose roots, along with the surrounding soil, form a solid clump. If you want to harvest right away, it is best to buy finished plants with balls thoroughly permeated with roots. Garlic chive (needs same care as chive), a white-flowering cross between chive and garlic, does not form bulbs. Garlic chive grows about 16 to 20 in. (40–50 cm) high.

Blooming Season: June to July.

Family: Liliaceae (lily family).

Origin: Europe, Siberia, East Asia, North America.

Location: Bright to partially shady, better fresh and cool than sunny and hot.

Potting Soil: All-purpose mix or loamy, humus-rich garden soil; work in some slow-release fertilizer before sowing seeds or planting.

Raising: Sow chive in spring (harvest the first year and subsequent years); garlic chive, from March to May (harvest the first year and subsequent years).

Watering, Feeding: During the growth period, keep evenly damp. Avoid standing water. From spring to fall, feed every 2 weeks.

Further Care: When harvesting, cut little tubes off to about 1 in. (3 cm) above the ground, then wait until new ones have grown.

Overwintering: Keep plant in pot in the house, bright, cool, and almost dry. If you have a garden, take out of pot and set in bed.

Pests, Diseases: Aphids.

Propagation: From seed in spring (see Raising) or by division of the rootstock in spring or fall.

Decorating Tip: Chive, with its spherical pink flowers, is also a decorative plant for a box on a bright, but not hot, balcony.

Garlic chives array themselves in white flowers.

Anethum graveolens var. hortorum
Dill

Dill germinates at soil temperatures above 46°F (8°C).

As the popular saying goes, "Dill does what it wants," meaning that it germinates erratically and will not sprout everywhere you want it to grow. Because dill forms taproots (the container should be at least 8 to 10 in. [20–25 cm] deep), even young plants may have initial difficulties when transplanted. The plants, therefore, should be no more than 6 in. (15 cm) high. Nevertheless, this annual aromatic plant over 3⅓ ft (1 m) high, with its finely pinnate foliage and decorative yellow inflorescences, belongs on every kitchen balcony.

Blooming Season: July to August.

Family: Apiaceae (celery family).

Origin: Original form, Near East, India, Mediterranean area.

Location: Sunny to partially shady, sheltered from wind.

Potting Soil: All-purpose soil; loamy, humus- and nutrient-rich garden soil and sand in equal proportions. Mix slow-release fertilizer with soil.

Raising: From April on, sow directly in a container that is at least 8 in. (20 cm) deep and cover lightly with soil. Dark germinator. Seeds sprout only at ground temperatures exceeding 46°F (8°C). To prevent problems in transplanting, thin out seedlings slightly. Helpful: Sow among other plants. Dill loves company.

Watering, Feeding: Never let soil dry out completely, but avoid standing water. Do not feed.

Further Care: Leaflets can be harvested at any time; seeds, in August or September.

Overwintering: Not applicable.

Pests, Diseases: Aphids.

Propagation: From seed in spring (see Raising).

My Tip: If you mix mineral powder with the potting soil, it will benefit the growth and aroma.

Borago officinalis
Borage

Levisticum officinale
Lovage

The bees are overjoyed at the sight of borage flowers.

Lovage is robust and grows quickly.

Borage, with its brilliant blue flowers that grow at the tips of the shoots, is one of the most attractive potherbs and, moreover, a valuable honey-producing plant. This annual plant grows 20 to 39 in. (50–100 cm) high, depending on the container size. Its stalks, covered with dense hair, bear large, vivid-green, hairy leaves that have a refreshing cucumber taste.

Blooming Season: June to early August.

Family: Boraginaceae (borage family).

Origin: Mediterranean.

Location: Sunny and warm. Also tolerates partial shade.

Potting Soil: All-purpose mix or loamy, sandy garden soil.

Raising: In spring, sow seeds directly in the container you plan to use ultimately, which should be at least 8 in. (20 cm) deep. Dark germinator. Thin out, putting 1 to 2 plants in each pot, depending on its size.

Watering, Feeding: Water abundantly on hot days; otherwise, the plant will droop. Every 4 weeks, apply a tea brewed from horsetail, stinging nettles, or comfrey, or use an organic mineral fertilizer. The plant has a great need for minerals.

Further Care: Cut flowers off before they wither, in order to stimulate a second bloom. For consumption, remove only young leaves and shoot tips.

Overwintering: Not applicable.

Pests, Diseases: Frequently aphids, mildew if placed too close together.

Propagation: From seed in spring (see Raising).

Decorating Tip: Especially beautiful in large containers in combination with low marigolds, which need the same care.

Lovage is a perennial herbaceous plant that grows as high as 5 ft (1.5 m) in the garden. It forms tubular stalks on which coarsely pinnate, firm, dark-green leaves grow. The reddish spring flush and the golden-green umbels of this plant are quite beautiful.

Blooming Season: July to August.

Family: Apiaceae (celery family).

Origin: Iran.

Location: Sunny to partially shady.

Potting Soil: All-purpose mix or loamy, rich garden soil.

Raising: Sowing is worthwhile only with very fresh seeds. Preferably, buy a nursery-grown young plant. You need only one, because lovage is exceptionally vigorous. Use a large container (at least 12 in. [30 cm] in diameter).

Watering, Feeding: Water abundantly in hot weather. From April to August, feed every 1 to 2 weeks. High nutrient requirement.

Further Care: Unless you want the flowers to serve as honey-producing flora, cut them off; the foliage will develop more vigorously.

Overwintering: Hardy in wind-sheltered locations and in a large container; otherwise, wrap it up (see pages 28–29). Cut off yellow stalks. Water a little from time to time. In March, repot, water more, and remove winter protection.

Pests, Diseases: Rare.

Propagation: By division of stems, which must be at least 2 years old.

My Tip: The taste of lovage is quite strong, so use the leaves sparingly. If you find the aroma too intense, in place of lovage sow the more restrained celery in spring. Celery grows 12 to 20 in. (30–50 cm) high and is tended and used in the same way as lovage.

Melissa officinalis
Lemon Balm, Bee Balm, Balm, Balm Mint

Lemon balm is particularly easy to tend.

The attractively dented fresh-green leaves of this celebrated medicinal plant grow on four-sided branching stems and exude an exquisite scent of lemon, particularly when rubbed between 2 fingers. Lemon balm grows up to 39 in. (1 m) high in a bed; in a tub or box, it reaches a height of about 20 in. (50 cm) and a width of approximately 12 in. (30 cm). This herbaceous plant, with its luxuriant growth, easily can overrun its neighbors in a balcony box. From the upper leaf axils, it produces small, unobtrusive, white to pink-hued flowers. Two forms are differentiated: one erect and small-leaved, the other, decumbent and large-leaved.

Blooming Season: June to August.
Family: Labiatae or Lamiaceae (mint family).
Origin: Southern Europe, Mediterranean region, Near East, and Central Asia.
Location: Sunny and warm, sheltered from wind.

Potting Soil: All-purpose mix or loamy, sandy garden soil.
Raising: In spring, sow seeds directly in container. Because you need only one plant, it is best to buy a young plant.
Watering, Feeding: Keep young plants damp, water older ones moderately. From April to August, feed every 2 to 3 weeks.
Further Care: None.
Overwintering: Outdoors, with winter protection if in drafty location. Alternative: bright and cool, inside the house. Before moving plant indoors, cut it back and water it moderately. From April on, stand out of doors.
Pests, Diseases: Rare.
Propagation: From seed sown in spring (see Raising), by cuttings in spring or summer, or by division in spring.
My Tip: Harvest the young leaflets before the bloom.

Ocimum basilicum
Common Basil, Sweet Basil

Without sunshine and warmth, basil will not prosper.

Basil is an upright, branching annual with squared stalks and oval to oblong-ovate leaves. The leaves, which bulge as if blistered, have a peppery, sweet taste and aroma. The white to pale-pink flowers grow in whorls at the shoot tips. There are large-leaved forms that grow up to 20 in. (50 cm) high, with green or red-brown leaves, such as 'Genoveser' and 'Opal', as well as small-leaved, low cultivars that grow rounded and bushy, only 8 to 10 in. (20–25 cm) high, such as 'Balkon-star', which is highly suitable for container culture.

Blooming Season: June to August.
Family: Labiatae or Lamiaceae (mint family).
Origin: Tropical Near East.
Location: Full sun, sheltered from wind and rain. The plant has an extreme need for warmth. Do not move out of doors before June. Basil will cease to grow at a temperature below 57°F (14°C).

Potting Soil: All-purpose mix or humus-rich, loamy, and sandy garden soil.
Raising: Sow on surface of potting soil in spring. Do not cover with soil—light germinator. When seedlings are about 4 in. (10 cm) high, set them in clusters in pots or boxes.
Watering, Feeding: Never allow potting soil to dry out, but avoid standing water; otherwise, leaf drop will occur. Feed every 4 weeks.
Further Care: Pinch shoot tips to promote improved branching.
Overwintering: Not applicable.
Pests, Diseases: Aphids; leaf margin damage due to cold, drafty air, or too much rain. Also slugs!
Propagation: From seed in spring (see Raising).

Origanum majorana
(Sweet) Marjoram

Origanum vulgare
Oregano

The shoot tips are particularly aromatic.

☼ ✋ 💧 ⌂

Oregano spreads out rapidly, in large clusters.

☼ ✋ ⌂ 🪴

Marjoram, an aromatic and honey-producing plant, is a perennial, but because of its sensitivity to cold, it usually is treated as an annual. This medicinal plant and potherb grows 8 to 20 in. (20–50 cm) high and up to 16 in. (40 cm) wide. On tough, squared stalks, it produces ovate leaflets covered with fine hair, which taste strongly aromatic and somewhat peppery. The white or pink flowers grow in capitulumlike spikes and are surrounded by round involucral leaves.

Blooming Season: June to August.
Family: Labiatae or Lamiaceae (mint family).
Origin: North Africa, southwestern Asia.
Location: Sunny, warm, and sheltered from wind.
Potting Soil: All-purpose mix or loamy, sandy, and humus-rich garden soil.
Raising: Sow seed indoors from mid-March to late March. Do not put young plants outdoors before late May. Alternative: Sow seed directly in the box in May. <u>Do not cover seeds with soil</u>—light germinator.
Watering, Feeding: Do not let young plants dry out until they have taken root; thereafter, water less. <u>Avoid standing water.</u> During the growth period, feed two times, about 6 weeks apart.
Further Care: Remove flower shoots if you would like to prolong your harvesting of leaves.
Overwintering: Move indoors in fall at temperatures below 41°F (5°C); the plant is sensitive to cold. Put in a bright, cool place, water little.
Pests, Diseases: Rare.
Propagation: From seed in spring (see Raising) or by cuttings in spring or summer.

Oregano gives many favorite Italian dishes their typical taste. This perennial brother of marjoram, 16 to 28 in. (40–70 cm) high, does more than provide large numbers of soft-haired, gray-green leaflets for seasoning; with its lush, pink clusters of flowers, it also is a pleasant way to enliven the masses of green herbs on a kitchen balcony. Because it tends to spread fairly wide, it does best in a bowl with a large diameter.

Blooming Season: July to October.
Family: Labiatae or Lamiaceae (mint family).
Origin: Europe, Asia.
Location: Sunny.
Potting Soil: All-purpose soil. Loamy, sandy, that contains some lime garden soil.
Raising: Sow seed indoors in February and put outdoors from early spring on; alternatively, sow seed directly in container in April. <u>Do not cover seeds with soil</u>—light germinator.
Watering, Feeding: During the growth period, water little. <u>Do not feed</u>.
Further Care: Cut off flower shoots from time to time, so that new, leafy shoots will form and the plant will stay more compact.
Overwintering: Possible outdoors in sheltered position. In late fall, cut back almost level with the ground and supply winter protection (see pages 28–29). Alternative: Keep in a frost-free, not necessarily very bright location.
Pests, Diseases: Rare.
Propagation: From seed in spring (see Raising) or by division of older plants.
My Tip: The leaves can be harvested continuously, but their aroma is best during the blooming season.

Oregano contains essential oils, tannins, and bitter substances. It not only flavors foods, but also makes a tea that is used to remedy digestive complaints.

Petroselinum crispum ssp. crispum
Parsley

Rosmarinus officinalis
Rosemary

Curly parsley is milder than the flat-leaved type.

Rosemary can live to a ripe old age in a tub.

The biennial parsley, along with chives, is one of the most used potherbs. Depending on the cultivar, its tripinnatifid leaves may be curly or fairly flat, and they have a bitter aromatic taste. The flat-leaved varieties are more aromatic than those with curly leaves. The umbels appear the second year, and thereafter the plant becomes unpalatable. Well-known cultivars are 'Einfache Schnitt' and various types of 'Mooskrause'.

Blooming Season: June to July.

Family: Apiaceae (celery family).

Origin: Mediterranean area.

Location: Bright to partially shady.

Potting Soil: All-purpose mix or loamy, humus-rich, and permeable garden soil. Enrich with mineral powder or shake diatomaceous earth over the top.

Raising: From March on, sow directly in container. Cover seeds lightly with soil—dark germinator. In April, put outdoors.

Watering, Feeding: Keep damp, but not wet, at all times. Apply low dose of fertilizer every 2 weeks.

Further Care: None.

Overwintering: Outdoors with winter protection (see pages 28–29) or indoors in a bright, cool place. Keep slightly damp.

Pests, Diseases: Aphids.

Propagation: From seed in spring (see Raising).

My Tip: Do not cut the leaves until the plants are fully developed. Fresh parsley contains large amounts of Vitamin C.

Rosemary is an evergreen shrub. Properly tended, it can grow old and stately even in a tub. Planted in the garden, it grows to 6½ ft (2 m) high. Rosemary forms needlelike leaves with blue-green upper surfaces and soft, silvery undersides. The sky-blue flowers (see photo, page 217) appear in spring and are popular with bees. Rosemary exudes a sweetish, rather camphorlike fragrance. The leaves taste acrid and bitter.

Blooming Season: May to June.

Family: Labiatae or Lamiaceae (mint family).

Origin: Mediterranean area.

Location: Sunny, hot, and sheltered from wind. Heat intensifies the aroma.

Potting Soil: All-purpose soil. Loamy, sandy, humus-rich, and not overly heavy garden soil. Blend in substantial amounts of peat or sand if the soil is heavy.

Raising: Growing from seed is quite tedious. It is best to buy a nursery-grown young plant.

Watering, Feeding: During the growth period, water little, but do not allow to dry out completely. From March to April, feed monthly. Beneficial: Using fertilizer with a high potash content.

Further Care: Plant can be cut back after flowering.

Overwintering: Move indoors at temperatures below 23°F (–5°C); overwinter in a frost-free, bright place. After the last frost date in May, move plant outdoors again.

Pests, Diseases: Rare.

Propagation: By cuttings in July or August, or from seed in early spring (see Raising).

Decorating Tip: Rosemary is particularly lovely in a glazed tub or in a terra cotta-colored tub.

Salvia officinalis
Sage

Sage can be overwintered outdoors.

How can you die if sage grows in your garden? Freely translated, this is an aphorism from the Roman medical school at Salerno. Sage is in fact one of our most valuable medicinal plants, as well as a headstrong potherb and a decorative subshrub. It grows outstretched, about 12 to 20 in. (30–50 cm) high. Its oblong-ovate leaves are gray-green in the pure species, white-margined and tinged with red in the cultivar 'Tricolor'; they have an astringent, bitter taste. The blue-violet, sometimes white flowers grow in whorls at the shoot ends and provide a playground for bees and bumblebees.

Blooming Season: June to August.
Family: Labiatae or Lamiaceae (mint family).
Origin: Northern and central Spain, southern France, western Balkans.
Location: Sunny, warm, and sheltered from wind.
Potting Soil: All-purpose mix or loamy, sandy, and lime-rich garden soil.

Raising: Sow seed outdoors in April or May, or even earlier indoors. Cover lightly with soil—dark germinator.
Watering, Feeding: During the growth period, keep more dry than damp, and feed every 4 to 6 weeks.
Further Care: Cut back by one half in fall.
Overwintering: Outdoors with winter protection (see pages 28–29). Possibly cut back once more in spring.
Pests, Diseases: Mildew, if grown in too damp and shady a position and too peaty a potting soil.
Propagation: From seed in spring (see Raising) or by cuttings in late summer.
My Tip: Harvest young leaves. To soothe sore throats, use tea brewed from dried leaves as a gargle or chew raw leaves.

Thymus vulgaris
Thyme

Summer thyme brings the scent of the Mediterranean.

This strongly aromatic subshrub from the sunny Mediterranean countries has a bushy growth habit. It reaches a height of 8 to 12 in. (20–30 cm) and has narrow, elliptical, gray-green leaves that are slightly involuted at the margins. The flowers are pink to violet. There are two varieties, English or winter thyme—which is hardy when planted in the garden—and summer thyme, which is frost-tender.

Blooming Season: June to September.
Family: Labiatae or Lamiaceae (mint family).
Origin: Western Mediterranean region to southeastern Italy.
Location: Sunny and hot.
Potting Soil: All-purpose mix or loamy, sandy, humus-rich garden soil. Loves lime. Mix some mineral powder with the potting soil.
Raising: Sow seed from March to May—light germinator. It is better to buy precultivated young plants.

Watering, Feeding: During the growth period, water little. This plant will tolerate dryness. Feed overwintered plants once, lightly, in April and after the first cutting back.
Further Care: None.
Overwintering: Keep bright and cool, almost dry. Cut back in spring to stimulate new growth.
Pests, Diseases: None.
Propagation: From seed in spring (see Raising), by cuttings or layers in summer; old plants, by division in spring.
My Tip: When harvesting, do not cut too deep, so that the plant can shoot forth again.
Plant thyme beneath or beside other plants. Its strong aroma will keep plant lice away.

Small and pale pink— thyme flowers.

Beta vulgaris var. flavescens
Mangel

Cultivars such as 'Feurio' are extremely decorative.

☀ 💧 **1**

Did you know that sugar beets, butter leaves, and red beets are descended from the same wild species as mangel? They all are varieties of *Beta vulgaris*, whose change-ability was known even in ancient times. Mangel is a biennial that generally flowers the second year, but it is treated as an annual, because only the leaves and stalks are harvested. It is especially suitable for container culture (choose tubs at least 12 in. [30 cm] deep and wide!): Not only does it have an abundant yield, but it also is exceptionally handsome. There are green-leaved cultivars and extremely decorative cultivars with fiery red stalks and black-red leaves veined with bright red, for example, 'Feurio' and 'Vulkan'.

Blooming Season: Summer (when grown as a biennial).
Family: Chenopodiaceae (goosefoot family).
Origin: Original form, probably eastern Mediterranean area and Near East.

Location: Sunny.
Potting Soil: All-purpose mix or loamy, humus- and nutrient-rich garden soil.
Raising: From April to July, broadcast seed directly into container. Thin out to distance of 10 in. (25 cm).
Watering, Feeding: Keep potting soil slightly damp at all times. Water daily on hot days. In summer, feed once or twice.
Further Care: Gradually separate leaves, going from outside in. When harvesting, make sure the core is left intact. New leaves will arise from it.
Overwintering: Not applicable.
Pests, Diseases: Rarely, downy mildew.
Propagation: From seed (see Raising).
Pointer: A relative, the spinachlike leaf mangel (*Beta vulgaris var. vulgaris*), which also can be sown in a box, is treated in a similar manner.

Capsicum annuum
Peppers

The fruits need a great many sunny days to ripen.

☀ 💧 **1** ☠

If you have a balcony or patio with full sun, you can grow peppers there successfully. The modern breeds will ripen even in our latitudes and are, moreover, quite attractive. The erect, bushy plants reach a height of 10 to 18 in. (25–45 cm) and have beautiful, shiny-green leaves. From the small white flowers arise, depending on the cultivar, medium-sized round to squared fruits. Green at first, they later turn red or yellow. Suitable for the balcony are: 'Merit', 'Golden Bell', 'Puszta-gold', and the ornamental pepper 'Festival' with edible fruits.

Blooming Season: June to September.
Family: Solanaceae (nightshade family).
Origin: Probably Mexico.
Location: Sunny and warm.
Potting Soil: All-purpose mix or loamy, humus- and nutrient-rich garden soil.
Raising: Sow seed in warm propagating bed in February or March. Put young plants singly in large pots. Do not move outdoors before the end of May.
Watering, Feeding: Keep soil slightly damp at all times. Water daily on hot days; as soon as the flowers develop, feed weekly.
Further Care: Because of the heavy fruits, tie the plant to a bamboo pole.
Overwintering: Not applicable, because it is treated as an annual in most areas.
Pests, Diseases: White-flies, aphids, spider mites; wilt diseases (fungi).
Propagation: From seed (easy).
My Tip: Peppers can be harvested from August to October. From September on, protect against cold, for example, with tomato hoods (see drawing, page 26).
Warning: With the exception of the fruits, all parts of these plants are poisonous.

Cucumis sativus
Cucumber

There are cucumber cultivars that do well in tubs.

○ ⚎ ➴ **1**

Thanks to modern breeds that grow tendrils only 24 in. (60 cm) long and are compact of habit, cucumbers will also fruit abundantly on balcony or patio boxes. The container should be wide, but not deep. Suitable cultivars are, for example, the outdoor salad cucumber 'Bush Champion', the F_1 hybrid 'Sandra', and the mildew-resistant 'Bella'. The F_1 hybrids are parthenocarpic; that is, they need no other pollination. With 'Bush Champion', however, the pollen of the male flowers has to be transferred to the stigma of the female flowers by hand if the bees flying around your balcony do not do the job for you.
Blooming Season: Summer.
Family: Cucurbitaceae (cucumber family).
Origin: India.
Location: Bright, but not full sun, warm, and sheltered from wind.
Potting Soil: All-purpose mix. Loamy, humus-, and nutrient-rich garden soil or compost soil.

Raising: From mid-April to late June, sow 2 to 3 seeds per pot and put in warm propagating bed. After germination, leave only the strongest seedling in the pot.
Watering, Feeding: Water abundantly with sun-warmed water, but avoid standing water. Apply a low dose of fertilizer weekly.
Further Care: Provide a support for the twining tendrils—strong twine or a lattice. Cut back overly long shoots to two leaves above the outermost cucumber.
Overwintering: Not applicable.
Pests, Diseases: Spider mites; cucumber mildew, botrytis, cucumber mosaic virus.
Propagation: From seed (see Raising).
Pointer: The related muskmelon (*Cucumis melo*) and zucchini, zucchetti, or squash (*Cucurbita pepo*) are raised and tended the same way.

Lactuca sativa var. crispa
Leaf Lettuce (Picking Lettuce, Cutting Lettuce)

Leaf lettuce will renew itself after being cut.

○ ⚎ **1**

Although head lettuce (*Lactuca sativa var. capitata*) forms satisfactory heads on a balcony or patio only when grown in fairly large containers, leaf lettuce can be easily raised in boxes. The variety harvested by cutting (head lettuce) is ready only 4 to 6 weeks after it is sown; it is harvested only once. The variety meant for picking (leaf lettuce) will regenerate several times if you leave the core untouched. It forms a stalk 12 to 20 in. (30–50 cm) high, on which the leaves grow and are picked from bottom to top. Subsequent sowings until June will ensure that this lettuce is available well into late fall. Recommended cultivars: 'Grand Rapids Salli' and the highly decorative 'Red Salad Bowl' (red-leaved oak-leaf lettuce), 'Lallo Rosso', and 'Red Sails' (picking leaf lettuce).
Blooming Season: About 3 to 4 months after the first harvest.
Family: Aster or Compositae (aster or composite family).
Origin: Uncertain. Probably Egypt or western Asia.
Location: Sunny to partially shady.
Potting Soil: All-purpose mix or loamy, humus-rich garden soil.
Raising: From mid-March on, sow seed for head or cutting lettuce broadcast and densely; sow seed for leaf or picking lettuce in 2 rows per box. When the leaves are about 4 in. (10 cm) high, both types are ready for harvesting. In the case of leaf lettuce, leave one plant every 8 to 10 in. (20–25 cm) for further culture. Protect first sowing against frost.
Watering, Feeding: Keep damp; do not allow to dry out. Fertilize after the first harvest.
Further Care: None.
Overwintering: Not applicable.
Pests, Diseases: Aphids. Infestation less heavy in red-leaved and dark-leaved cultivars.
Propagation: From seed (see Raising).

Lycopersicon lycopersicum

Tomato

The following tomatoes are suitable for container culture:

- Bush or balcony tomatoes ('Balkonstar', 'Tumbler').
- Trellis or currant tomatoes ('Gartenfreude', 'Sweet 100', 'Bistro').
- Pot or cocktail tomatoes ('Tiny Tim', 'Phyra').
- Pear tomatoes ('San Marzano', 'Roma').

Blooming Season: Summer.

Family: Solanaceae (nightshade family).

Origin: Peru, Ecuador.

Location: Sunny, warm, sheltered from wind. In fall, protect against rain.

Potting Soil: All-purpose mix enriched with slow-release fertilizer. Loamy, humus- and nutrient-rich garden soil.

Raising: From seed, from early March to mid-March, in a warm propagating bed. Transplant and later transplant again to larger pots. Keep quite bright and warm until planting outdoors after the last frost date in May.

Watering, Feeding: Keep well dampened at all times. Feed weekly in July and August.

Further Care: Tie taller cultivars with thin shoots to a stake. Remove side shoots periodically. From time to time, shake plants in bloom so that they will pollinate themselves. From late August on, use tomato hoods (see drawing, page 26) to protect the plants from cold.

Overwintering: Not applicable.

Pests, Diseases: Whiteflies, aphids, spider mites; rot, botrytis.

Propagation: From seed (see Raising).

Warning: With the exception of the fruits, all parts of tomato plants are poisonous.

Phaseolus coccineus
Scarlet Runner Bean

Even children can raise scarlet runner successfully.

Scarlet runners creep quickly and profusely up all possible climbing aids. This property makes them popular with gardeners who want an area green quickly. The plants grow as high as 8 ft (2.5 m) and are generally tougher and more robust than pole beans. Less affected by wind, they flourish also in harsh climates and flower freely. From their white or fiery-red flowers develop strong, slender pods (legumes). Stringless cultivars: 'Hammond's Dwarf Scarlet' (fiery red, low, and bushy, for boxes), 'Desiree' (white), 'Butler' (red), and 'Red Knight' (red).

Blooming Season: June to September.
Family: Fabaceae or Leguminosae (pea or bean family).
Origin: Probably Mexico to Central America.
Location: Bright to partially shady and airy. Not too warm or in close, stale air.
Potting Soil: All-purpose soil (can be enriched with slow-release fertilizer) or loamy, humus-rich garden soil.
Raising: With preliminary culture indoors, mid-April; outdoors, from mid-May on. In either case, sow seed directly in container, leaving 2⅓ to 2¾ in. (6–7 cm) between seeds. Surround young plantlets with hills of soil.
Watering, Feeding: Never allow to dry out. Do not water with cold water and do not cover foliage with netting. During the growth period, feed weekly.
Further Care: Prompt harvesting will stimulate the setting of new flowers.
Overwintering: Not applicable.
Pests, Diseases: Bean aphids; fungal infections.
Propagation: From seed (see Raising).
My Tip: Underplanting with savory will prevent bean aphids.
Warning: Eat only cooked beans; they are poisonous when raw.

Pisum sativum conv. axiphium
Sugar Pea

Sugar peas have to be harvested early.

Peas are annual climbing vegetables, common worldwide. Their pods may be eaten raw or cooked. The delicious sugar pea is best for growing on balconies and patios. Well-known cultivars are 'Denise Knackerbse' (24 to 32 in. [60–80 cm]), 'Früher Heinrich' (28 in. [70 cm]), 'Graue Buntblühende' (20 in. [50 cm]), 'Nofila' (32 to 39 in. [80–100 cm], stringless, needs little support), 'Oregon Sugar Pod' (32 in. [80 cm]).

Blooming Season: June to September.
Family: Fabaceae or Leguminosae (pea or bean family).
Origin: Eastern Mediterranean region, Near East, and Asia Minor.
Location: Sunny and airy.
Potting Soil: All-purpose mix (can be enriched with slow-release fertilizer) or loose, rich garden soil. Mix with diatomaceous earth.
Raising: From April to May, sow seeds directly in container, ¾ to 1⅕ in. (2–3 cm) apart. Once the young plants are 4 to 6 in. (10–15 cm) high, surround them with hills of soil; this will give the tender plants a firmer foothold.
Watering, Feeding: Do not allow to dry out, but avoid standing water by all means. During the growing period, feed weekly.
Further Care: Provide a climbing aid. Spray with horsetail concoctions (see page 35) or aromatic sprays (see page 30) to prevent diseases and pests. Dill and fennel make good neighbors.
Overwintering: Not applicable.
Pests, Diseases: Pea bugs, pea moths, pea thrips; downy mildew.
Propagation: From seed (see Raising).
My Tip: Sugar peas are harvested when the pods are still pea-green and the peas are completely flat.

In restaurants, this tasty vegetable is served in small quantities. Your own harvest will let you enjoy twice as much!

Fresh from the balcony to your table. A small culinary garden above ground level that will eliminate the need for many a trip to the grocery store.

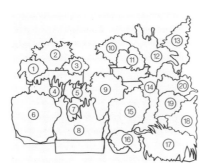

1 Monkey flower, *Mimulus* hybrids
2 Basil, *Ocimum basilicum*
3 Curly-leaved parsley, *Petroselinum crispum*
4 Lavender, *Lavandula angustifolia*
5, 6 Rosemary, *Rosmarinus officinalis*
7 Scented geranium, *Pelargonium odoratissimum*
8 Garlic chives
9 Nasturtium, *Tropaeolum* hybrid
10 Common sage, *Salvia officinalis*
11 *Asteriscus maritimus*
12 Sage, *Salvia patens*
13 Thornless blackberry, *Rubus* hybrid 'Thornfree'
14 Tomato, *Lycopersicon lycopersicum*
15 Chervil, *Anthriscus cerefolium*
16 Savory, *Satureja hortensis*
17 Chives, *Allium schoenoprasum*
18 Nasturtium, *Tropaeolum* hybrid
19 Marjoram, *Majorana hortensis*
20 *Asteriscus maritimus*

INDEX

V

W

Y

Z

SOURCES

Bibliography

Azaleas
Darden, Jim, *Great American Azaleas: A Guide to the Finest Azalea Varieties,* Greenhouse Press, Clinton, North Carolina, 1986.
Fairweather, Christopher, *Azaleas,* Globe Pequot Press, Chester, Connecticut, 1988.
Galle, Fred, *Azaleas,* Timber Press, Portland, Oregon, 1987.

Bamboo
Farrelly, David, *The Book of Bamboo,* Sierra Club Books, San Francisco, California, 1986.
Takama, Shinji, ed., *Bamboo: One Hundred Paths to Beauty,* 2nd ed., Books Nippan, Carson, California.

Begonias
Catterall, E., *Growing Begonias,* Timber Press, Portland, Oregon, 1984.
Haegeman, J., *Tuberous Begonias: Origin and Development,* Lubrecht and Cramer Ltd., Forestburgh, New York, 1979.

Bonsai
Ainsworth, John, *The Art of Indoor Bonsai,* Trafalgar Square/David and Charles, Inc., North Pomfret, Vermont, 1989.
Anderson, Charles and Anderson, Ruth, *The Care and Feeding of Bonsai,* HarborCrest Publications, Bainbridge Island, Washington, 1988.
Daute, Horst, *The Macmillan Book of Bonsai,* Macmillan Publishing Co., Inc., New York, New York, 1986.

Cacti
Benson, Lyman, *The Cacti of the U.S. and Canada,* Stanford University Press, Stanford, California, 1982.
Cullman, Willy, *et al. Encyclopedia of Cacti,* Timber Press, Portland, Oregon, 1987.
Gibson, Arthur and Noble, Park S., *The Cactus Primer,* Harvard University Press, Cambridge, Massachusetts, 1986.
Haselton, Scott E. *Cactus and Succulents and How to Grow Them,* Desert Botanical Garden, Phoenix, Arizona, 1983.

Camellias
Noble, Mary and Graham, Blanche, *You Can Grow Camellias,* Peter Smith Publishing, Inc., Magnolia, Massachusetts, 1983.

Chrysanthemums
Brock, Wallace, *Growing and Showing Chrysanthemums,* David and Charles, Inc., North Pomfret, Vermont, 1984.
Randall, Harry and Wren, Alan, *Growing Chrysanthemums,* Timber Press, Portland, Oregon, 1983.
Skeen, Bruce, *Growing Chrysanthemums,* International Specialized Book Services, Portland, Oregon, 1985.

Citrus
Ray, Richard and Wallheim, Lance, *Citrus,* Price Sloan Stern, Inc., Los Angeles, California, 1980.

Ferns
Brooklyn Botanic Garden, *Ferns,* Brooklyn, New York.
Cobb, Boughton A., *Field Guide to Ferns and Their Related Families: Northeastern and Central North America,* Houghton Mifflin Company, Boston, Massachusetts, 1977.
Foster, F. Gordon, *Ferns to Know and Grow,* Timber Press, Portland, Oregon, 1984.

Geraniums
Shellard, Alan, *Geraniums for Home and Garden,* David and Charles, Inc., North Pomfret, Vermont, 1984.
_____, *Growing and Showing Geraniums,* David and Charles, Inc., North Pomfret, Vermont, 1984.
Yeo, Peter F., *Hardy Geraniums,* Timber Press, Portland, Oregon, 1985.

Herbs
Brooklyn Botanic Garden, *Culinary Herbs,* Brooklyn, New York.
Clarkson, Rosetta E., *Herbs: Their Culture and Uses,* Macmillan Publishing Co., Inc., New York, New York, 1990.

Freeman, Sally, *Herbs for All Seasons: Growing and Gathering Herbs for Flavor, Health, and Beauty,* NAL/Dutton, Div. of Penguin, USA, New York, New York, 1991.

Zabar, Abbie, *The Potted Herb,* Stewart, Tabori & Chang, Inc., New York, New York, 1988.

Lilies

Jefferson-Brown, Michael, *The Lily: For Garden, Patio and Display,* Trafalgar Square, North Pomfret, Vermont, 1982.

Redoute, Pierre, *Lilies and Related Flowers,* Overlook Press, New York, New York, 1982.

Palms

Blombery, Alec and Rodd, Tony, *Palms,* Salem House Publications, Harper & Row, Scranton, Pennsylvania, 1983.

McGeachy, Beth, *Handbook of Florida Palms,* Great Outdoors Publishing Co., Saint Petersburg, Florida.

Rhododendrons

Clarke, J. Harold, *Getting Started with Rhododendrons and Azaleas,* Timber Press, Portland, Oregon.

Cox, Kenneth and Cox, Peter, *Encyclopedia of Rhododendron Hybrids,* Timber Press, Portland, Oregon.

Greer, Harold E., *Greer's Guidebook to Available Rhododendrons,* Offshoot Publications, Eugene, Oregon, 1987.

Roses

Brooklyn Botanic Garden, *Roses,* Brooklyn, New York.

Gibson, Michael, *Growing Roses for Small Gardens,* Timber Press, Portland, Oregon, 1991.

Reddell, Rayford C., *Growing Good Roses,* HarperCollins Pubs., Inc., New York, New York, 1987.

Stump, D.S., ed., *Roses,* Brooklyn Botanic Garden, Brooklyn, New York, 1989.

Taylor, Norman, *Taylor's Guide to Roses,* Houghton Mifflin Co., Boston, Massachusetts, 1989.

Addresses

American Bamboo Society
666 Wagnon Road
Sebastopol, CA 95472

American Begonia Society
P.O. Box 1129
Encinitas, CA 92024

American Bonsai Society
Box 358
Keene, NH 03431

American Camellia Society
Box 1217
Fort Valley, GA 31030

American Conifer Society
P.O. Box 242
Severna Park, MD 21146

American Fern Society
Pringle Herbarium
Department of Botany
University of Vermont
Burlington, VT 05495

American Ivy Society
P.O. Box 520
West Carrollton, OH 45446

American Poinsettia Society
Box 706
Gloucester, VA 23061

American Rhododendron Society
P.O. Box 1380
Gloucester, VA 23061

American Rock Garden Society
221 West 9th Street
Hastings, MN 55033

American Rose Society
P.O. Box 30000
Shreveport, LA 71130-0030

Cactus and Succulent Society
of America
2631 Fairgreen Avenue
Arcadia, CA 91006

Gardenia Society of America
P.O. Box 879
Atwater, CA 95301

Indoor Citrus and Rare Fruit Society
176 Coronado Avenue
Los Altos, CA 94022

International Camellia Society
P.O. Box 750
Brookhaven, MS 39601

International Geranium Society
4610 Druid Street
Los Angeles, CA 90012

International Palm Society
P.O. Box 368
Lawrence, KS 66044

National Chrysanthemum Society
10107 Homer Pond Drive
Fairfax Station, VA 22039

North American Heather Society
62 Elma-Monte Road
Elma, WA 98541

North American Lily Society
P.O. Box 476
Waukee, IA 50263

Primula Society
6730 West Mercer Way
Mercer Island, WA 98040

CREDITS

The Photographers:

Apel: page 155 top left; Becker: pages 16, 18, 39, 100 top right, 148 left; Benary: pages 94 right, 95 bottom left, 103 top left, 136; Busek: page 223 top right; Eberts: page 197 right; Eigstler: pages 111 left, 129 left, 185, 221 right, 223 top left; Eisenbeiss: pages 157 right, 190 left, 219 left; Finkenzeller: page 141 left; Greiner & Meyer: page 107 left; Heitz: page 186 top; Ibero Import: pages 172 right, 178 left; Kögel: pages 49 left, 138 right, 153, 163 top left, 215; König: page 133 right; Kordes: page 130 bottom; Lamontagne: page 149 right; Layer: page 13; mein schöner Garten (msG)/Fischer: pages 93 left, 225 right; msG/Graham: page 95 bottom right; msG/Gross: page 187 left; msG/Kögel: page 183 right; msG/Stehling: page 110 right; msG/Stork: page 152 middle top, right bottom; msG/Wetterwald: pages 100 top left, 111 right; Nickig: page 19; Reinhard: pages 92 right, 106 right, 141 right, 151 right, 170 top right, 173 left, 174 top left, 180, 187 right, 202, 203 left, 205 left, 207 left, 210 left, 217, 227 left; Riedmiller: pages 122, 124, 125 bottom, 126 middle top, middle bottom, top right, bottom right, 129 right, 151 left, 178 top right, 218 top left, 224 left; Rohdich: page 30; Sammer: pages 182 top right, 189 bottom, 225 left; Scherz: pages 2/3, 48, 49 top, middle left, middle right, 156 right, 158 right, 186 bottom, 193 right, 194 left, 195; Schlaback-Becker: pages 49 bottom, 109 left, 171; Schrempp: page 119 right; Seidl: pages 144, 150 top right, 155 bottom, 160 top right, 163 bottom, 184 top left, 189 top right, 199 bottom, 212 left; Silvestris/Bieker: page 116 right; Skogstad: pages 199 top right, 218 top right, 221 left, 223 bottom; Stork: pages 168, 199 top left, 201 right; Wetterwald: pages 38, 118 bottom, 135, 191 left, 198 bottom, 201 left, 204 left; Willemse: pages 116 left, 138 left; Wolff: pages 108 top left, 127 left, 131 right; Friedrich Strauss: all other photos.

The Artists:

Ushie Dorner: pages 36, 37; Christel Langer: pages 14, 20, 35, 228; György Jankovics: all other drawings.

A scented box with lavender, basil, heliotrope, mignonette, scented geraniums, and white tuberoses. For directions on planting and care, see pages 56–57.

English translation © Copyright 1992 by Barron's Educational Series, Inc.
© Copyright 1991 by Gräfe and Unzer Verlag GmbH, Munich, West Germany
The title of the German book is *Balkon und Kübelpflanzen*
Translated from the German by Kathleen Luft

All inquiries should be addressed to:
Barron's Educational Series, Inc.
250 Wireless Boulevard
Hauppauge, New York 11788

Library of Congress Catalog Card No. 91-38256

International Standard Book No. 0-8120-6278-7

Library of Congress Cataloging-in-Publication Data

Heitz, Halina.
 [Balkon- und Kübelpflanzen. English]
  Container plants : for patios, balconies, and window boxes Halina Heitz ; translated from the German by Kathleen Luft.
      p.   cm.
  Translation of: Balkon- und Kübelpflanzen.
  Includes bibliographical references
(p.) and index.
  ISBN 0-8120-6278-7
  1. Container gardening.   I. Title.
SB418.H4513   1992
635.9'86—dc20   91-38256
                                                   CIP

PRINTED IN HONG KONG

45   098765432

Important Note

This book deals with the care of container plants, in addition to ornamental woody plants, herbaceous plants, grasses, and flowering bulbs that are grown in pots, as well as in gardens. Some of the plants described are lethally toxic, others are poisonous to varying degrees. In the introduction to the plant portraits (see page 88), reference is made to the health hazards posed by certain plants. The major toxins are listed, and examples of plants containing them are given. In addition, in the descriptions of the individual plants (see pages 86–227), the specific type of physical danger or effect is pointed out under the heading **Warning**. Poisonous plants and plants that contain skin irritants or allergens are marked with a skull-and-crossbones symbol. Make absolutely sure that children and pets do not eat the plants that carry these warnings and the symbol. Store fertilizers and pesticides out of reach of children at all times. Anyone who suffers from contact allergies should wear gloves when handling these plants.